# Temporary Stages II

# Temporary Stages II:
## Critically Oriented Drama Education

Jo Beth Gonzalez

**intellect** Bristol, UK / Chicago, USA

First published in the UK in 2013 by
Intellect, The Mill, Parnall Road, Fishponds, Bristol, BS16 3JG, UK

First published in the USA in 2013 by
Intellect, The University of Chicago Press, 1427 E. 60th Street,
Chicago, IL 60637, USA



A catalogue record for this book is available from the British Library.

Series: Theatre in Education
Series ISSN: 2049-3878
Cover designer: Holly Rose
Copy-editor: Emma Rhys
Production manager: Jessica Mitchell
Typesetting: Contentra Technologies

Print ISBN: 978-1-78320-011-5
ePDF ISBN: 978-1-78320-089-4
ePub ISBN: 978-1-78320-090-0

# Contents


Foreword xi

Acknowledgments xv

**SECTION ONE: Critically Oriented Drama Education Shapes Growth** **1**

Chapter 1: Stepping From *Temporary Stages* to *Temporary Stages II* 3

Rethinking Power Relationships in the Theatre Classroom and Rehearsal 6

Sections of the Book 6

Promoting Critical Consciousness: The CODE Classroom and Rehearsal 8

National Trends Demonstrate Need for Critical Investigation of Secondary Theatre Education 10

Seven Guiding Concepts of *Temporary Stages II* 11

Power 11

Authority 12

Student Artistry 13

Incomplete Understandings 14

Change 14

Privilege 15

Place 17

The Adventure of Teaching Theatre for Self-Agency and Critical Consciousness 18

Chapter 2: Characterizing CODE Classrooms and Rehearsal Spaces 21

Self-Reflection: The Gateway to Critically Conscious Classrooms and Rehearsals 24

Qualities of a CODE Classroom 24
Positioning the Listening Ear 26
Reflection as Evaluation: What About Grades? 27

Chapter 3: Balancing Passion and Censorship 29
Promoting Critical Consciousness Through Drama/Theatre Education 31
Daily Demands and Tradition Hinder Change 34
Language and Homosexuality Prompt Censorship 36
Plays With Themes of War Prompt Censorship 39
Treading the Divides of Partial Understanding 41
Personal Commitment to the Social Cause Contributes Conditions for Change 44

Chapter 4: Discovering CODE in Musical Theatre 47
Critical Directing Challenges Conventional Hierarchies in Musical Theatre 49
Challenge #1: Asking "Where Are the Stars?" 52
Challenge #2: Involving Students in All Aspects of Artistry and Production to Strengthen the Whole 53
Challenge #3: Securing Confidence in Collaborative Leadership 54
Challenge #4: Steering Away from Stereotypes by Designing Rehearsals that Foster Critical Consciousness 55
Challenge #5: Questioning Assumptions of Privilege: Dramaturgy Unveils Identity 57
Challenge #6: Contemplating Complexities of Cultural Border-Crossing 61
Postscript 65

**SECTION TWO: Critically Oriented Drama Education Alters Traditional Power Dynamics 67**

Chapter 5: Examining Power Dynamics in a CODE Theatre Design Classroom 69
Perpetuating Dominance In Spite of Principles 71
Evolution of a Design 72

Resisting Authority and Authorizing Resistance: Students and Teachers Negotiate Control 74
Whose Vision Is This? On Artistry and Compromise 75
Co-Authored Vision: *The Winter's Tale* 75
Teacher's Vision: *Much Ado About Nothing* 77
Artistic Compromise and Compromising Artistry 79
Much Ado About Trees 79
The Winter's Tale of Trees 81
A Midsummer Night's Nightmare 83
Binaries Blend When Students Exercise Power 84
The Teacher/Student Binary 84
The Actor/Crew Binary 85
The Leader/Follower Binary 86
Chapter 6: Emerging Conflict, Paradox, and Social Change When Students Exercise Power 89
Multiple Perspectives Fuel Power Struggles 91
Paradox: Democratic Teacher and Director Authority 93
Conflict Arises from Paradox: Democratic Teacher or Authoritative Director? 94
Social Change Evolves from Conflict: Democratic Teaching Strengthens the Co-curricular Theatre Program 95
Conventional Mindsets Rear Heads When New Ideas Depart From Tradition 97
Chapter 7: Shaping an Ensemble Approach to Casting Understudies with a Mindset for CODE 101
Critical Partnership versus Conventional Substitution 103
Conditions for Understudy/Principal Critical Partnership 105
Technique #1: Play Selection 106
Technique #2: Terminology 106
Technique #3: Shadowing 108
Technique #4: Ensemble Roles 110
Technique #5: Ensemble Improvisations and Workshops 111

Technique #6: Switching Out 112
Technique #7: Added Time 113

Chapter 8: Adjusting to a New Theatre with Critical Awareness 115
Adjusting With Unease to a Place of Privilege 118
Effective Power Dynamics Manage Transition into a Performing Arts Center 121
Scheduling Activities in the New Performing Arts Center: Feminist Leadership Involves All 122
Top-Down Management Seeps In 123
The Politics of Danger: Technology Presents New Cautions 124
Evaluating Co-Governance in a Technological Environment 126
A State-of-the-Art Space: The Creativity/ Technology Binary 128
Technology and the Spirit of Theatre 129
Technology: The Science/Theatre Binary 130
Performing Arts Center-Turned-Classroom Engages Science Students in a Fresh Way 131

**SECTION THREE: Critically Oriented Drama Education Examines Controversy and Oppression 133**

Chapter 9: Establishing a Foundation for Examining Tough Issues 135
Evolution of Original Scripts with Controversial Themes 138
Leading Discussions of Controversial Subject Matter 139
Exploring What Works ... And What Doesn't: Sometimes Traditional Teaching Methods Are Best 142
Testimonies Contribute Substance to Research 143

Chapter 10: Unfolding Ongoing Reflective Practice Through Five CODE Strategies 145
Students Resist Teacher-Fed Script 147
CODE Conditions in a Classroom Support Student-Written Scenes on Hot Topics 148
Strategy #1: The Spoonful of Sugar—Incorporate Satire to Advance Serious Work 149

Scene 1: "The Best Drunk Driver" 150

Scene 2: "Fagzilla" 150

Strategy #2: Invite Self-Disclosure 151

Strategy #3: Build Trust to Raise Social Consciousness and Express Emotion Honestly 153

Strategy #4: Integrate Teacher Voice to Model Vulnerability as Strength 157

Strategy #5: Involve Tempered Teacher Authority as Process Evolves into Product 159

Chapter 11: Investigating Student and Teacher Identity 165

Positioning Student Identity in the Classroom 167

Positioning Teacher Identity in Rehearsal 168

The CODE Classroom: A "Safe Space" *With Consequences* 171

Seeing the Opposite Reveals Identity 173

Strong Critical Classroom Experience is an Ongoing Process 174

Unveiling Whiteness in a "Safe Space With Consequences" 176

Positioning Whiteness in Performance When the Joke is on *Who?* 178

Chapter 12: Preparing for the Audience 181

Working Through the Audience "Fear Factor" 183

When Emotions Aren't Enough: Integrating Facts for Healthy Digestion of Controversial Material 186

The Responsibilities of Democratic Teaching Include Preparing for the Audience 190

Postscript 194

Epilogue 197

Works Cited 203

Index 213

# Foreword

Each year, I teach a class titled "Teaching Theatre Methods" to a small group of brave teacher-education students who, despite their knowledge of the fact that they will likely be hired for their certifications in English, social studies, or other core curriculum subjects, are working on a second certification in Theatre. These students also know that in many future job contexts they could teach a theatre elective or direct the school play without theatre certification, but they want thorough training because they want their work to be good. They know from their own experiences in theatre that the rehearsal space can be intimate and scary, and they want to make sure they are ready to take on a leadership role as director and teacher. And they want their artwork to have meaning and be worth their time and the time of everyone who will work so hard on it. In short, they are believers. They are theatre people. And they are teachers.

I think high school theatre teachers are extraordinary. They prepare, design, build, and rehearse plays alongside full teaching schedules. They must sometimes be their own technical director, their own stage manager, and their own fundraiser. Sometimes they provide choreography. They have to make an art product that will be well received by family audiences, but still critically engage students, both in the audience and onstage. They must navigate the complicated terrain of teenage identity with appropriate casting choices that validate individuals, and they must take student actors on the challenging emotional journey of creating a good production. Finally, they do all of these things knowing that if their school faces budget cuts, they will be in jeopardy because theatre is not a core curriculum subject. Who would choose this job?!

The people I have witnessed willing to juggle all of these pressures are individuals who know that the transformative power of theatre has a unique capacity for elevating our human existence and helping us understand one another across great divides. They know that experiences in theatre can be opportunities for teenagers to understand themselves and the world around them in new ways, opening the door not only to artistic expression, but also meaningful socialization and more authentic understanding of their own identity.

Across the United States, high school theatre teachers are taking calculated risks and examining boundaries so that their students may engage with material that meaningfully interacts with the current events of their lives. But risk-taking is not always welcomed in schools, and teachers' First Amendment rights are a bit muddy when they are working in a school context.

The First Amendment to the U.S. Constitution protects citizens' right to freedoms of religion and expression; the Fourteenth Amendment protects such rights from interference by state governments. Freedom of expression includes the rights to freedom of speech, press, assembly, and to petition the government, as well as the implied rights of association and belief. Freedom of speech includes all mediums of expression that communicate a message.[1]

The Supreme Court interprets which speech and other forms of expression are protected by the First Amendment, and has made important rulings in its application to public school contexts. The 1969 ruling on *Tinker v. Des Moines Independent School District* established that First Amendment rights are applicable within public school contexts, as long as the form of expression does not pose a possible threat to other students or a disruption to school activities.[2] In 1988's *Hazelwood School District v. Kuhlmeier*, the Supreme Court ruled that "educators do not offend the First Amendment by exercising editorial control over the style and content of student speech in school-sponsored expressive activities so long as their actions are reasonably related to legitimate pedagogical concerns" in response to arguments over journalism students' articles about pregnancy and divorce.[3] Finally, in 1998, the U.S. Court of Appeals ruled in *Boring v. Buncombe County Board of Education* that a high school theatre teacher's academic freedom and freedom of speech rights were not violated when she was dismissed for directing/teaching Lee Blessing's *Independence* (1985), a play that includes divorce, homosexuality, and unwanted pregnancy.[4]

*Boring v. Buncombe* is the only federal court case about a high school theatre project. Clearly, the federal government has established that high school theatre teachers must have the support of their principal and possibly their local community when it comes to production choices. The Courts have ruled that it is not a violation of First Amendment rights to censor teachers or students in public high school theatre contexts, and has demonstrated that not all subjects are available for the high school theatre stage. Across the United States, high school theatre teachers know this. They know that it is not enough for them to make good curriculum choices for their students; those choices must also meet the expectations of their community.

Clearly, high school theatre today is positioned in the middle of a complicated nexus of power struggles. Parents, teachers, administrators, and community members often all have a stake in the theatre teacher's curriculum. Conflicts can lead to censorship, a narrow repertoire of play selections, and pedagogical choices that fail to put students' needs first. Arguments against producing particular play titles often cite the potential for "harm" done to students onstage, or in the audience. Marjorie Heins argues that historically, indecency laws and other regulating actions that cite something as "harmful to minors" are more often about preserving adult perceptions of children/childhood than they are about actually protecting young people (*Not in Front of the Children* 3–36). Heins's point can be applied to high school theatre pedagogy; ideas about "who" high school youth "are" can regulate popular choices for high school theatre production, determine what language and content might cause them "harm," and produce the ideological boundaries of what is thought of as "reasonable" acts of censorship in public schools.

I believe that one of the strongest contributors to teachers' inability to take risks is their isolation from one another. So many high school theatre teachers face similar obstacles, and yet because of busy schedules and isolated teaching conditions, they are forced to "reinvent the wheel" over and over. This is why it is so important for teachers to tell their stories in published works. It is teachers' individual stories that reveal the variety of complications within high school theatre curricula. Collectively, individual stories can guide us toward the critical questions that are so easy to miss when you're in the thick of activity in your own classroom.

In this second edition of *Temporary Stages*, Dr. Gonzalez shows us how high school theatre teaching and learning, as well as community expectations, are greatly impacted by resources and space. She continues to reflect on how to best construct a "critical pedagogy" in high school theatre education. And she re-examines her idea of the "democratic classroom," now faced with new challenges to overcome. Like the first edition, the strength of this book is that it is one teacher's story. It is not a prescription or "how-to" manual. Out of this single, specific, localized story, Gonzalez encounters questions that have broader implications for teaching and learning in high school theatre in the United States. If you've read the first edition of this book, don't skim this one. It's a new story, and worth a careful read. And if you're in my class, keep reading. Chapter 1 is due tomorrow.

— Jennifer Chapman, Ph.D.
Associate Professor and Director of Theatre Education
Department of Music and Theatre Arts
University of Wisconsin-Eau Claire
October 2012

## NOTES

1 For an extended explanation of the First and Fourteenth Amendments, including their history, important Supreme Court Rulings that have cited them, and how they have been interpreted in various situations, see the Cornell University Law School Legal Information Institute Website: http://www.law.cornell.edu/constitution/constitution.amendmentxiv.html. For an explanation of the implications of Supreme Court rulings on contemporary art, literature, and scholarship, see the Free Expression Policy Project Website: http://www.fepproject.org/index.html.

2 To read the entire transcripts of the case, see http://www.firstamendmentcenter.org/faclibrary/case.aspx?case=Tinker_v_Des_Moines_Independent_Community_School_Dist.

3 To read the entire transcripts of the case, see http://www.firstamendmentcenter.org/faclibrary/case.aspx?case=Hazelwood_v_Kuhlmeier.

4 For a summary of the Court's ruling, see http://www.firstamendmentschools.org/freedoms/case.aspx?id=1682.

## Acknowledgments

A friend once advised me, "You can do everything you want in this life, just not at the same time." Thus, I am foremost grateful to the Bowling Green City Schools Board of Education for approving my request for a semester leave of absence to complete the first edition of this book. I am grateful to summer vacations for time to write the second edition. I thank Aunt Lute Press and the Educational Theatre Association for permission to reprint three portions of articles originally published through them. I thank Intellect for recognizing the value of theatre education and supporting authors in our quest to wrestle with big ideas through publication.

I am indebted to many friends and colleagues whose incisive feedback on drafts of both the first and second editions, and one-on-one conversations, pushed me to think, question, clarify, and probe more deeply. I thank the following for their keen insights: Ann-Elizabeth Armstrong, Megan Arnold, Lisa Barnett, Lynda Belt, Max Bush, Linda Cantú, Sarah Caserta, Jennifer Chapman, Pam Christian, Bradford Clark, Leda Cooks, William Donnelly, Abigail Doust, Susan Enders Fronek, Lorenzo Garcia, Tempe Goodhue, Kathleen Juhl, Trese Kaspirik-Postellon, Jeanne Kleine, Patty Kubow, Ellen Larrabee, Joan Lazarus, Mary Lenning, Karen Libman, Ione Lloyd, Christina Marin, Bobbi McKean, Jessica Mitchell, Jim Palmarini, Roxanne Schroeder-Arce, Jess Simmons, Diane Tache, Gus Weltsek-Medina, and my ten EdTA 2007–2008 Critical Links partners.

I am grateful for the support of the Bowling Green City Schools Central Administration, and the administrative staff, teachers, guidance counselors, custodians, and secretaries past and present of Bowling Green High School and Bowling Green Middle School. Advice and encouragement, cautions and go-aheads mark my relationships with all of you.

I recognize the American Alliance for Theatre and Education for its conferences, which give colleagues opportunities for rich contemplation and inspiring discussions, some of which resonate in these chapters; the Children's Theatre Foundation of America for a generous financial gift that made it possible to write the first edition; and the Education Theatre Association for the conference, performance, advocacy, and leadership experiences it offers to middle and high school students and teachers.

I warmly thank my parents, Mary Lee and the late Bud Enders, for championing me always. I thank my daughters Monica and Veronica, for teaching me about balance in life. With deep respect, love and appreciation, I thank Al for a critical perspective that feeds my intellect and a trust that feeds my soul.

Finally, I thank my students at BGHS who have enrolled in theatre classes and participated in productions, workshops, conferences, and community events during these past nineteen years. I commend your willingness to experiment, to speak out honestly, to reflect, and to stay in touch. You will always have my deepest gratitude.

# SECTION ONE

## Critically Oriented Drama Education Shapes Growth

# Chapter 1

## Stepping From *Temporary Stages* to *Temporary Stages II*

In 2006, two days before I hosted a book signing party for the publication of the first edition of *Temporary Stages*, a high school student in one of my theatre classes committed suicide. Who would have thought that on my way to this celebration I would attend the wake of a student who had taken his life? This event cast the title of my book, *Temporary Stages*, in a light I hadn't considered.

Since writing the first edition, other conditions at my school have changed. *Temporary Stages* was originally titled in part because students in my drama program performed in a wide array of venues because we had no permanent home. Every stage we performed on was quite literally temporary. Throughout the writing of that book, I could only dream of what it would be like to teach and direct teenagers in a state-of-the-art performing arts center, never expecting I would, half a dozen years later, write a second edition to my book precisely because this dream came true. A new stage was born; yet it, too, remains a temporary stage: temporary for students who move on after graduation; temporary for fine arts faculty and staff who enter and exit variously, depending upon yearly supplemental contracts and teaching assignments; and temporary for the drama program itself, always susceptible to cutbacks due to failing tax levies and state budget constraints.

Change, an inevitability of living, makes all experience temporary. My work as a critical theatre teacher has been challenged and rewarded since working in the new facility. In *Temporary Stages II: Critically Oriented Drama Education*, I deepen my inquiry into the application of critical pedagogy in secondary theatre classrooms and rehearsals. I do this by examining the essential qualities of the first book—student self-agency and power relationships—by exploring the significance of a performance *place* in public school theatre and analyzing the competing opportunities and restrictions that accompany it.

Throughout the book, I have omitted, tweaked, refreshed, or rearranged material from the first edition. Additional chapters deepen the themes. This analysis includes reflections on events described in the first edition in light of the passage of time, expanded theoretical roots, and perceptions influenced by transitions to the new stage. In this second edition, I investigate how working in a top-notch facility complicates a critical approach to teaching and directing. I analyze how experiences in the new Performing Arts Center place previous experiences in relief. Committed still to the cause of student self-agency, I examine moments of new tensions that arise because of increased attention, raised stakes, greater danger, more expensive equipment, and broadened opportunities. I compare the process of teaching and directing before and after the construction of my high school's Performing Arts Center to strengthen my ability to teach theatre through a critical feminist lens—at times in spite of, and at other times solely because of—the new facility.

## RETHINKING POWER RELATIONSHIPS IN THE THEATRE CLASSROOM AND REHEARSAL

As I investigate the impact that the new Performing Arts Center makes on the pedagogical approach to my overall drama program, I question how altering power relationships guide theatre students toward greater student-driven learning in public high school. I examine the kinds of engagements associated with these efforts and question how teachers and students navigate together though these encounters. I suggest what theatre teachers, students, administrators, parents, and community residents can learn from the pursuit of risk-taking that transforms high school theatre practice. Reflection through the lenses of critical and feminist theory increases my understanding of how the teaching techniques and directing strategies that I employ and enjoy lead to innovative and meaningful learning experiences for both my students and me.

## SECTIONS OF THE BOOK

Throughout all three sections of this book, I investigate critical and feminist theories of pedagogy by probing key teaching and directing moments within three theatre courses and several theatre productions. The primary investigation of the book is how I tend to the critical-inquiry strategies that nurture my high school theatre program while it functions in a conventional institution. Specifically, I investigate the ways each participant exercises power in a classroom, rehearsal, and performance space to either promote social change or maintain the status quo. These moments occur when standard practice—which upholds cultural values that marginalize and silence—collides with alternative procedures that foster student self-agency for social justice. Each section of the book explores a component of Critically Oriented Drama Education. Section One looks at the value of teacher, as well as student, reflections, because reflection is a primary tool for growth in theatre education. Next, I examine accounts of high school principals who censor plays with contemporary political themes. These accounts are touchstones to the major thematic question of the book: How does power work both to constrain and liberate students, teachers, playwrights, administrators, and all others with vested interests in secondary theatre classwork and production? The first section concludes with an analysis of directing high school musicals within the construct of a critically oriented approach to drama education. I point out moments of tension in the search for pockets of resistance against stereotype and other potentially marginalizing conventions of musical theatre.

Section Two explores conditions that arise when teachers alter traditional classroom and rehearsal methods to increase conditions for student-driven learning. Included in this section is an evaluation of pitfalls and achievements in a theatre design and construction course. In this section, I offer new methods for notifying students of casting decisions and experimenting with understudy casts. I contemplate the sense of loss experienced by students and teachers who move out from comfortable and familiar rehearsal and performance spaces into expansive and newly equipped auditoriums. Finally, I rationalize the reservations teachers hold when considering the new power structures that are sure to accompany their new theatres.

In Section Three, I examine class projects and play productions that tackle controversial topics. I study the impact of these experiences on students, teachers, and community members. Included in this section are techniques for carefully engaging students in devised theatre for social change. Additionally, this section analyzes whiteness as a position of dominance, as manifested through choices by playwrights, actors, and directors in high school theatre classes, rehearsals, and performances. The final chapter probes the augmented responsibilities placed upon students and directors when they invite audiences to watch the plays they stage that hold serious social significance.

The book does not progress chronologically, nor do I discuss the critical impact of the Performing Arts Center sequentially in "before" and "after" segments. Rather, the focus remains on the opportunities for critical inquiry—some examined, some missed—that continue to emerge in my teaching and directing. I discuss these occasions in relationship to topic and theme, not necessarily by the order in which they occurred, to achieve a thorough investigation of praxis. It is my hope that readers will relate some of the questions I pose for myself, as I reflect on my own practice through the lenses of critical and feminist pedagogy, to their own classroom and directing environments. I hope that this book will prompt more questions, like those I model in this book, to enrich readers' reflections and deepen their own understandings of what, how, and why they teach theatre in high school.

## PROMOTING CRITICAL CONSCIOUSNESS: THE CODE CLASSROOM AND REHEARSAL

Public perception holds that drama/theatre experiences in the public school are alternative to "regular" classroom instruction. Drama teachers work collaboratively with students who participate actively, and curricula encourage creativity and self-expression. I believe the collaborative process of play production is what prompts education researcher Theodore Sizer to remark that drama is one of few activities in high school through which students and teachers get to know one another (Sizer 1984, 82). Sustained conversations about the connection between theatre arts and students' life experiences often lead to self-disclosure uncharacteristic of regular classrooms.

But do these differences necessarily lead to a critical theatre pedagogy? On the surface, theatre arts classrooms look and sound different from many non-arts classrooms, but methods of teaching and play selection typically uphold dominant ideologies embedded in standard schooling. What models inspire us to reconceive our drama programs as sites for resistance, critical inquiry, and social change?

A critical pedagogy helps students learn to perceive social, political, and economic contradictions that surround them (Freire 1970). A critical pedagogy transforms practices of standard education, which originate from an ideology that favors white, middle-class, European-descended, able-bodied, heterosexual Americans (hooks 1998, 12; 1994, 26–27). Gordon Berry and Joy Keiko Asamen claim that "critical consciousness" engages students in the collective work of changing the conditions of people in our society who have often been excluded, misrepresented, victimized, and marginalized (2001, 359). Theatre teachers who embrace a critical pedagogy seek production styles and classroom projects that help students see how to change existing systems of inequality—both visible and invisible—in their schools, their communities, and their nation.

> Theatre teachers who embrace a critical pedagogy seek production styles and classroom projects that help students see how to change existing systems of inequality—both visible and invisible—in their schools, their communities, and their nation.

Self-agency in the classroom contradicts traditional notions of education, where the teacher is the only individual who operates with authority. Self-agency breeds a form of democracy that alters the power of the teacher's authority. In a true democratic classroom, students would devise, lead, and execute all of their projects without the presence of an authority figure. This form of idealistic authority will not take place in a high school classroom because 1) since students are minors, a teacher must always be present, and 2) the teacher ultimately determines how students earn grades.

Throughout this book, I use the words *democracy*, *democratic classroom*, *democratic theatre design*, and other variations of the term to mean a form of social interaction among students and teacher that guides students toward self-agency. When the teacher purposely adopts a teaching style and establishes a classroom or rehearsal atmosphere that requires teens to make decisions that affect the outcome of projects, they become actively engaged in the teaching and learning process alongside the teacher. This form of engagement holds the potential to foster critical consciousness in students.

The second edition replaces the wordy "critically conscious production-oriented classroom," or "CCPOC," with the streamlined term "critically oriented drama education," or "CODE." For the second edition, I rename the term I give for the tone and design of the classes and rehearsals discussed in the book. As I inquire about critical moments in my practice, I invite readers to wonder with me and reflect on their own experiences in relationship to CODE.

A CODE classroom or rehearsal is one where

1. class work or rehearsal is aimed at presenting original live theatre to the (sometimes paying) public;
2. altered power relationships between teacher and students make students central to the artistic evolution of the production;
3. a "democratic" construct operates in the classroom, whereby the teacher's voice is not *the* voice of authority, but one authority among many;
4. tacit knowledge that students bring into the class or play combines with group dialogue, team writing, designing, constructing, and planning. As a result, understanding about theatre, self, and humanity not only emerges from but also prompts continued student inquiry; and
5. action for social justice is a goal of the course and is fostered through group dynamics that promote students' awareness of societal difference and privilege.

The three CODE courses that I discuss in the book are Theatre Design, Play Production, and Social Issues Theatre. These three courses, though different in purpose, represent in structure and style the five tenets of a CODE classroom. Each is an elective; students meet for 50 minutes a day, five days a week, for 18 weeks. Students who enroll in CODE courses range in age from 14-year-old inexperienced freshmen to 18-year-old drama club officers. Finally, in the second edition, I draw upon several co-curricular plays that the Drama Club has produced that involve students within the same age range, which are rehearsed solely after school. For example, often the theatre courses and drama program reflect more diversity, such as gender-orientation, race, ethnicity, class, academic strength, and weight, than found in the overall student body.

## NATIONAL TRENDS DEMONSTRATE NEED FOR CRITICAL INVESTIGATION OF SECONDARY THEATRE EDUCATION

Creativity, a primary feature of arts education, is a key component of the competencies necessary for student success, identified as 21st Century Skills (Ballanca and Brandt 2010). President Barack Obama advocates, "In addition to giving our children the science and math skills they need to compete in the new global context, we should also encourage the ability to think creatively that comes from a meaningful arts education" (BarackObama.com 2009). The College Board likewise recognizes that commitment to strengthening the arts in all schools will lead U.S. education in a new direction. The College Board asserts that arts programming is "an effective tool to improving education in general and as a solution to achieving access and equity for all students" (*Arts at the Core* 2009). At the same time, Secretary of State Arne Duncan addressed a letter to school and education community leaders across the nation announcing a forthcoming survey of arts education. He wrote, "The arts can help students become tenacious, team-oriented problem solvers who are confident and able to think creatively. These qualities can be especially important in improving learning among students from economically disadvantaged circumstances" (*Arts at the Core* 2009).

A 2012 survey, conducted by the National Center for Education Statistics, released dismaying findings:

- The number of theatre programs available to teens in high schools decreased by 3 percent in the last decade.
- Only half of secondary theatre programs are taught primarily in dedicated rooms with special equipment.
- The percentage of schools with theatre specialists is small compared to teacher specialists for music and visual arts.
- Lower income children are 28 percent less likely to have access to theatre arts instruction in their schools compared to affluent school districts. (*Arts Education in Public Elementary and Secondary Schools* 2012)

Despite support in word by political leaders, research points to widening discrepancies in theatre education among school districts across the country. This is all the more reason to scrutinize the ways we teach theatre, better guiding all students toward self-agency for transformative social equity. Therefore, the theatre classroom/rehearsal space is a logical site from which to write about restructuring power in the public school. Self-expression and teacher/student bonding are primary features of the theatre-education process.

These same features should make drama a mainstay for experimentation with alterations in the *placement of power*, in the *expressions of conflicting or ambiguous identity*, and in the exercise of *student independence*.

Some high school theatre education programs across the country are led by teachers who make student-developed, socially critical theatre central to their practice (Lazarus 2012; Lement and Dunakin 2005; Ressler 2002). Other theatre teachers have documented experiments that pursue the notion of participatory relationships in classroom and production (Stevenson and Deasy 2005; Conrad 2004). For the most part, however, theatre programs reflect the values of a dominant ideology that privilege students commonly viewed as "normal" (Seidel 1991, 3–5; Strut and Fret 2012, 20).

Great disparity exists in the quality, depth, and breadth of high school theatre programs in the United States (*Arts at the Core* 2009; Consortium of National Art Education Associations 1995). If contemporary high school theatre textbooks are evidence, most high school theatre programs retain the presentation of "safe" and non-controversial plays from the high school canon, use teacher-instructed skill and technique, and rely on standard rehearsal procedures. Alternative approaches are alluded to, but rarely detailed. It is idealistic to hope that what I envision in this book is attainable in every system of formal education. In fact, in this second edition, I question to what extent attaining this vision is hampered or ushered forward by a rags-to-riches upgrade in facilities. Though I write from a specific and localized perspective, I hope other drama teachers can adapt portions of this vision to suit their individual contexts.

## SEVEN GUIDING CONCEPTS OF *TEMPORARY STAGES II*

Seven concepts guide my interpretation of a critical secondary theatre pedagogy.

### Power

Power is different from authority. When I first began teaching, I had authority vested in me automatically by the institutionalized position of teacher, but I didn't have power because students weren't sure if I was "on their side." (As a novice theatre teacher, I was too overwhelmed to be on anyone's side but my own.) Over the years, I gained students' trust. As they ascribed power to me in my classroom and rehearsals, I exercised my power in the service of their increasing self-agency. Thus, I don't believe that if I give my students power, I have less of my own. Power is not something we gain, steal, own, or choose to give up or parcel out like bread. The French theorist Michel Foucault conceptualizes power as something that individuals exercise in different ways and in different settings (McNay 1992, 148). Instead of thinking about power as teachers *with* and students *without*, I consider that teachers exercise power in relation to students who exercise power in relation to the course, the classroom learning environment, and the climate of the school. These contexts, and the events that occur therein, impact the work of teachers and students daily.

The central markers of power in my community's high school are skills, age, class, and gender. Adolescents exert their powers in ways that contrast shortcomings. A student struggling to maintain a C in sophomore English might be a fine public speaker in her church; an excellent student in Public Speaking might not make the basketball team; a leader of the Drama Club might be suspended for bringing alcohol on a school trip. Age difference divides teachers from students, and divides students who can drive and hold jobs from those who cannot. The kinds of clothes and hairstyles kids wear, the cars they drive, and the after-school activities in which they participate are manifestations of class difference. Gender difference causes students to be targets of ridicule when their appearances and/or behaviors conform closely to what students perceive as negative gender stereotypes. These stereotypes prompt them to target others with words like *slut*, *cheerleader*, *fag*, *dyke*, and *jock*. Although skills, age, class, and gender are more subtle than "big issues" like race and poverty, Elizabeth Ellsworth contends that teachers and students nevertheless use these as a basis for sorting, grading, rewarding, ignoring, celebrating, marginalizing, and disciplining (1997, 2).

## Authority

Authority is a position of self-government through which one develops new knowledge and aids others to develop new knowledge for themselves (Britzman 1991, 230). In the classroom, my authority as teacher takes various forms: I am the person who knows more about the course subject than the students, has the maturity to set realistic boundaries, has experience to determine when a risk is too dangerous, can view the course or production as a whole, and has confidence that students will become proud of their work. At the same time, I am a guide of students' exploration into theatre, not claiming to know (and claiming not to know) everything, willing to take risks for and with students, creating a classroom where they learn to depend more on each other and themselves than on me, and engaging them in projects of social significance that speak to them in order to encourage them to notice and resist oppressive forces in their lives.

I want students to experience an authority in my classes that is based on cooperation among and between themselves and me. I want to nurture students' confidence to implement their own plans for learning about theatre. I don't want students to become independent thinkers by following directions for my productions on my terms. I want to begin from a standpoint of collaboration: I want to see my students as independent rather than subordinate on the first day of class or rehearsal (Belenky et al. 1986, 224). In other words, I want my authority to come from shared experiences rather than through exertion of my power or status.

I want students to experience an authority in my classes that is based on cooperation among and between themselves and me.

## Student Artistry

Concepts of power and authority in a democratic high school theatre program are not without contradiction and paradox. The very idea of collaborative teacher/student artistry poses a contradiction. As an artist, I like to experiment with concept and style. When I conceptualize a production (casting the character of Prometheus in *Prometheus Bound* with five half-masked actors who speak in collective voice, for example), am I imposing my authority on students by asking them to go along with me? Sometimes students will work democratically on a production in class while I am directing actors conventionally after school. What kind of authority do I have then?

Contemplating teens' theatrical artistry prompts teachers to ask what the primary purpose of secondary theatre education is. Can students develop artistic quality when the skills they learn for making that art come from each other rather than from professionals? When a democratic approach intentionally minimizes competition associated with attention to the so-called top performers, does the product suffer in quality? Or can students who are not receiving professional training achieve a quality product because they invest in shared ownership resulting from effective cooperative learning?

How do the politics of a school influence students' artistic freedoms? How do economic conditions enhance or hinder the artistic potential of students? How much theatre training by professionals in the field can students receive in a high school theatre program managed by one theatre teacher? How much theatre training will students absorb over the course of four years in school districts that offer theatre experiences only to high school students?

## Incomplete Understandings

Because the knowledge that students generate leads to more questions, the learning process is constantly activated. Therefore, my understandings and my students' understandings are always only partial. When I presume full knowledge, I stagnate, and I can do little more than replicate past productions. Because I can never know all of what my students think, and they can never know all of what I am thinking (and none of us thoroughly knows what we ourselves are thinking), our understanding agitates questions. This state of unrest gives momentum to novelty and innovation. I don't want students who will echo me (Belenky et al. 1986, 225); I want students who will create new sounds.

Many of us learned, and were taught to teach, in ways that provide a sense of security through conformity and imitation, as in, "If we learn this, then we can pass that." But teaching, directing, instructing, guiding, listening to, and engaging adolescent students in the discovery and self-understanding of the dynamics of human interaction through the medium of drama is sometimes incomplete and seldom linear. Personal bias, an unclear direction, and even a tone of voice taken the wrong way create multiple interpretations that complicate understanding. We move forward and backward, sideways and diagonally. We wait, hesitate, stop, start over. As others have noted, it is unsettling to consider that knowledge production operates on ambiguity and indecision.[1] In this book I analyze the inconsistencies, breakdowns, and breakthroughs that occur in teaching theatre, for unless I understand the ways in which I exercise my own power and understand the implications of that exercise, I limit my ability to assist students as they exercise the power that they own.

Unless I understand the ways in which I exercise my own power and understand the implications of that exercise, I limit my ability to assist students as they exercise the power that they own.

## Change

While conservative educators have historically perceived the public school as a potential site for transformation, they have also found the liberating, secular forces of public education dangerous. This view has led to reactionary and repressive reform movements. Ira Shor describes the framework of our working environments as "entrenched traditionalism." He asserts that most of those with whom we work (colleagues, administrators, parents, and students) come to our programs with fixed expectations and values, and with experiences that have taught them that schooling is something to tolerate as best they can, in a place where questions are answered more than asked (1992, 96–99). Jennifer Gore observes that teachers who consciously "decenter" their authority still find students looking to them for approval, guidance, and assessment, even when the teacher downplays the influence of grades. Gore surmises that the "progressive pedagogical practice of 'negotiating' with students is frequently much less open than we pretend or believe" (1993, 143).

The location from which I reflect on the content of the first edition of *Temporary Stages* is radically altered. My students and I have access every schoolday to the new Performing Arts Center. Preparations for the upgrade in status—for example, moving props and costumes from a musty, smelly, flooded storage space under a junior high bathroom to a large, open, airy loft above a spacious scene shop in the new Performing Arts Center—were accompanied by reservation and tension on my part, and envy on the part of others. One colleague, who coaches basketball in both gymnasiums at our school, labeled the new auditorium the "Taj Mahal."

I also use the word *change* in the context of critical pedagogy. Critical theorists scrutinize inequalities of power in educational systems and question conditions which reinforce beliefs that have become "internalized to the point where [students] abandon the very aspiration to question or change their lot in life" (Barbules and Berk 1999, 50). Transformative education is a titanic concept. If a solitary theatre teacher like me questions the impact that a major change in location makes on my pedagogical approach to teaching and directing, it is no wonder that shifting the power-center of the national education system to make room for greater equity for all is a slow and challenging effort. However, we can contribute to change one theatre program at a time.

## Privilege

To promote change and embrace difference, I have to unlearn my own privilege; I must question what I am biased toward and how my biases manifest themselves in classes and rehearsals. Interrogating my biases means I have to give up the desire and security to believe that I am right. Critical self-assessment of characteristics that place me in positions of some privilege in the United States—that I am white, heterosexual, Christian, middle-class, able-bodied, educated, and supported by family—not only keeps me humble and skeptical, it tempers my temptation to feel safe in being right and knowing the answers (Tatum 1997, McIntosh 1998, Denevi 2004). The fact is, although I can now catch myself in my own assumptions, there are many times when I teach in what Ellsworth calls "the state of unknowing" (1989, 110).

In a democratic society, people make decisions after assessing multiple points of view. Information we glean from various perspectives remains partial because complete knowing is impossible, yet we are obligated to take action. Therefore, when I make my "unknowing" known to my students, I begin a communication that moves beyond information exchange and into the realm of questioning. Performance artist David Gonzalez told a recent conference audience that Ancient Greece bore twins to the world—theatre and democracy.[2] Even as I teach with the aim of fostering democratic theatre classrooms, I wonder if democracy itself is an ideal that upholds dominant ideology—just as theatre productions can reinforce hegemonic notions as much as challenge them. Democratic dialogues offer opportunities for students to recognize—and for me to remember—that understanding privilege doesn't provide answers; it positions us for inquiry. It is from this place of questioning that students and teachers can become agents for social change.

As I write about diversity in this book, it is with an awareness that Americans, myself included, are quick to categorize ourselves into binaries that allow for facile judgment. When describing the dimensions of lesbian and homosexual relationships to students in a recent Social Issues Theatre class, guest speaker Sandy Mencer explained:

> There is a continuum, I believe, that all people sit on. Some are extremely straight, and some are extremely gay. Some know early on; others suppress and deny for a long time. Some are bi-sexual and can be as attracted to a man or a woman. Some women can be attracted to and have relationships with men, even though they are lesbian; some men can be attracted to women, even though they are gay.
>
> (Mencer, February 28, 2012)

Such spectrums apply to all categories of labeled individuals. When we think about diversifying our theatre programs in schools dominated by students appearing to be Caucasian, we might check ourselves before signifying race as the defining element of diversity. Our ethnic and racial make-up is marked more by hybridity than singularity, and categories of race and ethnicity are often contested and always changing. Students heading into college are challenged to think about race and ethnicity in terms of a spectrum of power and mixed identities because the politics of affirmative action require them to pack their cultural identity into a tiny, labeled box. I remind myself to consider diversity in terms of gender, age, physical ability, fitness level, academic acumen, socio-economic class, and interests, as well as race and ethnicity. Still, I wonder: can we cultivate enough diversity in our school's arts programs to stage *Ragtime*?

## Place

Critical secondary theatre educators who are committed to producing theatre productions with teenagers that unequivocally lead toward self-agency and social justice work within systems that inherently restrict. Even when conditions in such spaces are altered to give voice to others, all participants may not feel equal safety to speak, nor may all voices be respected and engaged with by others (Redmond 2010, 8). A new theatre intensifies restrictions while simultaneously widening opportunities for student liberation.

An aesthetically pleasing 738-seat theatre designed with the latest in theatre technology is valued, admired, celebrated, communal, and educational. It is also tradition-oriented, dominated, envied, dangerous, territorial, and disrespected.

An aesthetically pleasing 738-seat theatre designed with the latest in theatre technology is valued, admired, and celebrated; it is communal and educational. It is also tradition-oriented, dominated, envied, dangerous, territorial, and disrespected. Ng points out that teaching sites in the public school are not by definition democratic spaces. He asserts, "To pretend that [they] can be is to deny that hierarchy and institutional power exist. It is to delude ourselves that democracy and empowerment can be achieved by goodwill alone" (1995, 140).

A theatre teacher in a new auditorium will be confronted by new technologies that may require the advice of and training by theatre technology professionals; events in the facility may be run by a business manager; and the facility itself may be managed by others who have authority to approve or deny use. The more complex power structures that accompany a new theatre alter conditions in which critical theatre educators interact with colleagues, administrators, and students.

Pedagogy of place shares tenets of critical theory. David A. Gruenewald explains:

> Human communities, or places, are politicized, social constructions that often marginalize individuals. [...] If place-based educators seek to connect place with self and community, they must identify and confront the ways that power works through places to limit [their] possibilities. [...] Their place-based pedagogy must, in other words, be critical.
>
> (Gruenewald 2003, 315)

Place-based pedagogy primarily examines educational programs that take place in natural surroundings such as parks, preserves, and nature sanctuaries (Redmond 2010; Stevenson 2008; Ruitenberg 2005; Gruenewald 2003). But I believe any space—natural or constructed—reserved for theatre that is crafted, rehearsed, and performed under the abiding grace of the creative spirit is a sanctuary. A new theatre fundamentally changes the surroundings in which theatre teachers and students study, rehearse, and perform. Therefore, place-based pedagogy helps unpack the additional conflicts, missed connections, disconnections, and competing goals that a new performing arts center fosters in high school theatre education.

## THE ADVENTURE OF TEACHING THEATRE FOR SELF-AGENCY AND CRITICAL CONSCIOUSNESS

Cindy Brown describes the near-perfect teaching environment that the subject of her study enjoyed for much of her 30 years teaching in the public schools:

> I got into a position where I had autonomy; I mean it was like no one could touch me. [...] No one ever censored me. I've never had a principal that read my plays or even asked to. [...] I knew I would never be questioned. Certainly I've been called up because they thought that something was too adult or something, but I've always been backed up by my administration. (Anonymous 1999, 38)

Likely, many high school theatre teachers will never find ourselves in the teacher's situation that Brown describes because we might change school systems during our careers, stop teaching and change careers, or lose our jobs because of decreased arts education funding. While longevity at a single institution fosters a seniority status that can envelop a high school theatre teacher in an aura of the "magically untouchable," the community's conservative and/or dominant ideology upon which one's public school institution sits often grounds his or her "dynasty." Staging edgy material without thoroughly preparing ourselves, our students, their parents, our administrators, and/or our community may put our jobs at risk. Even with strong administrative support, the public school system becomes at once a liberating and confining place to teach and create theatre. Recognizing the potential for secondary theatre programs to become sites for altering traditional modes of power to benefit student self-agency, Brown comments, "Empowering students is the essence of education and few have the opportunity to empower students as theatre teachers do" (37).

If we want to help our students exercise power, we will come upon times as we teach when we are confident enough to take a risk, and likewise so unsure that we seek—often from a patriarchal authority figure—permission to take the risk. A supportive administrator once advised me that it is sometimes better to ask for forgiveness than permission. When do we take that chance? The mainstream is wide and alive, but its by-waters are also active. As we cross from mainstream theatre teaching into currents of critical pedagogy, we may slip into turbulence. We must climb out and cross again, on a different pattern of stones. With persistence, we can discover new territories that celebrate the full potential of high school theatre education. Making opportunities for our students to gain and practice critical self-agency is the purpose of the adventure. This book is a tour through the temporary changes and different stages of one teacher's adventure with her students and their parents, her administrators and community … thus far.

## NOTES

1 Excellent inquiries into how the physical positioning of furniture and equipment in public institutions revises constructions of power from a feminist perspective include Gore (1992, 1993), Luke (1992), Ellsworth (1997), and Lather (2001).

2 David Gonzalez delivered a keynote address at the American Alliance for Theatre and Education National Conference in Louisville, KY, August 12, 2012.

# Chapter 2

## Characterizing CODE Classrooms and Rehearsal Spaces

The self-dubbed "Theatre Studio," an oversized classroom where I teach most classes, is sandwiched within the math and science corridor. In addition to the 24 black bucket-seat chairs that I arrange in four sets of six chairs, each divided into two rows of three and angled toward the center, the "studio" includes a teacher's desk with a backless swivel chair, a short blackboard, a glass-window storage booth that houses an old dimmer board, a dozen infrequently used Fresnel lights hung over the center of the room, an eight-inch-high platform stage measuring 10 × 16 feet, computers, and a computer-linked projector and screen. Before the Performing Arts Center was constructed, it was in this room that all co-curricular production work took place. The Theatre Studio was adapted for all needs theatrical: academic classes, rehearsals, set construction, properties and costume construction and storage, meetings, and performances all took place in this room.[1]

The new Performing Arts Center includes a postage-stamp-sized office which I utilize most often during after-school rehearsals and performances. The day-to-day management of activities, however, takes place in the Theatre Studio that allows no privacy and few secrets. Discussions over grades, student behavior, peer issues, letters of recommendation, rehearsal schedules, agendas, and other significant responsibilities that comprise the inner workings of the drama program are transparent to students, parents, and administrators. The open space reinforces the notion of democratic engagement.[2]

For the most part, however, as I work in this classroom within a modest school building built approximately 40 years ago, I conform to the routines of public schooling. Day by day, evening by evening, I plan activities to suit 50-minute class periods, grade papers and projects with conventional rubrics, meet with parents, follow procedures for student discipline, comply with school rules, learn to incorporate new technologies, unpack the latest state mandates for English and theatre arts education, and prepare students with test-taking strategies to help them pass rigid, point-assessed standardized tests.

## SELF-REFLECTION: THE GATEWAY TO CRITICALLY CONSCIOUS CLASSROOMS AND REHEARSALS

When I refer to Critically Oriented Drama Education or CODE throughout this book, it is with the understanding that I strive to engage students in theatre arts experiences that challenge them to think about the positions of privilege and oppression they occupy each day. Amid the daily constraints of my school environment, I struggle to make ever-present a spirit of equity. This spirit manifests itself in various ways: when a senior class leader, making a wasteful computational error, follows the advice of a freshman; when a Latina's brief script unpacks resentment of dominant white ideology; or when students, knowing that sarcasm is a popular tool for communication among young people, write satirical scenes that clearly point to the senselessness of driving intoxicated. These engagements always arrive sporadically; they are always fragmented, and always short-lived. The forthcoming chapters describe moments of collision in one public school theatre program and present a collage of *critical possibility*.

The forthcoming chapters describe moments of collision in one public school theatre program and present a collage of critical possibility.

A CODE classroom/rehearsal is not inherently critically conscious, but it contains aspects that complement critically conscious teaching and directing. Students who enroll in a CODE class or accept a role in a play commit to public performance, and this aim heightens their desire to achieve high standards. In traditional classrooms where students work only for a grade, typical grading scales allow students to achieve an "A" at 90 percent. When theatre students prepare for a public performance, 90 percent effort is not good enough to shape a quality, polished production and to give performances fueled by the contagious energy that the pride of hard work generates.[3] I often tell ensembles that if each of them is not pushing themselves to 150 percent, the show will be less than stellar; theatre students understand full and complete commitment, and a production-oriented classroom, like rehearsals, generates this energy.

## QUALITIES OF A CODE CLASSROOM

Because a production-oriented classroom is fueled by the looming display of teens' self-image, students work hard to do their best. They have more riding on the line than in a typical class where they are working for a letter that appears on a computer screen. Students from disparate social groups collaborate in small groups to create an artistic performance. Dialogue in small groups fosters “reflection on students’ own values, perspectives, and biases in a safe and comfortable setting” (Kumagai and Lypson 2009, 784). These conversations often include self-disclosing vulnerabilities which invariably touch upon inequities related to race, ethnicity, class, gender, sexual orientation, religion, appearance, and/or language differences. When part of a project breaks down, the crisis is intensified; as students work to rebuild, their assumptions, biases, and values are often challenged. The reflection questions posited at various stages through the course capitalize on these challenges. They ask students to shift their gaze from themselves to others and to contemplate conditions of injustice among their classmates and, by extension, their school and community. Carefully constructed reflection questions nudge students toward critical self-awareness.

A good critical reflection question is open-ended, because if I am to model justice and equity in a CODE classroom, students must trust that I am listening to their multiple points of view. Reflection questions, as Phillip Taylor points out, are best when phrased broadly, which keeps responses to various categories “open to the multiplicity of happenings and events that can occur” in the classroom (2003, 120–121). For example, “Please describe a decision we made as a class that you were initially skeptical of? What factor(s) influenced a change in your perception?” are open-ended questions that ask students to evaluate the process of collaboration. I seek diverging opinions to account for students whose perspectives are different from the majority (108–09). As some of the comments in this book demonstrate, the lone voices of dissent make me reflect the most as a teacher and director, and often those who are most critical instigate action for change in my teaching and directing methods.

A good critical reflection question is open-ended, because if I am to model justice and equity in a CODE classroom, students must trust that I am listening to their multiple points of view.

Teachers may award points to reflection writings that contribute to a final course grade. In a CODE classroom, abundant self-reflection dominates tests, quizzes, research papers, and other traditional forms of evaluation. Yet reflections can be evaluated for depth, thoroughness, and clarity. In a CODE class, students are unlikely to earn points by correctly answering test questions, but they earn points by contemplatively and completely responding to reflection questions. Reflective writing suits an unconventional course—one without tests and research papers—to a conventional educational system that requires grades.[4]

Reflective evaluations are evidence, and evidence is the seed of theory. Students’ personal narratives and teacher observations comprise the evidence that supports the critical and feminist theories I use in this book to discuss critically conscious teaching in rehearsals and production-oriented classwork. In a self-energizing cycle, these theories inform my practice, my practice responds to observations, and observations question the theories.

## POSITIONING THE LISTENING EAR

I have learned to listen to my students. My interpretations are highly subjective, as I am influenced by past experience, ingrained notions of authority, mandates to enforce school policies, and individual relationships with students. My reflections are valuable, but I strive for *objectivity* by weighing my subjectivity against the collective outcome of students' self-reflections. This objectivity makes teaching and learning bi-directional (Kumagai and Lypson 2009). When I read students' reflections with a willingness to accept their criticism, I maintain the flexibility necessary to the ongoing improvement of the courses and drama program. This openness, Taylor asserts, "can remove the stifling shackles of expertise […] and revise conventional understandings of authority" (Taylor 2003, 132).

I am a teaching artist committed to examining the theatre work that I and my students engage in, to better understand how my intuition, beliefs, and values shape my choices as a teacher and director. Reflexivity supports my decisions on a daily basis. I want my students to practice reflexive thinking in order to better understand the deep-seated beliefs and desires that drive their actions and fuel their dreams.

I read students' reflective responses, curious as to how they do the following:

1. recognize ways new knowledge emerges from the group;
2. observe how power circulates in different social settings to foster or hinder efforts for fair and equitable treatment of all members of society;
3. notice the relevance of learning to their lives;
4. understand that collaboration requires all participants to be co-learners; and
5. perceive multiple ways that theatre can function.

Broadly-worded but framed specifically for each class and occasionally a drama club production, good critical reflection questions draw responses from students that address altered power relationships, co-authority, student artistry, unfixed understandings, change, privilege, and significance of place. Critical reflection questions I asked students whose comments contributed to this book include variations of the following:

1. In what way(s) do you think differently about theatre, yourself, education, and/or your school and/or community as a result of taking this class?
2. What were some decisions that you had to make as a class before you could begin to write, sketch, or construct?
3. Describe some of the challenges that you encountered and/or observed other groups encountering. Consider a variety of variables, such as individual differences, team communication, territoriality, foresight, strengths and weaknesses of team members, trial and error, and the constraints or dangers of your work environments. Why do you think these challenges/setbacks occurred?
4. What insight have you gained about your peers?
5. From which student in the class did you learn the most? Why?
6. What have you learned about yourself from working collaboratively with your peers?
7. How did performing in the new auditorium complement or complicate your efforts?
8. What suggestions can you offer so that the course can be stronger for the next class?
9. Describe one time when you felt privileged or oppressed in this class. What factor(s) contributed to that feeling?
10. At what point in the semester do you believe you and your classmates shared the greatest equity? Why?

## REFLECTION AS EVALUATION: WHAT ABOUT GRADES?

Grades are necessary cogs of the system, and after years of formal schooling students enter a CODE class expecting to earn grades conventionally. But because CODE approaches learning unconventionally, alternative assessment strategies deviate from the norm. In CODE, the detail and depth of students' ongoing assigned reflections comprise a third of their grades. Another third is students' participation in the final production. Individual assignments that contribute to team and class decisions, as well as points for daily focused on participation, constitute the remaining third.

Because my students and I often drift into new "learning terrains" in CODE, what students are learning can be new knowledge for me, too. Thus, I withhold my comments and the points I award for their efforts until after they have evaluated their own work. Because CODE aims to promote students' self-constructed knowledge and agency to change oppressive social conditions, I respond to their reflections with comments and probing questions. Reflections become a series of evaluations that chart the *dimensions* more than the progressions of students' development.

In a reflective evaluation, students contemplate peer interactions, tacit knowledge, misjudgments, discoveries, ownership of and public response to projects, and benefits and drawbacks of democratic theatre education. Conventional educational systems mandate evaluation in the form of letter grades. In the CODE classroom, assignments requiring thoughtful and thorough written reflections give students points toward their mandated grades. Reflection writings enable the mainstream (graded) and the alternative (self-teaching) to coexist when students use reflexivity to evaluate emerging critical consciousness.

## NOTES

1 For a detailed list of qualifications that should be evident in a working theatre classroom, see Bennett (2001, 3). For a comprehensive description of facilities for optimum secondary theatre education, see "Opportunities-to-Learn Standards for Arts Education" (1995).

2 For descriptions of school spaces that foster democratic pedagogy, see Holt (1982).

3 I acknowledge an anonymous theatre teacher for this point, which he stated with eloquence and passion in a late-night open-mic session that featured teachers and teaching artists during the 2012 International Thespian Festival.

4 Some teachers nurture critically conscious students by getting the grade out of the way on the first day of class with a contract that guarantees an A or a B. If I am to uphold an atmosphere of critical consciousness, students cannot be second-guessing my agenda, because assessment in critical classroom practice is a team effort between students and teacher. Joe Norris (1995) believes the contract alleviates student anxiety that blocks attention to the work, explaining, "Was I the coach encouraging them to do better or was I a reminder that their marks were going down? The contract of the 'A' removed this fear and enabled them to do 'A' quality work" (302).

# Chapter 3

## Balancing Passion and Censorship

In 2011, the United States honored the tenth anniversary of the September 11th tragedy. In the fall of that year, the drama program at Johnstown High School in Johnstown, Pennsylvania, faced community uproar over their plans to produce the musical *Kismet*. Set in ancient Baghdad, *Kismet* features Muslim characters, and Johnstown is the community over which Flight 93 flew and crashed during the 9/11 attacks. The principal's rationale for censoring the production was to protect students from public criticism. Instead of *Kismet*, the school's drama director opted for a solid component of the high school musical theatre canon, *Oklahoma*. National Public Radio reporter Scott Simon queried:

> But does the [Johnstown] school district know that one of the signature characters [of *Oklahoma*] is a peddler who comes to the Oklahoma territory of gushers and sodbusters to find freedom and his own fortune? He's from Persia. His name is Ali Hakim.
>
> (Simon 2011)

Because *Kismet* and *Oklahoma* were popularized during the "Golden Age of Musicals," they emerged from the same cultural milieu. Both shows draw upon Arab stereotypes, but because of its obvious reference to Arab culture through setting, *Kismet* was censored. *Oklahoma* was permitted, apparently because its reference to Arab culture through a supporting character was more subtle. Through both censorship and sanction, the institutionalized system of public education often forces high school theatre programs to uphold dominant ideologies embedded in U.S. culture. Drama teachers need models that inspire us to reconceive our drama programs as sites for true resistance, critical inquiry, and social justice.

## PROMOTING CRITICAL CONSCIOUSNESS THROUGH DRAMA/THEATRE EDUCATION

In *Acting, Learning and Change*, Jan Mandell and Jennifer Lynn Wolf recount how urban, immigrant students responded to traditional musicals by recreating them to fit their own lives (2003, 66). It is interesting to note that the author introduced original scriptwriting to her students only after she recognized a clash between standard storylines and musical styles and the interests of her inner-city students. Why is the status quo invisible when students represent mainstream America? Secondary theatre educators must teach and stage plays in rural and suburban areas, as well as in inner cities, in ways that aim to liberate consciousness. Otherwise, high school theatre education will perpetuate norms that silence.

Secondary theatre educators must teach and stage plays in rural and suburban areas, as well as in inner cities, in ways that aim to liberate consciousness. Otherwise, high school theatre education will perpetuate norms that silence.

One play at a time, high school theatre programs are changing community opinions on topics of social import, including suicide (*The Girl in the Mirror* by Bruce Jacoby, 1980), bullying and homophobia (*The Wrestling Season* by Laurie Brooks, 2001), school violence (*Bang Bang You're Dead* by William Mastrosimone, 1999) and sexual abuse (*Good Boys and True* by Roberto Aguirre-Sacasa, 2009 and *Spring Awakening* School Edition, licensed by Music Theatre International, 2011). Michael Peitz, former executive director of the Educational Theatre Association (EdTA), contemplates:

> There are times when we think students aren't ready to handle these issues and, in some ways, doesn't that deny the reality of the world the students live in since they deal with those issues every day? In all of these [works], the teachers are looking for plays that challenge their students' minds, as well as those of their audience.
>
> (Peitz, quoted in Loschert 2004, 22–23)

Edgy plays stir controversy often because they underscore difference. One "school edition" of a musical with edgy themes about drug addiction, sex, and AIDS is *RENT* (Jonathan Larson, 2009). The school edition is tamer, with most of the profanity removed. Nevertheless, for high school culture, the play's compelling questions provide fertile ground for bullying. Angel remains a cross-dressing homosexual in the school edition. After a performance of the play at San Mateo High School in San Francisco, a city with a large gay population, the actor who portrayed Angel was physically harassed and called "faggot." The director's original choice for that season's musical was *Dames at Sea* (book and lyrics by George Haimsohn and Robin Miller; music by Jim Wise, 1966), but he reflected that producing *RENT* is a "safer way than some of the ways some of the kids find out their information" about threats to their health caused by poor decision-making (Gallagher 2008).

Edgy plays stir controversy often because they underscore difference.

More and more schools are presenting contemporary plays that contain progressive messages. But as the Johnstown High School example demonstrates, reports are also on the rise of protesters, district refusals, angry phone calls, and other forms of community criticism of high school productions that deal with sensitive topical issues (Loschert 2004, 23). According to the 2012 Educational Theatre Association Survey of Theatre Education in United States High Schools, nearly one-fifth of the thousand teachers who responded to the survey reported the experience of administrative or community challenge to a show title. Furthermore, two-thirds of respondents dropped or changed language and/or other aspects of the show when pressed about the choice of the show (Ellis 2012). Teachers who attempt staging serious, meaningful plays that are subject to challenge (and especially those who succeed) are to be admired. But is it possible to incorporate elements that stir critical consciousness into productions of plays that represent the traditional high school canon?

To avoid bastardizing a "traditional, canonized" play, the effort must begin with a script that lends itself to critical inquiry. One Broadway musical often produced by high schools that centers on oppression is *Fiddler on the Roof* (lyrics by Sheldon Harnick; music by Jerry Bock; book by Joseph Stein, 1964). The typical staging of this popular and appealing show approximates the choreography, stage effects, and publicity reflected in Broadway productions, and acting styles often mimic inflection patterns of the professional adult actors who made the play famous. A critical approach to this musical turns some aspect(s) of the production around, inverting expectations. It invites students to investigate their own communities and act upon heightened awareness brought on by their inquiry.

The following suggestions can engage students in a critical approach to producing this musical. Critical theatre teachers might ask students to try these activities:

- List the differences between themselves and the characters in the play.
- Examine the power dynamics—both seen and unseen—among characters in the play, improvise scenes that connect those dynamics to their own lives, and incorporate an element of their improvised work into the show.
- Integrate visuals that provide a commentary on contemporary politics.
- Follow the production with a talk by displaced people from their community, or by community members whose Arab American families are disadvantaged by American–Israeli politics.
- Take collections at the door, or gather signatures on a petition, in support of an oppressed group in their community.

However, no matter how critically a high school stages *Fiddler on the Roof*, the production runs a great risk of 1) perpetuating elitism among cast members, as it features one major star, Tevye, and 2) marginalizing students from non-European cultures, for although its characters are oppressed Jews, they validate the experience of white Europeans.

Furthermore, directors must be cautious of taking liberties with any play that requires copyright permission, as the repercussions of copyright infringements by high schools can be expensive and embarrassing. More importantly, it is simply unethical to change a play without permission. It is an exciting challenge to stage popular plays with critically conscious overtones while keeping intact the integrity of the playwright and adhering to the publisher's contract. However, teachers can steer clear of the ethics dilemma altogether if they select canonized plays to adapt that are in the public domain (for example, the works of Shakespeare, Moliere, and Aeschylus), or guide students, as Mandell and Wolf do, in writing their own shows. Yet this is much easier said than done, and even harder to do consistently.

## DAILY DEMANDS AND TRADITION HINDER CHANGE

Because theatre teachers are immersed in the daily demands of teaching, staging, conferencing, and grading within a conventional education system, they often lack the time or energy to attend to factors that exclude underrepresented populations. For instance, when I wrote the first edition of this book in 2005, I had to consider that the classroom in which we often presented our plays was not handicapped accessible. I worried about the three narrow steps, guarded by a rail, that usher students and guests into my theatre studio/classroom. Anyone who is in a wheelchair must enter from a door behind the stage, and this requires securing ramps in two different places so the person can move from the classroom behind our stage into the audience area. In other words, my classroom is not handicapped accessible.

So, even as I search for pockets in my program where students can gain agency, I marginalize other students. I could blame my school district for constructing an entrance that restricts people with disabilities, but in my school district it is up to the teachers to point out problems with our classroom facilities and fill out work requests. Thus far, I haven't made that task a priority because almost all of the people who come into my classroom are able-bodied. As a result, immediate concerns arrest my attention, and I think infrequently about the obstacle the stairs present to others. Each of us must work within the bureaucratic systems that support us, and therein lies the great tension of critical educators: as we work daily in environments that confine and regulate, we must constantly seek "openings" and create therein occasions when students can develop and practice self-agency.

Thrilled that the new Performing Arts Center would endorse the theatre program and excited for the expanded opportunities it would give my students, I simultaneously held reservations that the autonomy I enjoyed would be curbed and the creative energies weakened that drive programs to be inventive when they have little at their disposal but an empty space. What new freedoms and constraints would I encounter as I continued to educate from a critical, feminist perspective in the new theatre?

Change is ongoing. From a Zen perspective, it is good that change is constant. This means that all social change, reactionary or progressive, is temporary. My predecessor had organized the standard school desks (seat and table top) in the room to face the curtains that had outlined a stage space. As soon as I took the job, I rearranged the desks into four quartets so that the center of the room was open. However, the standard desks were burdensome because we had to move them several times a day to make room for theatre activities, and whenever we performed a play in the room we had to lug the desks out of the room and down the hallway. I requested bucket seats that take up little space and stack neatly, and purchased clipboards for students to use as a writing surface. The difference satisfied me and pleased many students.

I took a semester's leave of absence to write the first edition of *Temporary Stages*, and the person who replaced me during my leave was my predecessor who had taught English and theatre in that room for 27 years. The first comment she made when she stopped by the classroom was "Well, these chairs have to go. Where are all the desks?" Although she didn't find the standard desks, she located six tables for students to sit behind in a conglomeration of seats that included metal folding chairs, the new bucket seats, and chairs with folding desktops. When I would walk into the room I felt claustrophobic. There was no room to walk! Students stared at the backs of heads! This configuration didn't reflect the openness, the democracy, of the theatre program I had worked to shape for more than a decade.

When I think about it, the evolution of my classroom seating plan is a spatial metaphor for the evolution of my democratic theatre pedagogy. The shifts in my classroom space—from desks-in-rows to bucket chairs and back to tables-in-rows—symbolize how conventional practices are always available to replace new models of non-traditional teaching. This is a warning. I accept temporary progress as I and my theatre students exercise power unconventionally. The two following in-depth accounts illuminate my point.

## LANGUAGE AND HOMOSEXUALITY PROMPT CENSORSHIP

One spring, the president of the Drama Club asked if she could take on an independent project. Tina wished to direct *The Shadow Box* (1977), a Pulitzer Prize-winning play by Michael Christofer. I read the play and was drawn to its moving portrayal of three families: a middle-aged man, his wife, and their son; a grown daughter and her aging mother; and a thirty-something homosexual couple. The play depicts each family in separate scenes, struggling to grasp the meaning of life as one member of each family faces death in a hospice-like retreat. Tina told me she had begun volunteering at the regional hospice to better relate to the play. I knew immediately that the mature language and homosexuality would be issues if a high school drama club were to produce the play in my community.

My school district is supported by a conservative-leaning, middle-class community that employs citizens through a mix of agriculture, light industry, and university-related jobs. Audiences here respond to plays performed by teenagers differently from audiences in more liberal or urban, or more conservative or rural, areas. Besides high school plays and musicals, live theatre is presented in my town by the university's theatre department and several community theatre companies. In my community, "adult" language in live performances by and/or for teenagers is generally considered vulgar and unacceptable; *hell*, *whore*, *damn*, and *shit* are acceptable. *Fuck* and *goddamn*, which are used throughout *The Shadow Box*, pose a risk. My students are aware of this. For example, when teens use obscenities in the school hallways and I tell them to "watch your language," most times they apologize quickly. Yet, like most American adolescents, they live in a world of contradiction. Social networks, Internet sites, television, film, and radio programs, and magazine content, promote the same styles of dress, codes of behavior, and language that schools often set rules against. At the same time, more and more teachers are integrating technology into their classrooms. Every two or three years, school administrators update rules that permit and restrict student access to the most recent innovations, leaving students to navigate between the permissiveness of popular culture and the restrictions of school policies as they try to make sense of the world.

Moreover, I held serious reservations about the breadth of Tina's request to direct the play. In a production that has strong direction and solid acting, mature language becomes an element of the drama that an audience is likely to absorb as an integral part of the story. In a weakly directed and acted drama, the audience may be less emotionally engaged, and raw content may stand out. As Tina and I discussed the parameters of the project, I offered to sit in on rehearsals and provide lots of notes, but Tina wanted to direct the project with as little teacher intervention as possible. I asked if she would be willing to cut much of the R-rated language.

Furthermore, the potential ramifications of sponsoring a student-directed play in my school that featured a homosexual couple concerned me. Tina and I talked about the conflict between a student's desire for artistic freedom and how the community might respond to a high school play with adult language and the characterization of a homosexual couple. Tina's rationale for keeping the language was deeply rooted in respect for the playwright's work and the development of its characters, but eventually she understood that I must be very careful about producing plays with mature themes and language at our high school. Despite my reservations, I drafted a contract that indicated Tina's and my mutual responsibilities. Then I wrote to the publisher of the play, Samuel French Inc., and received permission to cut 18 lines that contained the words *fuck* and *goddamn*. But I was still unsettled. Students whom Tina was encouraging to audition were carrying uncut scripts around school that contained the language identified as offensive, and I worried that they were sharing them with other students not connected to the play.

I informed the principal of Tina's project, and his response was positive, but he thought we should run the idea past our superintendent. The superintendent, however, denied my request on Tina's behalf, explaining that students should not perform plays that need to be rated for characterization, content, language, or other components an audience might find objectionable. After receiving this notification, the principal told me that next time he would trust my professional judgment. Was I flattered or left hanging? Perhaps both. In a predominantly white, heterosexist, patriarchal education system, denial of my student's request to produce *The Shadow Box* represents one way the school upholds the dominant ideology of my community, i.e., "public space is heterosexist space." Nevertheless, the principal's willingness to accept my professional judgment from then on is an example of compromise, a crucial component of democracy.

I was wiser to deal with Tina's disappointment than lose administrators' confidence, or worse, my job, had I produced the play without inquiring first. In *Secondary Stages: Revitalizing High School Theatre*, Jeff Bennett sagaciously counsels teachers to follow school regulations regarding censorship. Bennett suggests it is better to change the language of a text—*as long as the teacher has received permission in writing from the publisher*—than risk losing one's job. He celebrates those administrators who give their theatre teachers professional latitude to set reasonable limits regarding content. But he asserts that too much leeway can lead to a downfall, justifying, "You [could] risk venturing too far, forgetting, after all, that it's children you're working with" (2001, 13).

I continued to wrestle with the censorship my students encountered, so I used an electronic mailing list on the Internet to query high school theatre teachers across the country who have faced similar situations. Regarding homosexuality, one teacher reported that her principal cautioned that the homosexual characters not "come off as flaming gays." Did the principal worry that overt homosexuality might draw attention to a subject the high school was not prepared to address? A teacher at a different school shared that his principal advised him to make sure that the homosexuals were "as gay as they could get." Did this principal hope that overt homosexuality might humiliate and thus silence students' serious endorsement of gay rights? The principals' polarized comments suggest that in a public school, homosexuality is still an issue that is best ignored, or laughed about. In her workshops on anti-homophobia, Paula Ressler has witnessed young people sharing stories that depict the shame and embarrassment they endure because of their fear of being stigmatized as belonging to a sexual minority (2002, 2). Chapman, Sykes, and Swedberg suggest that our field "totters on the edge of an ideological precipice of intolerance for students and teachers who identify as lesbian, gay, bisexual, or transgender" (2003, 29). The dialectical perspective of two principals on how to characterize homosexuals in a high school play is a case in point.

The principals' polarized comments suggest that in a public school, homosexuality is still an issue that is best ignored, or laughed about.

Jonnette DeMarisco, a public high school theatre teacher in Port Orange, Florida, asserts that high school theatre teachers live with live ammunition in our classrooms and theatres daily (e-mail correspondence, November 9, 2002). Some teachers who produce "adult-themed" plays in their high schools cut potentially offending language. Some bring in experts to hold post-show conversations with the audience on the subject of the play. Others send the script home so parents can read it and give their teens permission to act in it. Ron Santoro, who teaches at an all-boys private school in Danvers, Massachusetts, advises, "Make sure [the administrators] know exactly what you're doing and be able to defend yourself if challenged" (e-mail correspondence, September 2, 2002). Reflecting on the results of the Educational Theatre Association's 2012 survey, Johnny Saldaña comments:

> The social issues addressed in the plays we produce excites me: we've grown up as an art form at the secondary-school level. Teachers have become more brave and socially conscious (as have at least a few administrators, school boards, and parent organizations).
>
> (Saldaña 2012, 46)

I don't take this observation as a signal for teachers to tackle tough topics freely. Rather, it reinforces the wisdom of Santoro's advice.

## PLAYS WITH THEMES OF WAR PROMPT CENSORSHIP

A high school theatre class in Wilton, Connecticut prepared to stage a play titled *Voices in Conflict* (Playscripts, Inc., 2008), featuring monologues from soldiers who were serving in Iraq. In an interview, the principal said he was concerned the play might hurt Wilton families "who had lost loved ones or who had individuals serving as we speak" (Cowan 2007). According to students, their principal explained that the student body was not prepared to hear about the war from their peers. Supportive parents, however, spoke out, one complaining, "Here these kids are really trying to make a meaningful effort to educate, to illuminate their fellow students, and the administration, of all people, is shutting them down." Wilton High's drama director Bonnie Dickinson reflected, "If I had just done *Grease*, this would not be happening" (Cowan 2007).

The Wilton High incident prompts one to consider if plays with political dimensions may not be appropriate subject matter for high school actors and audiences. Max Bush, playwright of the award-winning *Kara in Black* (Dramatic Publishing, 2006),[1] about young people shaping points of view during the onset of the Iraq War, points out:

> High school aged people can and do vote. Some high schoolers have already begun a long journey into national and international business and politics. Health care, drug laws, educational reform, educational funding, unions, our shifting and increasing symbiosis with communist China, international business, interest rates on credit cards and student loans, gay rights, consumer rights, equal rights, abortion rights, government and corporate assault on privacy rights—these all affect their lives daily. Some will decide to go into the armed services. Within a year some will go to war. Some will die or return maimed. Others will be terrorized their entire lives because of their experiences on foreign soil at age 18 or 19.
>
> (Bush 2011)

The paucity of contemporary plays with political themes produced at the high school level is due in large part, Bush believes, to "a strong, concerned, *fearful* censorship at work." He asks:

> What is the nature of that fear? Where does it come from? Why does it exist almost universally across the United States? Whose responsibility is it to struggle

> to overcome this fear and make artistic choices the primary consideration? Who does this fear protect [...] and who does it victimize?
>
> (Bush 2011)

After Dickinson's principal told her that they were not to stage the play outside of the four walls of their classroom, she abided by his directive, explaining, "I can't have anything to do with [the play] because we're not allowed to perform the play, and I have to stand behind my building principal" (Cowan 2007). Perhaps she feared losing her job.

When administrators are leery of teens' examination of controversial public issues through drama, does it become the teachers' job to alleviate those fears? What is the price of this responsibility? The price may be an apprehension fused by merging freedom with constraint. I share Max's stance that adults should applaud the efforts of young people to counteract the constant barrage of, in Max's words, "political posturing from biased stances in the media" by exploring characters "of their own age and time, struggling to attain some reasoned, human clarity on a current social problem within the form of an entertaining, aesthetic, dramatic experience" (Bush 2011). I want my students to become self-learners by taking leadership in projects that they care about and that will challenge them intellectually, socially, and physically, for when students are passionate, they reach far beyond their present skill levels.

> When administrators are leery of teens' examination of controversial public issues through drama, does it become the teachers' job to alleviate those fears?

Yet, students empowered to be self-agents in learning, especially when the subject matter is edgy and current, may reach too far beyond their stages of mental, emotional, or skill development. One student, for example, had watched teen thespians practice a scene from the script *Danny and the Deep Blue Sea* by John Patrick Shanley (1983) in the television documentary *Thespians* (2011) and was motivated to rehearse an excerpt with a friend for a duet monologue entry in our State Thespian Individual Events competition. Their rehearsals were inconsistent, and I asked to read the script. The characters deal with challenging adult issues, and the language is peppered with expletives. While I did not discourage the team from pursuing an excerpt from the script that they could interpret comfortably, I found myself becoming reluctant rather than reinforcing. (Ultimately, due to lack of rehearsal, the duo withdrew from the competition.) In circumstances like this, I cautiously set up agendas that connect me more integrally to students' process, and my administrator-radar heightens because I don't want to jeopardize the drama program or my job security. Or both.

## TREADING THE DIVIDES OF PARTIAL UNDERSTANDING

High schools are administration-powered, but Elizabeth Ellsworth (1997) offers insight for teachers who dare to make space for students to generate socially critical perspectives. If our students become self-thinkers and self-learners, teachers will not know the exact content of students' knowledge; knowledge among students will differ as well. When my teaching techniques assist students' self-learning, I never have complete awareness of their gained knowledge. However, when I accept that unknown elements are factors in a self-learning environment, I reduce my anxieties about the future. Rationality feeds our desire to predict the future because foreknowledge establishes security. But predictability makes for uninteresting drama onstage, as in life, and also generates complacency, which in turn makes learning boring. Ellsworth characterizes a "pedagogy of the unknowable" as a classroom environment where each participant, fed through self-interest, brings contradictory and incomplete understandings to an issue (1989, 110). If I acknowledge a pedagogy of the unknowable as I teach, I can address challenges with the confidence that new knowledge will occur.

While one could say that Dickinson and her students "lost that round," I don't think of the interactions that I have with administrators as battles in the way some people refer to conflicts between, for instance, students and teachers, employees and bosses, and children and their parents. Ellsworth (1997) argues that self-agency in a classroom evolves only when individuals remain open to criticism, even antagonism; open to input and revision; and open to change in the ways students learn, teachers teach, and schools view the educational process (112). Our progress toward social change isn't about success versus failure. Rather, differences of opinion are steps toward what Britzman calls partial understanding (1991, 13). Contradicting points of view offer opportunities for dialogue among teachers, students, and administrators.

Ultimately, *Voices in Conflict* was performed by Wilton High's drama students in public at the Fairfield Theatre Company in Fairfield, Connecticut. Subsequently, students from Danville Community High School in Indiana performed the play at the 2012 International Thespian Festival. As part of their research, students contacted the soldiers they were portraying who had contributed material for Dickenson's scripts, gaining further insight into the multiple perspectives on contemporary military conflict. Steps toward adolescents' self-agency can advance despite temporary halts.

In 2003, at the onset of the Iraq War, I encountered one such halt. Max Bush and I had negotiated a respectful oral contract for the second production of his new play *Kara in Black*. All that remained was to run the project past my principal for approval. Max and my students and I were excited about the prospective collaboration. (The timing was critical, as the backdrop of the play was the impending invasion of Iraq. The publisher was confident that early publication would benefit the new play's release, but Max needed another production of the play to achieve that goal.) But after a couple of conversations with my principal, I, like Dickinson, adhered to administrative advice. I explained to Max why I felt pressure to withdraw from the project and described the discussion my principal and I had. Soon after, Max wrote a new scene into the play, including some of the dialogue verbatim that I had reported to Max.

In the added scene, Ms. Furman, a drama teacher, is asked to sponsor a silent, non-violent student protest against the war in Iraq. In the excerpt below, Furman explains her rationale for agreeing to advise the student organization, then explains why the planning meetings must take place off of school property:

> FURMAN: So, I've decided I'm a woman first and Jew second and I see mothers and children dying and grieving on both sides in Israel. And in Iraq and in America. And I'm afraid if we invade Iraq we'll be occupying their country and the same kind of situation will happen as in Israel. So, I went to the principal and asked if I could sponsor you.
>
> KARA: Oh, that's fantastic, Ms. Furman.
>
> JUANITA: Thank you!
>
> FURMAN: You're welcome. But our principal will not allow us to have these meetings on the high school campus.
>
> KARA: What?
>
> JUANITA: Why?
>
> FURMAN: He said he'd sponsor you if you were interested in something about the Vietnam War, or the Korean War, or World War II—even the Gulf War—
>
> JUANITA: But not this war.
>
> FURMAN: Exactly.
>
> KARA: Inappropriate? Kids from this school are already in Kuwait. And more will probably be going there.

FURMAN: That's what he pointed out. He thought this would show a lack of support for them. And their families.

KARA: I am their families. She's my sister.

FURMAN: And he said he doesn't want to divide the school. Or help divide the community. And, frankly, he thought it would be unpatriotic.

KARA: Unpatriotic? How can that be—

FURMAN: And then he said: "Off the record, I have to live in this community."

KARA: What does that mean?

JUANITA: We live in this community, too.

FURMAN: So if you think it's a good idea, we could hold the meetings at my house.

KARA: Sure, if that's alright.

FURMAN: Walk me to my car and we'll talk about it.

It is not surprising that school principals are reluctant to support theatre projects that aim questions directly toward a current political conflict, and instead suggest staging plays about war from previous generations. Even professional adult theatre companies are mindful of audience reception to plays about current military conflicts. Tom Morris, director of the World War I-era, Tony-winning play *War Horse* (Nick Stafford, 2007), opined, "We're sufficiently distanced from the First World War to convey the pure horror without getting messed up in the politics of it, and that makes it a more powerful way to discuss any war" (Goode 2011).

For the most part, my principal has supported teacher-sponsored student efforts that shed light on controversial topics. Granted, he followed the advice of *his* administrator, the superintendent, which stopped me from enabling Tina to stage Christofer's *The Shadow Box*. But he also backed my request to stage *Eric & Elliot* by Dwayne Hartford (Dramatic Publishing, 2004), a play about hope following suicide, in the midst of a wrenching rash of suicides among students in our high school.[2] And he is a strong advocate of my Social Issues Theatre class, out of which controversial-themed student-scripted plays are performed in public. So why didn't he give the OK for the Drama Club to produce Bush's *Kara in Black*? I had to wait for other opportunities to unfold before I could begin piecing together an understanding.

## PERSONAL COMMITMENT TO THE SOCIAL CAUSE CONTRIBUTES CONDITIONS FOR CHANGE

Six years after the *Kara in Black* episode, I was asked to read aloud a letter underscored by a composition played by our school band for a patriotic-themed concert. The letter was written by a mother to her son, a soldier fighting in Afghanistan. Band members were confused by the letter. Phrases beseeching the listener to "never forget my son and see my son beneath the uniform" struck them as maudlin; they didn't understand a mother's fear that her son becomes merely a number when he goes to war. Even I couldn't relate to the letter.

To gain insight into the persona of the mother, I shared the letter with my sister, whose son—my nephew—was currently serving in Afghanistan. My sister contemplated:

> Maybe the woman who wrote this is thinking of the Vietnam era, when soldiers who returned from the war were neglected [...] but even people I have come across who disagree with going over there are supportive of my son's decision and feel that our military deserve recognition. Maybe she is afraid that our country will make the same mistake again.
>
> (Fronek, e-mail correspondence, May 9, 2011)

I communicated her point of view with the band members, who appreciated the helpful perspective. I started to think about the relationship of Vietnam War veterans to the men and women who are serving today.

The following spring, Osama bin Laden was killed, and a citizen in our community wrote a letter to the editor criticizing the media for claiming credit for the killing. The writer expressed:

> "We" didn't do squat. "They"—the intelligence gathering community and the members of the Military and specifically one of the twenty-four members of Seal Team 6 "got him." It's easy to take credit for something from which "we" are protected when the news is good, and then change "we" to "they" when something not so glorious happens. Where was "we" when WE came back from Vietnam? Yeah, I'm a combat vet of Vietnam and one of "them." Ironically, "we" became "The Military" or "rogues in uniform" when the actions of a few tainted the majority.
>
> (Arnold "Letter to the Editor," 2011b)

I continued to ponder. How much has changed since Vietnam? In what ways? What is still problematic? And most importantly, can we address these issues in our school?

That summer, I told my principal that I wanted to stage Act I of the play *A Piece of My Heart* by Shirley Lauro (1998), about women who served in Vietnam. Aware of our previous conversations during the *Kara in Black* episode, he looked me squarely in the eyes and said, "Remember what I said—I don't want anyone hurt." I assured him that the play isn't anti-military, but a post-show discussion might invite us to remember why we can't forget our soldiers. I told him that I had located a former Vietnam nurse and author who accepted my invitation to work with the cast and speak to the school. He agreed that the military system remains imperfect. We planned to perform the play for the entire student body in November, reinforcing the meaning of Veteran's Day.

And this is when the nagging question resurfaced: Why didn't my principal give the OK for *Kara in Black*? But another question was rooted more deeply: Why didn't I push back more when he advised against the play? (By this time, my relationship with the playwright had frayed. Since I'd expressed such enthusiasm about the new play development project, withdrawing had been a disappointing frustration for him.)

These questions were in the back of my mind as I came across the article about producing documentary theatre around a controversial subject. In it, author Jennifer Little describes the risk that she took when her students tackled *The Katrina Project: Hell and High Water*, by Michael Meeks and Mackenzie Westmoreland (Playscripts Inc., 2006):

> Finally, we were ready to perform. That is when our administration got nervous. School leaders had concerns that the audience would be offended by some of the opinions stated in the play, such as the belief that racial or economic factors were behind what many saw as the Bush administration's slow response to the crisis in the Gulf. [...] [W]hy couldn't we perform something by Neil Simon or Shakespeare? Their concerns grew to such a level that during our tech week, they considered canceling the performance. While our students continued working, I started fighting. I stressed the educational value of discussing economic and racial disparities in our country, and how these harsh realities were perceived internationally. [...] [W]e finally got the go-ahead. The show went on.
>
> (Little 2010, 28)

And this is when I paused for serious reflection. If Jennifer Little fought back, why didn't I? Why didn't I fight back? How much had I let my students down?

Had I compromised my *principles* to assuage my *principal?* I noted that Little and her students were steep in production by the time she and her principal seriously discussed the potential implications of performing the controversial play. In a sense, Little approached the yellow light of caution more than half-way to her destination, whereas I had seen the yellow light of caution before I even began, and decided to slow to a stop right then.

Little, with her colleagues and students, had much to lose if they quit at the point at which administrators got nervous, and she was able to advocate on behalf of the work they'd already accomplished. On the other hand, I wasn't yet committed to the play itself at the time I asked permission. I was committed to being involved in a new-play-development *project* that would enable my students to work with an award-winning playwright. But I wasn't committed to the *play*. My relationship with my principal, and protection of the drama program, trumped my relationship with the playwright and opportunity for an exciting, educational exchange between him and my students.

Of course, even when students and teacher are committed to the cause of a play with controversial content, administrators may censor. Therefore, at the outset, we should directly explain to collaborators who work outside the school system the risks that we may be up against if the project involves potentially questionable content. We can take other steps to advocate for a play of political import: if a project is important, we need to make a case, and we can do this by demonstrating the number of other high schools that are staging the play. We can connect the plays to their historical significance. We can collaborate with faculty in other departments to integrate across the curriculum. We can describe the potential educational outcomes, emphasizing how these plays raise questions for discussion rather than promote a singularly ideological agenda. Finally, by cautiously picking the battles that put our drama programs on the line, we can invite our administrators to take the risk with us.

## NOTES

1 *Kara in Black* was awarded Best New Play 2006 by the American Alliance for Theatre and Education.

2 *Eric and Elliot* was awarded Best New Play 2004 by the American Alliance for Theatre and Education.

# Chapter 4

## Discovering CODE in Musical Theatre

The question dominating my thoughts when a bond issue passed in my school district to support the construction of a state-of-the-art performing arts center was, "How will settling into the new facility change my pedagogy?"[1] Could I continue to teach and direct "democratically," drawing from ensemble-based, eclectic, student-designed, and often original production concepts in this expensive, dangerous, and very public new facility? Always lukewarm about musical theatre for personal and pedagogical reasons, I preferred Shakespeare, Sophocles, Moliere, Durrenmatt, Max Frisch, Aeschylus, Josefina López, and other playwrights who challenged assumptions or broke from the traditional high school canon. But now the writing was on the wall: my fine arts colleagues and I would stage Broadway musicals every year.

Musical theatre is a traditional component of thousands of high school arts programs across the country. For some schools, it is the sole theatrical presentation of the year. Because of their often large scales, big budgets, complexity of elements, and popular titles, musicals draw more attention, bigger audiences, and higher ticket revenue than plays. Its appeals are numerous. Musicals offer valuable opportunities for students, school districts, and communities at large, including: participation for many at various age and skill levels; involvement of multiple school departments; attention to the educational strength of arts programs; celebration of the one truly American theatre art form; unification of skills gained from distinctive arts programs (vocal, instrumental, dance, visual, and dramatic arts); transferability of gained skills to other experiences (teamwork, self-confidence, commitment, self-discipline); and recognition that individual contributions are part of a complex whole.

## CRITICAL DIRECTING CHALLENGES CONVENTIONAL HIERARCHIES IN MUSICAL THEATRE

Theatre is the most collaborative of the arts, so by extension, musical theatre is the most collaborative of all forms of theatre. Ironically, by nature of its complexity, musical theatre lends itself to the formation of hierarchical power relationships, which are inherently hegemonic. Therefore, musical theatre can deny, reduce, and exclude. Musical theatre historically marginalizes artists of color. Robin Breon reminds us:

> When the white actor Jonathan Pryce was cast in the role of the Engineer in the New York production of *Miss Saigon*, a furor erupted from Asian American actors who challenged the choice. Playwright David Henry Wang and actor B.D. Wong were among the protesters likening the use of prosthetics to slant the actor's eyes as akin to blackface; they argued that an Asian actor be given the opportunity.
>
> (1995, 92)

| Hegemonic Patterns | | Critically Conscious Challenges to Conventional Hierarchy | |
|---|---|---|---|
| **#1** | Perpetuates a star system which relegates others to the chorus as exemplified by compliments like "the lead was amazing," and thereby minimizes the commitment and efforts of others | **#1** | * Is Inclusive<br>* Levels leading actors and ensemble performers<br>* Counteracts diva mentality |
| **#2** | Drives artistry and production through teacher decisions | **#2** | * Counteracts ego-oriented decisions<br>* Involves students in all aspects of production |
| **#3** | Reinforces hierarchical leadership | **#3** | * Shares decision-making among adult teacher-artists/directors<br>* Challenges students to self-discover during scene and character development<br>* Draws upon strengths of collaborating teacher-artists<br>* Counteracts ego-oriented decisions |
| **#4** | Enables shameless and abundant stereotyping | **#4** | * Carves time to create space and participation for typically under-represented and marginalized students<br>* Practices positioning self-identity in relation to others |
| **#5** | Elicits "feel good" responses in the audience, as opposed to enticing audiences to think | **#5** | * Stimulates students, faculty, and audiences to question assumptions of privilege<br>* Designs rehearsals that foster critical consciousness and simultaneously maintains standards of high quality |
| **#6** | Defines cultural borders simplistically | **#6** | * Explores rich cultural connections |

Yet, over time—though not without dissent and opposition—my colleagues and I have been developing a critical model of collaborative leadership for high school musical theatre. The chart (on page 50) identifies six indicators of conventional thinking about high school musicals. Accompanying the indicators are alternative precepts that point toward producing critically conscious high school musicals.

High school theatre experience occurs at a time when young people are vulnerably responsive to leadership styles that engage them viscerally. Theatre engages students with emotional intensity. If we want to shape future adult citizens as thinkers who can critique and deconstruct the conditions surrounding them, and then devise means to minimize social injustices, we must lead by example. We must create environments in our classrooms and rehearsal arenas that invite critical inquiry—not just by the students, but by teacher-directors as well. To direct and teach in any other way shapes passive consumers and popular conformists, and secures us within our own biases (Carr 2011, 106).

Bias has been intrinsic, for not only have onstage roles traditionally been limited to light-skinned performers, but social barriers have curtailed minority participation backstage as well. Breon asserts that "stage managers, understudies, grips, set designers, choreographers, costume designers, lighting designers, road companies; the whole enterprise has historically offered very limited choices for non-white performers and technicians" (1995, 91). Practices modeled in mainstream professional theatre trickle into high school theatre; inadequate opportunities for marginalized students is an unfortunate example. With this in mind, applying the following questions to high school theatre programs can help develop and sustain a critical model of collaborative musical direction:

- What are the best features of our musical theatre program? What can we do to make it a better place for all?
- What does the architecture of the space in which we teach and direct tell us about the values of our musical theatre program, community, and school district?
- Does the actual space in which we teach and direct uphold or break down barriers that have historically marginalized students within musical theatre programs? How do the tangible locations of rehearsal and performance enable or prevent easy entry into our programs? Why? What groups have difficulty finding entry? What groups are rendered invisible?
- What might we do through theatre to ensure a more inclusive and accurate record of community heritage in our school and community?
- What steps can we take to preserve the features of our musical theatre "home"—the rehearsal and performance spaces? What might we do to

keep the space(s) inviting for guests, safe to work in, technologically up to date, energy efficient, and sustainable for expansion?

- To what extent do the users and guests of our classroom, rehearsal, and performance spaces model and promote habits, and practice behaviors, that protect the space? What can be done to reinforce good habits?
- What are the social, economic, and cultural assets of our community? How fairly are these distributed? What can we do to work for a more just community? How are our classroom, rehearsal, and performance venues situated among these assets? How can our musical theatre program use these spaces to advance efforts toward social justice?
- Of those students for whom entry into our musical theatre program is available, which find access easier than others? Which students are marginalized or diminished? Of those with prior experience, which have benefitted from profitable and enjoyable opportunities? Which students have been isolated or ignored? Which have had no opportunities at all?
- Who gets to make decisions in our school, and in our program? Whose voices are largely unheard? What might members of our programs do to achieve a more democratic society?[2]

Constructing a transformative model for collaborative high school musical leadership can be compromised by competing pedagogies, insecurities, previous experiences, and preconceptions. Perpetuating its tenets demands constant self-scrutiny. It is in retrospect that I examine the attempts, breakdowns, obstructions, and temporary successes in the development of the model that I propose. This model remains a goal, not a reality. Striving to adhere to its tenets provides the progress I count on one rehearsal at a time.

## Challenge #1: Asking "Where Are the Stars?"

Casting decisions that are publicly announced can shape a diva mentality. I experienced early in my career one way in which the star mentality can evoke an aura of bullying. During my third year of teaching, I took a job with a high school that had a long tradition of staging musicals; here is where I became an unwilling participant in strategies that publically excluded many and placed others on the proverbial pedestal. The tradition in this school was to write the cast list on large panels of white paper and plaster them over the central office windows. On these panels, lead actors were boldly identified next to their character names, while chorus members were listed at the side in smaller letters, and the crew was not displayed at all. "Who got the leads?" the hopeful actors questioned as they aimed their eyes at the larger-than-life display, alongside teachers and peers who paused to look. Some students rejected by the bully-poster slinked away, whispering, while students with leads and supporting roles shrieked gleefully and hugged.

I recently attended the International Thespian Festival where one evening I was highly impressed by a top-notch performance of *The Drowsy Chaperone* (lyrics and music by Greg Morrison and Lisa Lambert; book by Bob Martin and Don McKellar, 2006). Creative sets and costumes, technically sound and team-oriented ensemble numbers enthralled the audience. The following day I saw a weary-looking young man wearing the performing school's show T-shirt. I congratulated him on a super job, and he replied, "Thanks, but I was just in the chorus. The real credit goes to—" and he named the actor who played the lead. I felt very sorry for this talented teenager, ingrained to believe that the chorus is second class. A few years ago I created a notification method wherein students receive sealed envelopes containing casting notices accompanied by evaluations of their auditions (described in Chapter 6). This is one strategy that curbs comparisons of personal worth, levels leading actors and ensemble performers, and counteracts diva mentality.

## Challenge #2: Involving Students in All Aspects of Artistry and Production to Strengthen the Whole

Anticipating the advent of the new Performing Arts Center a few years ago, our school district supported the collaboration of high school arts teachers to launch a tradition of staging musicals. Our pedagogical approaches, however, were at odds, and I was the teacher-director primarily attentive to issues that contribute to the critical model of collaborative musical directing. One issue in particular manifested at the first full-cast meeting of the first all-school musical, *Guys and Dolls* (lyrics and music by Frank Loesser; book by Jo Swerling and Abe Burrows, 1950). One of my colleagues welcomed the actors and emphasized how great it was that art students would be involved in the production. Aware that drama club students designed and built their own sets, created their own publicity posters, and constructed their own costumes and props, she stressed to the actors that for this all-school musical, "You can just concentrate on acting." It turns out the subtext of this statement was, "You do the acting; I'll paint your set." In the Theatre Design class, every step of the process is transparent because the discussions and group reports required students to uphold transparency. The design sketches of my colleague, on the other hand, remained hidden until I noticed them sitting on her work cart the day before the show opened. While 30 art students had joined the crew to paint benches and background flats, the detail painting was completed by two art teachers and a single college-bound student planning to major in art.

The sets turned out to be gorgeously colorful and fun, but the detailed artistry became the domain of two teachers and one elite student. When I asked why more students weren't onstage painting the set, my colleague explained that as she observed the show shaping up, she didn't think the students' work was going to match the caliber of the rest of the show. Hadn't we agreed to stage a musical that would involve students in all aspects of the production even as we strived for as professional quality a production as possible? In this case, the professional-quality detail on the sets, which the audience saw prominently throughout the show, was painted primarily by teachers. Because musical theatre productions highlight schools' arts programs in a highly visible way, I recognize that adults feel pressure to show off the best of their arts through a Broadway-style musical attended by a paying public. This pressure may consciously or unwittingly motivate teachers to set boundaries for student input. What factors limit the degree to which students execute the artistry when the goal is to achieve the highest standards of high school musicals?

The sets turned out to be gorgeously colorful and fun, but the detailed artistry became the domain of two teachers and one elite student.

## Challenge #3: Securing Confidence in Collaborative Leadership

I am self-conscious of maintaining an open mind while listening to student feedback connected to projects in which both students and I are emotionally invested. When receiving student feedback, I remind myself that their perceptions are not public; I can accept and contemplate, or dismiss, their criticisms. When students sense that teachers are open to evaluation of a problem for the good of the show, their energy becomes a forward-flowing undercurrent rather than an eddy of resistance.

Traditional educational frameworks cautiously regulate student-shaped instruction. Hearing honest criticism from students can be unnerving, especially when the project under scrutiny—like a large-scale musical—infringes upon personal time, expends stores of energy, and occasionally taxes emotions. The critical educator welcomes students' evaluative perceptions and puts some of their suggestions for improvement into place. Students gain ownership when they know they've been heard. Ownership breeds commitment, commitment generates strong effort, and strong effort improves quality. Changes prompted by student voice strengthen a program.

After the first all-school production, I created a feedback sheet that asked participants about their experiences with this first all-school musical. Opposition to this democratic strategy first emerged when a colleague criticized the questionnaire for incorporating "leading questions." I then had students fill out a revised evaluation form during strike. That evening, I read them with great interest. Eager to share the comments with my colleagues, I offered to put them in their mailboxes, but no one accepted. Why were my colleagues disinterested? Did they fear their students' criticism? Were they worried that students' suggestions reduced their control? With what frames of mind should a critical educator read student feedback?

Students gain ownership when they know they've been heard.

## Challenge #4: Steering Away from Stereotypes by Designing Rehearsals that Foster Critical Consciousness

"For there to be social justice," writes Carr:

> citizens, educators, students and decision-makers must be able to understand identity and difference, common and differing values, the problematic nature of finding a terminology to discuss issues, and also, significantly, the context to deal with issues of identity in a meaningful and critical way.
>
> (Carr 2011, 94)

The critical model of collaborative musical directing was challenged again the following year, when we staged *West Side Story* (lyrics by Stephen Sondheim; music by Leonard Bernstein; book by Arthur Laurents, 1957). We should have addressed the issue of diversity before we even began auditioning actors. But we didn't. Rather, when I suggested we might consider actors' ethnicities when casting, the vocal director guffawed, "That's what we have wigs and make-up for." The producer agreed with him, the choreographer agreed with me, and the orchestra director remained silent. End of discussion. End of opportunity for dialogue. We were in audition mode; we cast the play and moved forward.

A couple of weeks before the show opened, some of the Shark girls informed me that they were going to begin tanning. Because it was their idea—they were taking ownership of their characters and empowering themselves—I didn't pause; I didn't ask us to consider the ramifications of this choice. They began bed-tanning and applying lotion. The shift in skin tone was soon noticeable.

One of my colleagues was offended as she observed the handful of orange-toned girls sitting her classes, and she told our producer so during lunch one day.

At this juncture, it's important to note that the actress who played Maria is Arab American, and the actress who played Anita is Latina. Once under the stage lights without make-up during first tech, I saw a striking difference in skin tone between the white girls who were tanning and the actresses of color, who weren't. The actress playing Anita went home and asked her Mexican American dad, "Will you take me to get spray-tanned tomorrow after school?" Pause. (Now it's time to let you know that the actress who played Anita is *my* daughter.) My husband looked at her; he looked at me. Another pause. "*What*?" he asked.

When I shared this scenario with our production's hair stylist, she said she'd noticed the odd skin-tone variations, but there was actually little distinction between the Sharks and the Jets. She decided that hairstyles for the Sharks should include lots and lots of curls, while hairstyles for the Jets should be pulled back to appear sleeker. That, along with costumes, would accomplish the image of difference, she asserted. And she was correct. The show would not have suffered had no one altered her skin tone. On the afternoon of dress rehearsal, both actresses of color paid to get spray-tans. "We didn't feel good about it," my daughter later confessed.

We side-stepped a significant teaching moment for our cast and crew by avoiding a discussion about individual skin-tone and hair color variation. *West Side Story* is a musical that explores conflict between two antagonistic ethnicities and we had a predominantly white cast. This is theatre, where we accept the use of costumes and make-up to create character (see chart, Hegemonic Pattern 6, page 50). What is the difference between our actresses cast as Sharks who bound their breasts and applied side burns which they obviously couldn't grow themselves, or the actor cast as the 44-year-old Officer Shrank who added age lines to his face and white spray to his hair, versus white actresses tanning to look Puerto Rican? And actresses of color spray-tanning themselves to match the tanned bodies of white actresses tanning to look Puerto Rican?

> Where do we draw the line once we begin the process of altering an actor's natural physical characteristics for a role?

Where do we draw the line once we begin the process of altering an actor's natural physical characteristics for a role? Think of the padding that some actresses add to play the role of Tracy in *Hairspray* (book by Mark O'Donnell and Thomas Meehan; lyrics by Scott Wittman and Marc Shaiman; music by Marc Shaiman, 2002). Is the bottom line, "You can do anything but apply blackface" because skin color is historically embedded in issues of racism? How is spray-tanning to darken one's skin different from applying blackface? How is changing hair color to look "sexily-blonde" different from changing hair color to look black or Asian or white? Emotions and politics mix to create heightened tensions regarding issues of color. Yet our politically correct sensitivities likewise influence casting choices related to age, size, class, and gender orientation. Does context matter when we draw the line? And when do we draw the line?

## Challenge #5: Questioning Assumptions of Privilege: Dramaturgy Unveils Identity

Our collaborative team was comprised of individuals who were most comfortable with popular titles in the canon of high school musicals, so when it came time to select a musical for the following year, Meredith Willson's *The Music Man* (music and lyrics by Meredith Willson, book by Meredith Willson and Franklin Lacey, 1957) was suggested. We were mindful that whatever title we chose would be the first musical to be staged in the new theatre; we were even more aware that a week after the show closed, the community was to vote on a bond levy that would either eliminate or continue all extracurricular activities, including drama.

With the weight of the levy looming, we reasoned that the popular title and a cast that included a bevy of children would draw large audiences, so we all agreed to the show. I was lukewarm about the title, however. Compared to the meaty challenge and serious subject matter of *West Side Story*, the mainstream representation of community and character in *The Music Man* lacked edge. Characters of color aren't integrated into the story (unless you count the scene in which the town-girls dress up as stereotyped Native Americans and speak in exaggerated broken-English). Conducting research, I easily found a great quantity of historical references that students would need to understand in order to interpret their lines, construct costumes, and build props. But I was also seeking the *invisible*.

The winter we began rehearsals for the show, I invited a playwright to lead a playwriting workshop. I specifically invited this playwright because her identity—lesbian, homeless, African American—collided with the romanticized perceptions of River City citizens depicted in the musical. The musical is set in late-nineteenth-century Iowa, the state in which the playwright grew up. Our guest shared with students that she lived as a homeless teen in small-town Iowa and described the harassment she'd experienced there because of her race, class and sexual orientation. I wanted students to recognize that the production we were staging painted a picture that was relevant to a privileged class of United States citizens. After the playwriting workshop, rehearsals for the musical began in earnest.

Dramaturgy helps us locate pockets for critical inquiry. Once found, it becomes our responsibility to make time to open them for investigation.

The barbershop quartet was influential in popularizing *The Music Man* when it opened on Broadway because it featured a famous quartet of the 1950s called The Buffalo Bills. Thus, *The Music Man* contributes to "whitewashing a rich and complex history of American and vernacular four-part harmony" (Averill 2003, 180). Historians detail how barbershop revivalists commodified the barbershop quartet during the mid-twentieth century to represent a symbol of the Victorian era. The history of barbershop music is actually a rich by-product of American vernacular music including ragtime, black minstrelsy, doo-wop, and black sacred quartet traditions.

Dramaturgy helps us locate pockets for critical inquiry.

The barbershop quartet revival developed in the early twentieth century as nostalgia for a "simpler time," a reaction to the changing social landscape. That "simpler time" included a sentimental perception of black–white relationships that were rooted in southern white nostalgia. This view constructed blacks as being subservient, nurturing, or amusing, as opposed to the parallel discourse of being threatening and dangerous (Averill 2003, 68). References to "mammies" and "strummin' banjos" are prevalent in songs linked to the minstrel tradition that barbershop quartets sing today (151). In the face of world war, economic depression, women's rights, and festering civil unrest, singing in barbershop quartets allowed tens of thousands of middle-class white men to "construct a space of privilege [...] based on nostalgia for unchallenged and exclusive sociability and camaraderie located in the adolescent memories of middle-aged men" (91). As participation grew, the barbershop quartet revival developed undertones of racism. Membership in state chapters of the Society for the Preservation and Encouragement of Barbershop Quartet Singing in America (SPEBSQSA), formed in the late 1930s, all but excluded African Americans, even as the music performed by barbershop revivalists was greatly informed by the vernacular of black music. As a matter of fact, it wasn't until the 1970s that performing in blackface was banned by the organization.

For those approaching rehearsals of *The Music Man* through a critical lens, it is also noteworthy that research published in 2012 linked the ancestry of First Lady Michelle Obama to white slave-owners. Like many blacks who suspected their heritage included white slave-owners, Mrs. Obama and her immediate family have not chosen to discuss this aspect of their personal history. Journalist Rachel Swarms surmises that African Americans who emerged from the tumultuous twentieth century had challenge enough untangling their African American roots; to contemplate the additional complexity of white ancestors was agonizing. With access to DNA testing and online genealogical records increasingly easy, more black Americans are uncovering their racial composition. The Smithsonian Museum of Natural History highlighted the complexities of Americans' racial heritages in an exhibit that ran from June through December 2011 at the National Museum of Natural History titled "Race: Are We So Different?" The impact of DNA testing on racial identity "is a whole new social arena," describes Jennifer L. Hochschild, professor of African and African American studies at Harvard. She explains, "We don't have an etiquette for this. We don't have social norms" (Swarms 2012).

In this chapter, I wish I could discuss my students' reactions when I shared the barbershop quartet history with them that I'd found. But I cannot because I did not share the history with them. Staging *The Music Man* turned out to be a greater challenge than I'd anticipated; the music and book of the show are much more textured and complex than my preconceptions led me to believe. During the rehearsal process, I realized that before we could attack the invisible, students needed to understand the visible, and we focused on investigating the historical references. (What exactly is a *demijohn*? And what did you use *flypaper* for?) Time passed as we explored these questions and, like a well-conditioned and organized director, before long I was integrating choreography, set pieces, and orchestra into scenes. I ran out of time to open a pocket of critical inquiry into the racial politics of the most popular element of the musical, the barbershop quartet. How much of students' experience was undermined by attention to surface details rather than mining its deeper complexities?

What does this anecdote signify for critically minded high school theatre teachers? Meredith Willson's *The Music Man* continues to be listed by the Educational Theatre Association as one of the ten most popularly produced high school musicals (Strut and Fret 2012, 16). By directing *The Music Man* without engaging our dominantly Anglo European cast in a conversation about the complex history of barbershop music, I located their experience within the nostalgic framework of a Norman Rockwell painting. Instead of introducing students to hegemonic structures embedded in American culture, I subtly reinforced them. Just because a musical doesn't incorporate black or Asian or Arab or Latino characters, we shouldn't ignore issues of cultural dominance. In fact, that's when we should search for them the most, because "the history of the American musical, like any other American institution including schools, churches, barrooms, etc. is a history of segregation" (Breon 1995, 91). Our sensibilities about race have changed since the mid-twentieth century. High school theatre teachers must commit to following a fresh paradigm if we want our students to rehearse musicals from the past with full engagement and critical awareness today.

I let go of an opportunity to bring to students' attention a prime example of hegemony in the United States. But I like to believe that our production of *The Music Man* contributed to positive change in our community in another way. If staged well, *The Music Man* can't help but stir nostalgia with its gentle, romantic humor and sentimental reflection on hometown life. Each performance of this production began with a short speech by the president of the school's Parent-Teacher Association, encouraging audience members to vote. The audience of this musical—having sat comfortably for the first time in an air-conditioned auditorium with excellent sight lines; comfortable seats; clear, consistent sound; and enhancing stage lighting—began to write letters to the editor. Our principal wrote, "If this levy fails, we will eliminate all [...] athletics, music events, clubs, prom, tutors [...] and theatre events such as the wonderful performance of *The Music Man* that was performed last week for our community" (Dever, 2010). A parent of a cast member wrote:

> I would like to pass on that seeing *The Music Man* was what solidly convinced me to vote for the renewal level. [...] My entire extended family [...] felt they were at a professional musical! I think the PAC had much to do with how this production came through.
>
> (*Sentinel-Tribune* May 5, 2010)

The levy passed, and the severe cuts were avoided ... this time. I had originally dismissed *The Music Man* as fluff. I'd discounted its potential power to sway an audience, and more significantly, to contain pockets for critical inquiry during rehearsal. Each production presents itself in its own context accompanied by its own politics. Mining them for their riches of critical inquiry contributes to a theatrical piece filled with depth and thick with nuance. Teachers committed to discovering ways to carve out times and places for critical investigation in the rehearsal period practice this search as if it were an art itself.

Teachers committed to discovering ways to carve out times and places for critical investigation in the rehearsal period practice this search as if it were an art itself.

The hegemonic qualities of *The Music Man* fed our audience with nostalgic comfort and contributed, in a small way, to securing for a while our district's finances. But an unfortunate triumph it was. Unless we act within the pockets that challenge notions of hegemony within popular entertainments, we've not risked social change; we have only sustained the mechanisms that support a violent hierarchy of silence and oppression. How do we dwell in the pockets of critical engagement during rehearsals of complex Broadway musicals without compromising artistic quality?

## Challenge #6: Contemplating Complexities of Cultural Border-Crossing

The following year, we chose to stage Disney's *Aida* School Edition (lyrics by Tim Rice; music by Elton John; book by Linda Woolverton, Robert Falls and David Henry Hwang, 2000). As in *West Side Story*, two groups represent different races/ethnicities: the Nubians and the Egyptians. Our intent in selecting the show was not to confront racist attitudes in the United States, in our community, in our school, and in our classrooms. We selected it because of the unique cultural landscape, its contemporary pop-rock style, and its rich musical score. We had learned from our *West Side Story* experience to address all issues in advance of confirming the show, so I asked if we should be concerned about casting Nubians from among our predominantly Anglo European student body. One member of the team opined that *Aida* is primarily a love story, so how we cast wouldn't be crucial to the success of the production. I, on the other hand, believed that casting for color was something we could not ignore. I was, in fact, eager to discover how we might cast this culturally diverse show from within our school population.

*Aida* may be primarily a love story, but it is set in Egypt and Nubia, the area of Africa now known as the Sudan. *Aida* offers potential for teens to broaden their perception of cultural identity by learning about the hybrid quality of the ancient Nubian and Egyptian races. In the first scene, the Egyptians plunder Nubia, and a white Egyptian captain captures the Nubian princess. The racial overtones are obvious. A comparatively new musical (2000), the play was written long after the civil rights movement of the 1960s, only a decade after the Rodney King beatings launched three days of race riots in Los Angeles, and just eight years before the first black American president was elected. Turbulent race relations continue to unsettle the foundation of our country, even though most people deny that racism "is a major force in the society at large, much less that it is endemic to and perpetuated by schools" (Berlak 2004, 124). It's worth noting that the composer and lyricist of *Aida*, Elton John and Tim Rice, are from Great Britain, a nation that gained significant power and wealth in the nineteenth century through world-wide colonization. It's also important to know that historically, some Egyptians were black due to a long history of shifting power between Nubia and Egypt, opportunities for Nubians to earn leadership positions in Egypt, and intermarriage.

When researching the show, I wondered how others responded to the question of cross-color casting. Comments from an online blog included an array of thoughts. Some chose to ignore the race issue entirely, posting, "White people do *The Wiz* all the time [...] there's no use in fighting anymore [...] just cast white people" (*Aida* Opinions, 1 April 2009) and "I don't think race should really matter. The contrast between Egyptians and Nubians can be achieved through costumes" (*Aida* Opinions," 31 March 2009). Others felt strongly about casting true to color as much as possible, advising, "Stick to African Americans for the leads for believability. I think it would be extremely laughable to listen to a white Aida try to sing those songs" (*Aida* Opinions," 1 April 2009). Still others rationalized using mixed-race casting. One person wrote, "On Broadway, the layering of modern sets, lighting, music and VERY contemporary performances by several leads created a rather messy heterogeneous show, so more racially diverse casting would not have been out of place in the least" (*Aida* Opinions, 1 April 2009).

These comments centralize the relationship between cross-color casting and issues of race. A production like *Aida* is a hybrid of musical styles; its characters represent a racial hybrid as well. Yet those who talk of *Aida* describe it with polarizing identifiers, limiting our perceptions of the cultural. One former colleague demonstrates the alacrity with which some can react with cultural bias. In response to the announcement of our school's intent to stage *Aida*, he messaged on Facebook a query skeptical of our "white" school's ability to pull off the show.

The identifier "white" competes against other racial classifiers and problematizes white identity by illustrating its own complex hybridity. For example, every actor who auditioned for our show received a role, and from among the pool of potential leads, we cast a Korean American as Aida, a Filipino as the king, and a white actor as Mereb. All actors in the ensemble played both Egyptians and Nubians. We made this choice in part because we wanted all actors to participate in the "Dance of the Robe" and "The Gods Love Nubia." But I also wanted the full cast to explore the contrasts between oppressor and oppressed, and I believed that if all ensemble actors developed a character for each, their experience would be enriched. The insight we'd gained through *West Side Story* motivated us to rely on costumes and hairstyle to reflect the character change.

One African American actress whom I interviewed for this book, Colleen, shared that she'd anticipated that audiences who entered the auditorium would "be like, 'OK, Nubians. They are probably going to be the African Americans in the cast'" and wondered if assigning actors into two ensemble groups would have told the story more clearly. Should the casting of a production meet or confront audience expectations? Colleen believed that casting actors in roles that represent specific races is "almost like not our decision." She considered, "It's kind of like our society's fault, in a way." She has a point. Americans are inducted into the racial hierarchy in early childhood when "all sides of the racial divide were told or shown, implicitly and explicitly, that people with lighter skin are 'more than' […] and that the unequal treatment light and dark skinned people observe and receive is justified" (Berlak 2004, 133).

Yet this is the exactly why we should use musicals as fodder for critical inquiry into racial and other social inequities with our students. How can we use a musical to help students "receive information about how [they] might be seen and heard by others whose views [they] had been socialized to discount or not to hear at all?" (Berlak 2004, 131). We did not meet the challenge with *Aida*. The story presents plenty of opportunities to question assumptions of privilege. Furthermore, chances to link the story of oppression to students' lived experience abound. But for the most part, the story remained distanced from students' and teachers' actual lives, figuring more as exaggeration or exception than reality. First of all, the "race radar" of participants—youth and adult—was not dialed to "Activism." Although actors attended several drama workshops that introduced themes of privilege, class, oppression, and racial tension, most perceived the story as a representation of another culture. Because Colleen is African American, students wondered if she identified with characters in *Aida* any differently than those she played in Shakespeare's *Twelfth Night*, Roald Dahl's *James and the Giant Peach* (script adapted by David Wood and published by Samuel French Inc., 2004), or *The Music Man*. Colleen replied, "I think all of us did, 'cause [...] none of us were from Sudan."

On the other hand, actors gained deep respect for African dance, both its significance and its physical challenges. The most meaningful way that Colleen connected to the play as an African American was through the "Dance of the Robe," which was choreographed and taught by an African American college student and member of our local university's Africana Dance Troupe. Colleen compared the stance required of the dancers—the body alternately rooting toward the ground and reaching to the sky—to that of a praise dance in church, and she believed that most cast members understood that the "Dance of the Robe" represented Nubian spirituality. But beyond that, connections to contemporary black Americans and the lived experiences of our students was not even tangentially addressed.

After one rehearsal of "Dance of the Robe," an observing and sincere white undergraduate dance education major complimented the cast on their concentrated effort by describing in awe his perceptions of the dance as "so ... tribalistic ...so animalistic!" Immediately, *my* race radar went off. I thought of the FX documentary from 2006 titled *Black. White* (produced and created by Ice Cube and R.J. Cutler); the polarizing title itself signals the sensationalizing of race relations in the United States. The documentary follows two families, one black, one white, who enter and interact inside the others' cultures after their appearances have been altered by wigs, hairspray, and make-up. In one scene, after the white daughter has confessed to the college-aged students in a black poetry writing group she had joined that she is white, she invites her peers to her home for a poetry slam. The white mother listens to a young woman's original poem. Very impressed, she expresses to the assembled class of African Americans her admiration for the work of "this black creature." The shocked reactions of those in the room is palpable, and the party soon ends. Later, the heated, emotional confrontation between the black and white mothers is fueled by frustration and hurt. The white woman in *Black.White*, and the white college student who observed the dance, reinforce Berlak's assertion that "the most insidious forms of racism [...] are those that are unwittingly perpetrated by ordinary well-meaning people" (2004, 127).

When the white student made his comment, why did my race radar go off but no one else's did? Was I the only one who recognized the potential harm of that comment? Perhaps I had succumbed to the sensationalistic tone of the HBO documentary and become hyper-sensitive. Neither the African American choreographer nor any of the students brought to my attention their concern over the possibility for derogatory interpretation of his comment, and I chose not to bring it to the cast's attention. When I later brought the comment to Colleen's attention, she was very forgiving. "He might have been trying to label it, but those were the first words that came to him," she reasoned, adding, "Because we're not used to this kind of dance, we don't really know what to call it. But since we've gotten the background about it being a praise dance, we know what to call it now." If I was the only one who reacted sensitively to the college student's comment, did I do the right thing by ignoring it? (I did apologize to the choreographer the next day, who also was forgiving.) With complicated rehearsals in progress and a deadline looming, would bringing this topic up have strengthened the show? Possibly not. Would bringing this topic up have opened a pocket for critical reflection and perhaps made room for students of color to have voice? Yes! Though strong examples are often sensationalized, the circumstances exemplified by *Black. White*, for example, facilitate conversations about crossing borders and the challenges with classifying racial identity in the United States. I believe that sensationalizing racial conflict benefits teens engaged in theatre production. This dialogue is especially effective when moderated by a teacher-director committed to helping teens discover their own points of view.

> Confrontation leads to fissures: fissures open opportunities for students to shape, share, and listen to one another's developing, conflicting, and hopefully honestly expressed points of view.

If we had truly wanted *Aida* to be a vehicle for examining race relationships, we needed to foster an environment during rehearsals in which issues could emerge that stimulated confrontation. Confrontation leads to fissures: fissures open opportunities for students to shape, share, and listen to one another's developing, conflicting, and hopefully honestly expressed points of view. Only through conflict that seeps into students' visceral awareness will students' anchoring worldviews be disrupted. "Crisis is essential in order for cultural secrets to be revealed," states Berlak, and that process forges a path toward transformation (2004, 141). But our rehearsals brought up no such moments.

The *Adia* experience demonstrated that a different approach is necessary in order to increase participation of African American students in our musicals in a predominantly white high school. It is certainly not enough to choose plays that feature characters of color. We promoted the auditions for *Aida* widely. For two weeks, the colorful screen saver on every computer in the school announced a free African Dance workshop prior to auditions, but no African American students participated other than those who were already a part of the theatre, instrumental and vocal music, and art programs. Our student choreographer from the African Dance Troupe surmised that the black students we were trying to reach may have been intimidated by others who are confident performing, especially on the huge new stage. How do we start?

## POSTSCRIPT

The following winter I asked the only African American teacher in our school if he would partner with me to create a Black Poetry Ensemble. Actors would stage and recite poems they chose themselves and be featured as an act in our winter one-act play festival. After several attempts at gathering a group, three students participated. The trio rehearsed three poems, including one original, that directly addressed black perspectives on racial identity. We needed to start small, one-on-one, with material that spoke directly to the few students involved.

The Black Poetry Ensemble, comprised of three girls and three poems, was the first block of a foundation on which to build a more diverse theatre program. We must build it, and we must build it one small block at a time.

## NOTES

1 For a description of a developed inquiry into this question, google "EdTA Critical Links Gonzalez."

2 This set of questions is adapted from McInereney, Smyth and Down (2001, 12).

# SECTION TWO

## Critically Oriented Drama Education Alters Traditional Power Dynamics

# Chapter 5

## Examining Power Dynamics in a CODE Theatre Design Classroom

At the first meeting, ideas swarmed over the table of a local coffee shop. It was summertime, and five student designers and I met to discuss the concept for the play *A Midsummer Night's Dream*. After participating in several experimental approaches to staging and casting, students had asked if they could perform *A Midsummer Night's Dream* the traditional way. This meant an elaborate set, one actor per role, traditional staging, and no gender switching for the sake of experimenting with gender reversal. These enthusiastic teens—one scene and lighting designer and four costume designers—would lead a class of 27 peers during the upcoming semester class.[1] I was proud of their serious energy that evening.

Between the first and second meetings, my imagination as director kicked in and contemplated integrating a framing device that would precede the play with interpretive movement; I pitched this idea to my students at the second meeting. Brad, the set and lighting designer, firmly resisted. He asserted that there wouldn't be enough room to perform behind a scrim, and scenery would simply be in the way. The response from the costume designers was vituperative.

"You'll have to ask the actors if they'd be wiling to do this," they warned, adding, "That's why no one comes out to our shows—they're all so weird and … different. It scares people; they don't like it."

"Yeah," Brad chimed in, "doing abstract movement is awful hard." Their tirade against the beloved work I'm proudest of went on.

## PERPETUATING DOMINANCE IN SPITE OF PRINCIPLES

I came home bewildered. "What's going on here?" I thought. I am a teacher committed to seeking avenues for student self-agency. In the Theatre Design class, I want to dismantle the conventional top-down power structures of classrooms so that opportunities for students to exercise power come to be (Kenway and Modra 1992, 143). But hadn't I just "top-downed" them? As I thought about it, I realized that the framing device stemmed not from deep within the students' creative psyches, but mine; I had unwittingly usurped their role as designers. The design team interpreted my ideas of the scrim and framing device as specific design elements that stifled the evolution of their ideas. Although I had thought of these five students as the design team, my actions and language demonstrated that I thought I was still in control. I had not validated their positions as designers, to either myself or them. My teacher instinct—the energy that "drives us all to talk, to tell, and to solve"—had kicked in (Garan 1994). The contradiction between my intent and my actions begs this question: In a theatre process intended to centralize students in the artistic process, "how do our very efforts to liberate perpetuate the relations of dominance?" (Lather 1992, 122).

In my teaching, I try to remain cognizant of this question. In Section Two, I describe and analyze strategies that help to counteract this tendency. Topics include a method for "democratic" theatre design, an alternative means of announcing cast lists, an approach to enriching the contributions of understudies, and transitioning into a new, expansive theatre.

## Evolution of a Design

I met the *Midsummer* team in a third meeting, and we discussed our terms. Firmly committed to letting these students do the show their way, I presented my philosophical stance to the team:

> As long as your efforts are rooted in a thoughtful and responsible understanding of the play, and you are demonstrating original thought as you interpret this play with the integrity of the playwright foremost in your mind, how the play looks visually is your domain.

From that point on, tension dissipated. I would now be working collaboratively with student designers. Our negotiated power relationship served foremost to execute the production. Students were authorized as constituents in the process of producing the play. Because they had authority to change the process, I hoped they might be more likely to problem-solve than mutiny when faced with difficulties.

At the next meeting, we negotiated the relationship between me and the student design team.[2] The points below emerged through discussion, but we did not consider drafting them into a written agreement. The students wanted to

1. produce a play that they picked;
2. independently design and construct the sets, lights, costumes, and props;

3. create a set more elaborate than that of any production they had done before;
4. stage the play without the confusing imposition of multiple casting and gender switching just for the sake of gender switching;
5. determine what their costumes would look like so that they would feel comfortable in them;
6. allow the visual images of the play to evolve from their artistic vision, not mine.

To facilitate students' desires, I would

1. direct the actors;
2. engage in discussions with the design team about their ideas and interject insights from the directors' point of view when necessary;
3. advise the design team when they encountered challenges in peer leadership;
4. step aside so Theatre Design students, cast, and production crew would look to the design team students as leaders.

My responsibility as a co-governing Theatre Design teacher was to launch the process and maintain the progress, but not have primary authority over it.

One reality of promoting the self-agency of minors is that the teacher must remain in control of the learning environment, even if students ostensibly run the show. Hence, the democratic teacher must acknowledge her own self-interest, student authority, and teacher intervention. Correlation of these components gives way to co-authority in the Theatre Design CODE classroom.

As Brad contemplated ideas for the set during summer meetings, he first thought of a series of sliding flats. Although I had encouraged him to develop this idea, when he encountered logistical problems I did not keep my self-interest in check. Solutions involved math that I would find tedious and time consuming. Besides, I didn't really like the idea in the first place, as sliding flats are two-dimensional. Brad's perplexity, along with my disinterest in the sliding flats concept, afforded us an opportunity to co-learn. I suggested using a technique that I had wanted to try for 20 years—the triangular *periaktoi*.[3] I thought each side could represent one of three primary locations in the play: the palace, Quince's shop, and the forest. Brad became intrigued, and he dropped the sliding flats concept. As rehearsals proceeded, Brad designed and led the construction effort of seven 10-foot *periaktoi* that became actor-like additions to the play, turning and switching places as the play itself unfolded.

## RESISTING AUTHORITY AND AUTHORIZING RESISTANCE: STUDENTS AND TEACHERS NEGOTIATE CONTROL

When I slipped into the position of authority, I provoked students' resistance. Their opposition to my ideas is an example of an incomplete understanding. The Theatre Design CODE classroom requires extensive interpersonal communication, which makes the learning process in the course highly susceptible to communication gaps. These fissures can exasperate students and teacher because they often impede development of knowledge. But agitation energizes the process of understanding and contributes to collaborative, co-authored discoveries.

I established the expectation that students would have a full say in how the design process would run in the *Midsummer* project. In an effort to do this, I was practicing a way to disrupt authority's center of power from my standpoint as an authority without altogether giving up my authority (Wallace 1999, 191). The conflict between the authority that my role as a teacher/director naturally imposes and my commitment to a classroom where students collaboratively create and construct the design components of the play forms a dynamic that is unstable and fragmented. While I sought liberated students, I remained highly conscientious of the artistic outcome of the production and worried that student designs would be hackneyed and contrived. This tension points out the unsettled and untenable position of an authority who deconstructs her own authority. My status as "non-authoritative authority" exists in a state of constant flux as my artistic vision, my teacher's instinct, and my liberating tendencies combine to problematize a notion of democratic theatre design.

My status as "non-authoritative authority" exists in a state of constant flux as my artistic vision, my teacher's instinct, and my liberating tendencies combine to problematize a notion of democratic theatre design.

The *Midsummer* students embraced the opportunity to develop and express a collective student vision. However, a teacher who nurtures student agency must be vigilantly aware of potential obstacles. One barrier may be the students themselves, for as Seth Kreisberg contends, many may be unwilling to accept the change of routine. He explains:

> The typical high school student has spent his or her life in classrooms in which teachers make most, if not all, of the important decisions and are the source of all academically important information. He or she comes to accept this as the way schools are. Most adapt and learn to play the game. Thus, there is no reason to expect all, or even most, students to respond

> favorably or immediately to teaching that offers them a share of decision-making power.
>
> (Kreisberg 1993, 227)

Old habits and/or institutional regulations are embedded in teachers as well as students and can thwart attempts at co-authority and altered power relationships in the classroom. Thus, teachers who experiment with an alternative pedagogy face the nagging possibility of scrutiny from administrators and colleagues. Teachers' anxiety may pass to skeptical students, increasing their resistance.

## WHOSE VISION IS THIS? ON ARTISTRY AND COMPROMISE

The design concepts for *A Midsummer Night's Dream* were initiated by a team of five class leaders before the start of a single course. As the class became popular, enough students signed up to offer two sections each semester. However, increased numbers complicate the issue of compromise as more students collaborate to achieve artistic balance. Examining the dynamics of this complication in two Theatre Design CODE classes illustrates how student-generated new knowledge emerges from co-authority.

### Co-Authored Vision: *The Winter's Tale*

Even though there were nearly 40 students in the course, they arrived at the concept for *The Winter's Tale* democratically. After several discussions in which students debated possible settings and time periods, I mediated ideas between classes until they settled on one student's suggestion that Act I take place in the United States in the late 1940s and Act II take place in a 1960s-like commune. Students formed teams to create trees, fortress pillars, a Bohemian landscape, costumes, properties, and the sound plot. Next, the class contemplated how to represent the prison, the storm, and other secondary elements. Students brainstormed several ideas, all of which would increase the already daunting workloads for each group.

At this point, I pitched a favorite concept of mine, the "ensemble character," a team of actors who portray various character and set elements throughout a play.[4] In William Shakespeare's *The Winter's Tale*, those could include the transitional character "Time," a windstorm, prison doors, castle curtains, and passers-by. Students accepted the idea, and the props team stitched 5 × 8-foot lengths of blue sheer fabric that the ten ensemble character actors manipulated to communicate attitude, location, and energy. I kept my self-interest in check, suggesting the ensemble character idea in the midst of, rather than before, discussions with students, and not offering the idea until students had discarded theirs. This differs from the "coerced" concept for the *periaktoi*, which I introduced to Brad out of dislike for (and before he discarded) his sliding flats concept.

Students were generally positive about creating the designs from their own visions. A student wrote:

> It's much more fun and heartening to go in and make something that is your own idea than to do it because you were told that's the way it needed to be. I think people put more effort and heart into their work because it really was their own.

The comments of another student, however, intimated that some students felt that a traditional mindset prevailed and that I, their teacher, held the vision for the play, as opposed to a democratically shared vision. She wrote at the end of the course:

> Maybe the class didn't quite catch your vision of the show, so you never really got what you expected. Maybe you like that, but if not, kind of be more blunt on your vision and maybe [the classes] will catch it.

Yet another was satisfied with the distance I maintained, stating, "You wouldn't force certain ideas unless the class wanted them and you always gave the help when it was needed."

Comments from other students revealed their reservations about the amount of responsibility the course required of them—not because they weren't willing to take it on, but because they felt that greater authority from me would have made the process more organized. One highly motivated and dedicated student reflected:

> I understand wanting us to be able to explore our own creativities and not wanting us to feel choked or limited. For instance, I feel much more confident about myself and my artistic abilities now […] But I do feel that a bit more direction would bring about a better production and alleviate some stresses amongst the design team and cast. An example would be for the director to have a complete list of all the characters and costume changes […] for the costume team, before they start.

As others have noted, administrative support factors greatly in the degree of success that alternative pedagogies achieve inside a traditional school structure

(Britzman 1991; Kohli 2000; McNeil 1986). In an observation report, the assistant principal of my school noted the educational benefit that students appeared to gain from the democratic fashion of the class:

> This type of class closely emulates situations encountered in the working world [...] successes are attributed to the students, but the students must also be responsible for failures. It would be interesting to bring these educational ideals to other academic areas to see if this philosophy works. Some educational theorists believe it is the optimal environment for learning. I believe it works for this class.

Thus far, I have been fortunate that administrators with whom I have worked recognize the values of learning in democratic environments.

## Teacher's Vision: *Much Ado About Nothing*

In contrast to *The Winter's Tale*, where students conceptualized time and place, I created the concept of *Much Ado About Nothing* because performance dates mandated fewer weeks to design and build the show; we couldn't spare the two or three weeks it takes to democratically conceptualize a play. The concept examined how the play correlates with the kind of rumors contemporary media spread about celebrities. What if, I pitched to the classes, we create contemporary Hollywood wherein Leonato has just ended a media war and is filming a major motion picture that stars Beatrice, Benedick, Hero, and Claudio? We could cast, I imagined aloud, a group of paparazzi who would be omnipresent throughout the production. And we could add entertainment news-type characters whose reports transition us between key scenes.

During the class periods that I presented my concept, I was personally jazzed about the framework I'd devised as a director. But I also recognized that these classes would be successful only if students owned the production. How could I get them to own a concept that I had created? I anticipated concern over whether this angle would muddle a storyline that some audience members would find already challenging to follow, as this was Shakespeare. Perhaps students would say I was forcing the concept on them or giving lip service to the ideas they offered. I wanted to remain democratically open to suggestions and questions about the concept—in other words, ready and willing to throw my ideas out if they didn't pique the students' curiosity—even in the face of time constraints. Wallace cautions that to second-guess students is to "risk closing down something new and different and [restrict] our discussion to [the teacher's] own terms" (1999, 193). Thus, as I listened to, and for, students' resistance to my concept, I reminded myself to keep my own self-interest in check, struggling against my teacher's instinct for cohesive meaning and neat closure and my artist's affinity for innovative and non-period productions of Shakespeare's plays.

In reflections after the production, students admitted their initial disinclination when asked, "Do you think that the conceptual focus on how contemporary media spread rumors about celebrities helps communicate the story to your contemporary audience?" One student allowed, "At first I would have preferred to have it take place in Shakespeare's day. I was also worried that the audience wouldn't understand the paparazzi." Another disclosed, "I did wonder how we were going to portray to the audience that the characters all have to do with the movies." Another frankly asserted, "I have reservations about communicating that concept to the audience, and I still don't think we pulled it off." Yet, he reasoned that the concept worked overall because it "provided a way for the rumor to become a natural part of the play without resorting to the precise setting that Shakespeare probably intended it to be." Despite early tentativeness, students accepted the challenge to stage the play as a contemporary statement on how the media harangue celebrities, and soon they contributed original ideas that truly marked the play as their own. One example that shows how student ownership developed is the "living statue paparazzi."

Having watched the 1993 film version featuring Kenneth Branagh and Emma Thompson (Metro-Goldwyn-Mayer), students were enamored with the concept of a fountain, around which Branagh (also the director) staged much humorous action. Suggestions flew regarding size and shape, safety and security. Could we transport the completed fountain safely? What if the water leaks? Should the fountain have a statue? Who could design the statue? Eventually, though, they agreed that the fountain project would be overwhelming. But the statue idea remained alive until someone from one class suggested that the statue be human, a paparazzi disguised as a statue. When I shared this idea with the other class, someone in that class mentioned that there could be two or three paparazzi statues; another added that they could switch positions and even trade places during the show.

By this time, the play had been cast, so I asked who could play these roles. Students speculated that some actors cast as paparazzi could be recast as statues. Then a young man who had never participated in the drama club quietly volunteered. The next day, two students from the other class, who also had never been involved in the drama club, volunteered. These three actors—two

Then a young man who had never participated in the drama club quietly volunteered. The next day, two students from the other class, who also had never been involved in the drama club, volunteered.

senior boys and a junior girl—created moments of comic relief in rehearsals that we incorporated into the production. In performance, they smeared green make-up over all the visible parts of their bodies. If students and I had agreed from the outset that I would devise the overall concept for *A Midsummer Night's Dream*, I sense they would have worked with, rather than flat-out resisted, the framing device. By contrast, the statue example indicates that an initial strong artistic vision by the teacher-director does not diminish student ownership. From these experiences, I contend that student ownership develops from whatever point the students enter the process, as long as the teacher-director seriously considers, and works to integrate, the ideas that students contribute to the initial vision.

## ARTISTIC COMPROMISE AND COMPROMISING ARTISTRY

### Much Ado About Trees

Incomplete understandings complicate learning as students discover that the process of compromise in theatre design can likewise compromise the artistic quality of the production. Because understandings are always incomplete, interpretations of one another's points of view lead students and teacher to be uncertain about outcomes. This uncertainty compels us to compromise. An example of how incomplete understandings generate compromise occurs after students earn points toward their individual grades by fulfilling an assignment that requires each member of a group to draw thumbnail sketches of their design project. Then each group selects one sketch that they like best or (more typically) draws a composite of elements from several group members' sketches and shows it to both classes.

Students decided to construct two trees for the production and agreed that a team from each class would design and build one tree. This decision led to communication breakdowns and mismatched design ideas. We had discussed how the genre of *Much Ado About Nothing*, like much of Shakespeare, integrates serious drama and comedy. One class designed an oak tree, complete with real bark and realistic-looking foliage and flowers, to represent what they understood to be the realism of the garden. The other class designed a willow tree, weeping for Hero. To contribute comic flavor, students designed a cartoon-like tree, making foliage out of green crêpe paper and thin green plastic rope. As their work progressed, classmates and students randomly passing by the room remarked on the aesthetic appeal of the oak tree, whereas the willow tree team received comments like "keep trying." Though one student was common to both classes, her observations and occasional mediations attended to issues that, at the time, took precedence over the evolution of the tree designs. No one considered the ramifications of the obvious differences until both projects were too far along to start over. Then, disaster struck.

In transit to the auditorium where we performed the show, the willow tree survived the ride unscathed. However, the oak tree suffered an almost deadly punch in the trunk. How students reacted to this setback demonstrates the intensity of their ownership. Cast and crew members contributed advice, tools, and sympathy to the oak-tree-team-turned-tree-surgeons. At one point, one of the statue actors (and a member of the willow tree team) spent 45 minutes inside the trunk of the oak tree to stabilize it as the team stapled, glued, and nailed the tree back together. Voices were tense, hushed, and serious, but not a single student shed a tear, and not one student criticized another as they all worked diligently to repair the damage.

Voices were tense, hushed, and serious, but not a single student shed a tear, and not one student criticized another as they all worked diligently to repair the damage.

Once we placed the trees on the stage with the rest of the set, students (and later some audience members) commented that the trees didn't appear to belong in the same production. Tree team members acknowledged this criticism. But then they rationalized the positive aspects of the trees' opposing styles. "I heard that the trees actually made the play balanced," offered one student. Another shared that a friend saw "this green light shining on the willow tree and [said] it looked so beautiful!" A third student reflected:

> One of the compliments [...] [was] that the willow tree helped maximize the idea of the villain. Even though I thought that parts of the set seemed disoriented, I [had] never thought of the willow tree as an important prop to the villain.

Ultimately, students from both tree teams were proud of their teamwork, their collaborative abilities, and their friendships that formed from adversity. One student, referring to the democratic approach to the course, reflected:

> We were independent; we didn't have a teacher telling us what to do. [...] It was amazing how four teens took four different ideas and made them into a weeping willow tree. If a certain tree would have been assigned, we probably would have done a poor job.

"We were independent; we didn't have a teacher telling us what to do. [...] It was amazing how four teens took four different ideas and made them into a weeping willow tree. If a certain tree would have been assigned, we probably would have done a poor job."

Without chagrin, students advised that tighter communication between classes is an objective that the next Theatre Design classes should improve upon. The experiences of the *Much Ado About Nothing* tree teams illustrate that lack of communication between classes leads to mismatched images. However, collective ownership induces conscientious effort and reduces territoriality, which in turn encourages students to see their designs in light of the whole production. I like to think that compromise does not necessarily disadvantage art. Poor communication compromises the artistic and educational advantages that democratic teaching fosters.

## The Winter's Tale of Trees

Interestingly, the *The Winter's Tale* design classes encountered the same problem of uncoordinated trees. Like the experience in *Much Ado About Nothing*, thumbnail sketches by the two tree groups differed markedly. One was a tall, curving, palm-like tree in slightly muted colors resting on a platform with casters; the other was a straight, mushroom-shaped, brightly colored tree set on the ground. Students on each team were surprised by the difference between the two visions, and they began to protect their own designs. Two friends later told me that at this early point in the process they had agreed to not bring up the topic of the trees because it led to arguments. Other students took personal offenses at notes from one class to the other that depicted details that they liked or didn't like about the other tree. Soon team members were referring to the trees as either "our tree" or "their tree."

Territoriality, thumbnail sketches perceived as right or wrong, and gut reactions demonstrate the fragility of easily bruised teenage egos. These adolescent artists were insecure with themselves and about their ideas. Their doubts made them vulnerable, and the ambiguity of the final product—not knowing what the trees should or would finally look like—made them hesitant, protective, defensive, and quick to interpret difference as rejection.

Through trial and error with the shape and height of the trees, and my encouragement to communicate regularly, students achieved artistic balance. One tree was made from coffee cans, heavy cardboard, colorful wrapping paper, and glittered leaves; the other was constructed of PCV piping, foam-board, streamers, glitter, paint, and swim "noodles." Both trees sported colored lights, stood upright, were boldly colored, and were mounted on wooden platforms with casters. Because students agreed on the purpose of the trees and the general idea for color and size, they realized that there could be two different trees in the same forest. Undergoing the trial and error integral to theatre design, students discovered that they can give up elements of their original idea to strengthen the overall vision, while also retaining parts of their own. Coming to this basic agreement allowed these students to enjoy the freedom of their individuality, yet still feel secure that the trees were balanced artistically.

Undergoing the trial and error integral to theatre design, students discovered that they can give up elements of their original idea to strengthen the overall vision, while also retaining parts of their own.

The public performance aspect of the class contributes to teen designers' need, as evidenced in all three Shakespeare projects, to feel secure that the outcome of their productivity will warrant audience approval. As one student from the *The Winter's Tale* project stated, "It's all about embarrassment. I didn't want people to laugh [at our work]." Adolescents' extreme sensitivity to how the artwork they place onstage reflects on them compels them to work very hard. Students explained, "Having people see our work and enjoy it gives us a great sense of pride for our work," and "seeing [the audience's] response was the ultimate reward in this class." As students learned, in their words, "to work under an impending due date that mattered," they practiced time management and attention to detail, such as "adding all the extra stuff [like] glitter and flowers." The Theatre Design CODE course also illuminates the political implications of teen-empowered artwork. In the words of one student, "Older people can see teens' real talent, instead of saying teens are bad." Finally, the course motivates students to contemplate the value of an arts experience that goes public. One student explained:

> Designing, building, and finally showing your own images to an audience of complete strangers is hard. It's just like art. It is very personal, you have feelings within the piece and you're never sure if someone else will see what you see in it. So it always gives you a bit of added pressure to convey your images well. On the other hand, if we didn't have the added pressure of showing it to an audience, sets might not have turned out like they did. What good is a great painting locked up in the artist's attic? No good.

Advantages notwithstanding, compromise—a fundamental aspect of the democratic atmosphere of the class—heightens students' reservations about putting their artistic construction before a public audience.

## A Midsummer Night's Nightmare

The degree to which student artists must compromise to collaborate on design ideas magnifies the "unknowabilities" of a methodology that operates primarily to connect multiple perspectives into a unified whole. The *A Midsummer Night's Dream* Theatre Design class encountered a controversy during their process that further highlights the democratic principle of compromise in this CODE class.

It was Brad's idea to put up for a vote questions regarding the images that would appear on the *periaktoi*, a technique that revealed his own self-confidence as a student designer and leader. The images students voted on had been submitted by all students in the class through a project requiring them to design one of the three sets that they would paint on the *periaktoi*. The issues they discussed before voting were situated in serious questions that identified the nature and purpose of theatre design: How ornate should the "royal" feeling of the palace be? How whimsical should Quince's house be and why? If we draw fairies on the set, will they detract from or complement the actors? What is the tone of the forest flats—neutral, light, or dark? How can a neutral set complement the play? Why have a set at all if it doesn't complement the play? Students animated the classroom with ideas, and they began to monitor each other during the discussions. One criticized her peers, railing, "Would everyone be quiet so Sabrina can finish and you can listen to Brad and Dr. G? This is a discussion, so we need to hear each other!"

The voting was serious in tone. Brad instructed, "All those in favor of a plain grey set, raise your hands." A student asked, "Now what are our options again?" Brad repeated the choices, and then hands either shot up or remained still. There was total silence; the anticipatory tension was obvious. Within seven days, 27 high school students, led by a peer, democratically determined the designs for three different sets.

Still, the compromises required of the democratic approach led some to criticize the production's artistic vision. In a reflection paper assigned at the conclusion of the project, one student wittily expressed her dissatisfaction with democratic decision-making in the production-oriented classroom:

> I was slightly peeved when we voted for whether *Midsummer* was going to be "dark" or "light," in reference to the colors, shading, as well as the mood of it. Knowing it was a comedy, I personally voted for light. We began to take a vote, but as the second set of hands raised, there came the voice of someone [...] we shall call that person Destiny [...] from somewhere behind me.

> "Why," Destiny asked, "couldn't we have a little of both?"
>
> We asked Destiny what he or she meant. And this is where it happened.
>
> "Well, there could be some darkness, and also some light," Destiny explained. "The mood would be pretty light, but also kind of dark."
>
> My horror stirred as I saw heads nod in agreement and understanding. Of course, what had just been said made no sense and was utterly preposterous. It would make for a bland and mediocre production, obviously indecisive and hideously conservative. [...] Our scenery ended up being well-rendered, artistically beautiful, and dutifully constructed. However, the overall premise of the play was much less vibrant than it would have been, could we have been able to take a decent and conclusive vote.

Later in her paper, the student explained:

> There was an atmosphere of togetherness about the group, whether we liked it or not. We were all working on the same project, and we had to work together unless we all wanted to fail and look like fools. No one wanted that, and so we grudgingly banded together and buckled down.

In this student's opinion, the performance aspect intensified the students' frustration as the democratic procedure compromised the artistic product.

## BINARIES BLEND WHEN STUDENTS EXERCISE POWER

### The Teacher/Student Binary

As students begin to see themselves as artists in Theatre Design, I intentionally distance myself from their discussion about artistic choices. I do this to communicate that my voice is just one among the many of theirs. I want them to see, feel, and know that I am purposefully dissolving the student/teacher binary so prevalent in secondary schooling. Binary oppositions such as teacher/student, white/black, actor/crew, gifted/at risk, and leader/follower make both components essential, and often give privilege to the first over the second. This privilege has been used to justify and naturalize power relations (Orner 1992, 78). Thinking of teacher/student as a binary opposition limits my ability to think about how each simultaneously informs and exercises power for the good of the other.

As students begin to see themselves as artists in Theatre Design, I intentionally distance myself from their discussion about artistic choices. I do this to communicate that my voice is just one among the many of theirs.

Therefore, during these discussions I either sit on a stool to the side of the students or stand near a corner, indicating to all that I am primarily an observer who speaks up only occasionally to refocus designers on their goals and to advise caution. At one point during a discussion for *The Winter's Tale*, I interjected because I felt strongly as a director that a statue students wanted to place center stage would take focus away from the actors. After I explained why I felt the statue would steal focus, students voted again. Not one student voted for the statue the second time. I find it interesting that when I interjected a comment from the director's point of view, students accepted my perspective virtually without question. Why? Was it because we had engaged in a genuine dialogue about sensible design? Because I spoke so seldom that students perceived that what I had to say was important? Because students are trained to believe that teachers, and what they say, are "always more important than us?" Because students knew that I was tuned to the conversation with my director's ears? Was it because students appreciated my attempt to be fair and flexible, but also competent and in charge? This quandary points to the difficulty educators face when they attempt to "expand the horizons of students when existing school structures undermine the very conditions necessary to do so" (Boston Women's Teachers' Group 1983, 3).

## The Actor/Crew Binary

In addition to blurring the conventional teacher/student binary, a second binary that a democratic approach to theatre design dissolves is the status distinctions between actor and crew. A student who worked on *The Winter's Tale* recognized this and commented, "Theatre designers don't stop working, EVER;" "I have a deeper respect for the crew teams who make designs, not just the actors and actresses! In a way I think it's way more hard to be on a production team to make the set than to be an actor;" and "I guess I was just a conceited actress who thought the crew just showed up during tech week and was done." Another shared:

> This class has given me more things to sit and stew about than any other class this semester. When I began to realize the amount of work that was

involved, my brain was on overload when I saw Broadway's *Beauty and the Beast*. I know now that projects are just that, they are projects, undertakings that you will battle till the bloody end.

## The Leader/Follower Binary

A third binary that the democratic theatre class blends, that of leader/follower, increases student awareness of social justice. Some students learned that, in this class at least, they had to dismiss the dominant/subservient notion of leader/follower to work effectively in their groups. The democratic classroom refocuses attention from power (leader) and powerless (follower), which are clear oppositional stances, "to a problem of multiplicity and contradiction" (Gore 1992, 61). In CODE, I model a form of leadership that levels my authority. This model becomes a mirror in which students see in themselves qualities of both leaders and followers. Students from the Theatre Design CODE classes reflected, "I am both a leader and a follower," and "leaders need to be able to act as group members, and group members need to be able to act as leaders." One senior stated:

> Some people are leaders and some people are followers and for some reason at different times I can be both a leader and a follower. The follower's path is the much easier path and many people like to be the follower. It involves a lot of listening and following directions, while the leader's path is a little harder and involves a lot of open-mindedness and the ability to share your ideas, but still includes a lot of listening. I've learned that I am a follower mostly, but when a leader is needed I can easily play the part.

Another student, Ellen, commented on the design and construction of a large archway. Regarding wood alignment and stability, she reflected:

> I would always ask Todd, "Is that gonna be all right?" And he always answered that it would be fine, and I always believed him because he sounded so sincere. But he wasn't [right] all the time. I found out that as important as teamwork is, you have to trust yourself as well.

Ellen's thought indicates a changing perception. The "truth," that her peer had more knowledge than she, was inconsistent with the reality of Ellen's experience. The validity of assumptions such as "someone who sounds sincere really knows what he's talking about," is questionable. In CODE, students discover through teamwork that various truths, even contradictory points of view, coexist (Chow et al. 2003, 263).

## NOTES

1 In the class, students and I conceptualize the play together. Students divide into project groups, and then design the components of set pieces, costumes, puppets, properties, or other necessary elements. They set deadlines and order materials, then build, paint, glue, and stitch. Before access to the facilities in the Performing Arts Center existed, students worked in various locations, including the classroom, hallway, courtyard, art rooms, consumer sciences lab, and the agriculture department's power tools shop.

2 I recognize the adversarial connotation embedded in the word "negotiate." I believe we choose to negotiate authority with opposing forces or assumptions of opposition, rather than fight them.

3 A *periaktoi* is a three-sided set piece composed of painted flats atop a pivot. In our production of *Midsummer*, actors conveyed a new scene by pivoting the structures to show different faces of scenery.

4 For a detailed description of the ensemble character concept, see Gonzalez (1995).

# Chapter 6

## Emerging Conflict, Paradox, and Social Change When Students Exercise Power[1]

Increased self-confidence and the capability to simultaneously lead and follow are valued outcomes of critically directed theatre. These positive effects are nevertheless fraught with the "power differentials [that] exist in all social situations" (Wallace 1999, 184). Power is ubiquitous. No matter how educators attempt to alter it, the force manifests itself, if not as a struggle between teacher and students, then among students themselves.

## MULTIPLE PERSPECTIVES FUEL POWER STRUGGLES

Power dynamics were especially active throughout the work of the costume teams for *Much Ado About Nothing*. The two teams were comprised of five girls from one class and six from another. Problems surfaced immediately. In one class, a strong-willed, vocal student who portrayed a leading character in the play frustrated some team members who perceived her as trying to control the group. A student asserting that the girl breeched the democratic principles on which the course was organized acknowledged how power struggles sort people into binary oppositions of great/small. She recalled:

> [Her bossiness] made many people on the costume team and another team very angry. Especially since we were supposed to be democratic about our creations. To get back on track, all the 'little' people fought even harder to keep it democratic, as I did.

This team argued about style and color until they agreed to disagree; they never did compromise, so finally they asked the actors to supply their own costumes according to the contemporary "Hollywood star" concept. The other team encountered setbacks as well. A shirt designed and stitched by a student who, in the words of a teammate, "became territorial of [the shirt] and stopped talking with the group," fit an actress awkwardly. This required the actress for whom it was made to substitute it with a blouse from her personal wardrobe. Miscommunication and territoriality complicated the uncertainties experienced by the costume teams.

Because I consciously reduced my teacher power, students struggled to redefine and share authority. When power relationships reconfigure, vulnerability, ambiguity, and doubt enter, leaving open the question, "What kinds of power and authority are taken up and not admitted [in a democratic classroom]?" (Britzman 1991, 17). I could have stepped in, but I chose not to because I believed that students would learn more from this turmoil by working through it on their own than if I helped them fix the problem. This situation demonstrated the strength of students' self-commitment to the production, and caused students to re-evaluate their commitment to one another.

I believed that students would learn more from this turmoil by working through it on their own than if I helped them fix the problem.

In a post-production reflection, the student who designed and stitched the misfitting garment conveyed the vulnerability she felt when she was criticized by her peers. "I [...] [tried] my hardest to just keep my feelings to myself and [work] on the projects," she wrote. "I made my shirt and though we didn't use it, I am proud of what I made and that I finished it." The word choice "my shirt" rather than "our" or "the shirt" suggests the territoriality of which her peers were critical. About the shirt incident, one criticizing team member wrote that she learned to "work with people that have a negative attitude." The criticizing student did not understand that the reason the girl took on the shirt project in the first place (a point the girl shared in her final reflection) was to teach herself something new; the girl who made the shirt didn't understand why those on her team were exasperated by the sewing errors that resulted in the ill-fitting garment.

Instead of grading students' shoddy sewing (deducting points, for example, for uneven hemlines), or devaluing their decision that actors had to supply their own costumes, I evaluated the depth and breadth of their self-critiques. In the Theatre Design CODE class, outcomes are uncertain because students negotiate as they teach one another with skills they are developing together. This uncertainty leads to breakdowns that I ask students to reflect upon. This reflection raises insights that can lead to change. In the case of the misfitting shirt, the girls experienced the ramifications of poor communication and learned that early and ongoing communication is an imperative for effective team work.

The ambiguity that resulted from this power struggle cast doubt over team members' trust of one another and of their projects' success. Just in time, the team resolved problems for the good of the show, and the girls, in retrospect, realized that their conflicts were childish. The student who sewed the misfitting shirt testified, "I think that if we had just communicated to each other what needed to be done, and how we felt, things would have been a lot better."

The details of this conflict illustrate how all knowledge is situated. Different standpoints lead to confusions and contradictions that are a part of the instructional process (Orner 1992, 84). Truth is relative and partial, not absolute. The vulnerability, ambiguity, and doubt that accompany multiple interpretations of relative truth become assets to learning and understanding. Despite the fragmentations and instabilities of the democratic theatre design process, students strive to find unity, but not on the basis of 'sameness' (Martin and Mohanty, cited in Ellsworth 1989, 107). Observation and personal experience prompted one student to articulate the value of integrating portions of peers' vision into an image that is artistically balanced:

> [The democratic] approach [to theatre design] can greatly improve every aspect of the production because the project is seen through multiple eyes and ideas that no one person would have thought [to bring] to light. Therefore, the depth of the project can increase greatly because it will have been seen from many angles.

Students gained immense insight into themselves, the nature of teamwork, and theatre design because they occupied positions in a classroom environment that made power available to them (Kenway and Modra 1992, 146). Students discovered their human potential for equity that resulted from efforts to compromise. One student commented, "When you take students, all different kinds of students, put them together and make a set, it really amazes [the students] and the audience." This observation indicates that no matter how homogenous a student body might be or seem to be, high school students categorize themselves into groups. Struggling for compromise in a democratic theatre design classroom provides a means for students to learn how to work for equity later in their lives when differences will become more pronounced and political. As a student remarked:

"It took the process of letting even what you consider a great idea get remolded to form what will work best with the set. [This process,] in the long run, taught me to be humble, because even your best idea can still stand to have improvements."

> It took the process of letting even what you consider a great idea get remolded to form what will work best with the set. [This process,] in the long run, taught me to be humble, because even your best idea can still stand to have improvements.

## PARADOX: DEMOCRATIC TEACHER AND DIRECTOR AUTHORITY

When democratic principles become central to a high school theatre program, paradoxes create an energy born of conflict that generates social change. One paradox surrounds the role of the teacher. For instance, I intentionally teach

Theatre Design CODE classes during the same semester that I direct the play (after school) that students are working on in class. Everyone benefits from the interactions that take place five days a week for two periods a day among director, actors, designers, and builders. However, this choice requires me to wear two hats simultaneously: the democratic-classroom-teacher hat and the authoritative-director hat. The democratic classroom teacher is a guide whose path is driven by student need. The democratic teacher welcomes long, unexpected stops in the process because they invite opportunities for deeper student exploration that can lead to new knowledge. The authoritative director is a decision maker driven by deadlines. The director is the one who maintains the through-line of the play, orchestrates collaborative teams of artists and technicians, and whose own vested emotional connection to the play pushes everyone toward a quality production.

The democratic classroom teacher-director paradox is further complicated by an important fact about teacher power. When I want to perform the role of non-master, I have the choice to enact it or not, and having this option maintains my power over the students. It is this tacit advantage that causes resistance from students when I step into territory that I proclaim, and students believe, to be theirs. How then can a teacher undo authority from the position of authority "in a way that exposes the illusions of that position without renouncing it?" (Wallace 1999, 190). As I struggle to balance democracy and authority while directing a play, students struggle to perceive the difference. Reactions when the cast list of *A Midsummer Night's Dream* was posted epitomize these tensions.

## CONFLICT ARISES FROM PARADOX: DEMOCRATIC TEACHER OR AUTHORITATIVE DIRECTOR?

The Theatre Design class students who auditioned for the play, along with other members of the drama club, had clearly stated that they were tired of triple- and multiple-cast experiments; they wanted this play cast traditionally, with one actor per role. Half of the students from the Theatre Design class wanted to audition. Since I had promised them that this was their project, I dutifully auditioned students, held two callbacks, and cast the play. Students' serious auditions demonstrated an intense competition among them for the parts they coveted.

When I posted the cast list, students released an uncontrolled emotional charge that contradicted the mature prudence of their auditions. Two of the students approached me, grief-stricken, demanding to know why they didn't receive a fair audition. The athletic director commented on the foul language he had heard from a couple of students in the hall near the school office, where the cast list was posted. A teacher who had at least ten of these students in class the period after the cast list was posted explained that she was compelled to begin class with a free-writing journal entry to give students a chance to release their feelings silently and individually.

I had never, even with the high-stakes Broadway musicals I'd cast, witnessed the volcanic blowout that this group of students expressed. Having enjoyed the enthusiastic participation of the Theatre Design class for several weeks already, I posted the cast list, expecting the same sort of positive teamwork. But the Theatre Design class is structured to foster input and dialogue. Traditional casting is a competitive experience that operates with one-way communication. The vociferous reaction of the disappointed students occurred because they felt cut off from a project in which they had already invested emotionally, intellectually, and physically.

Traditional casting is a competitive experience that operates with one-way communication.

Once rehearsals got underway, students put aside their disappointments and committed to and immersed themselves in the work of putting on the play. But they hadn't forgotten the anxiety of the audition process. During the end-of-the-year awards supper, Brad reminded the Drama Club of the acute reactions displayed by some when the play they wanted cast traditionally caused many of them to face disappointment. Then he pointed out a freshman who auditioned for the role of Puck with exceptional intensity, was cast in that role, and played it with confidence, creativity, and complete commitment. Brad's public reflection was a sign that students had learned about themselves and the rigors of theatre production.

I believe that this rupture occurred because the construct of CODE separates my position as the high school drama teacher into two identities. In Theatre Design, I am a coworker, a conduit of information, a mediator of student differences, and an advisor. In rehearsal, I am the director, the person who says yes or no, right or wrong, keep or cut. The firm control over casting that I exert as a director creates great anxiety among the same students whose knowledge in class informs me. These two identities continually overlap, separate, and meld together in an unquiet relationship that energizes student self-agency and thrusts me into the teaching state of unknowing.

## SOCIAL CHANGE EVOLVES FROM CONFLICT: DEMOCRATIC TEACHING STRENGTHENS THE CO-CURRICULAR THEATRE PROGRAM

The collective resistance that students demonstrated in the hallway indicates that teens find it difficult to separate their identities as democratic theatre design student from that of actor. During the school day, they are co-authoritative designers. After school, they are actors: judged, evaluated, compared, and selected by the director during auditions. Some students who enroll in the Theatre Design class look forward to auditioning for the Drama Club play that they and their classmates are designing. The *Midsummer* casting response demonstrated that something would have to change if I continued to cast plays with actors simultaneously enrolled in the democratic Theatre Design class.

A few days after the explosive reactions to the *Midsummer* cast list occurred in the hallway by the main office, the athletic director and I had a conversation. "You know," he offered:

> what the basketball coaches do is we sit down with each player who tries out. We tell him what he did right, and we tell him what he needs to improve on. We encourage him to keep trying, or we tell him he made the team. The kids really appreciate that one-on-one communication.

I thanked him, of course. But secretly I was thinking, Are you insane? You have no idea how time consuming it would be for me. I teach academic classes all day and direct plays after school. There isn't enough time to sit down with every actor who auditioned. When would this possibly happen? I admit I also didn't relish facing the expressions on disappointed actors' faces when I told them they didn't get the part they wanted, or didn't get a part at all.

Four years later, my seventh-grade daughter decided to try out for the junior high school girls' volleyball team. She practiced for a month on her own, attended volleyball camp, and we even returned early from a family vacation so she could try out. At the end of the last day of tryouts, the coaches gave each girl an envelope. Inside was a letter inviting the student to join the team, or an evaluation sheet identifying her strengths and weaknesses, including a handwritten note of encouragement. Anxiously, I watched my daughter open her envelope. She received an evaluation form. After she read it, she placed it back in the envelope and stated firmly, "Hmm. I can get better!" That's when I realized the value of one-on-one feedback after a tryout. It took personal observation of my own daughter's experience to persuade me that the tradition of posting cast lists is inherently anti-educational. The athletic director was on to something important. My personal bias against the dominating attention that athletics received in my high school, if only by virtue of the material goods we possessed—two gyms, three tennis courts, a track, a soccer field, a baseball field, a practice field, and a football field, but no auditorium—closed my ears to a suggestion that held merit.

It took personal observation of my own daughter's experience to persuade me that the tradition of posting cast lists is inherently anti-educational.

Since then, I announce auditions this way: Each student who auditions receives two sheets of paper in an envelope. One is an evaluation form which includes a handwritten note, and the other is a letter indicating whether they've been cast. Preparing notes for some thirty auditions can require three hours or more, but spending this time is well worth the effort. I hand out the envelopes at the end of the school day; I don't post the cast list until all students have received notification. A colleague of mine casts this way now, too, but she asks her secretary to pass out the envelopes. It's a good idea. Not only does this keep the nervous students away from the director's classroom, the secretary enjoys interacting with the students, and the main office becomes the temporary center of current drama activity.

Although student resistance encouraged me to change the posting policy, the idea for how to change it did not stem from my own instinct or insight. In fact, when the athletic director had shared his knowledge with me, I dismissed the idea. I was in the privileged position to make social change, but was unable to make meaning of the idea until I vicariously experienced "supportive rejection" by observing my daughter read her volleyball tryout evaluation form. Democratic teachers who simultaneously wear the director's casting hat must alleviate the potentially damaging tension that builds during the casting process. Reminding designer/actors of their dual roles in advance can minimize the anxiety. Using personal letters to announce casting decisions shows the potential of a democratic classroom to impact social change.

## CONVENTIONAL MINDSETS REAR HEADS WHEN NEW IDEAS DEPART FROM TRADITION

After auditions for a production a few years later, I was sitting in a coffee shop filling out forms. An acquaintance in a university music program asked what I was up to, and when I described my notification process, she replied, "Humph. Kids have to get used to rejection sometime." I explained that teaching kids to accept rejection is not a feature of my drama program; teaching them to accept constructive criticism is. At that point, the acquaintance shared an anecdote about her high school experience. She was primarily a musical theatre performer, but decided she wanted to audition for a non-musical. She had her heart set on playing Anne in *The Diary of Anne Frank* (adapted by Frances Goodrich and Albert Hackett, 1955), but didn't receive the role. Because she was very upset, out of spite she did not audition for the school's musical that year, *Kiss Me, Kate* (lyrics and music by Cole Porter, 1949). After that show, the teacher-director asked her why she hadn't auditioned, adding, "I had you in mind for Kate!" If my acquaintance had received supportive feedback following the *Anne Frank* audition, would she have reacted more positively, auditioned for the musical, and landed the lead? Years later, this acquaintance still feels the sting of rejection from a *high school* theatrical role and asserts that "all kids must get used to it."

It is true that those students who pursue theatre in college and beyond are sure to find auditions and casting much tougher at those higher levels. They are not going to get handwritten notes after a Broadway cattle call. But that does not mean they have to *get used to* rejection—in school, in their work, or in life.

Therefore, when colleagues and I began staging Broadway-style musicals I introduced the non-traditional method of notifying actors of their roles in a sealed envelope accompanied by an evaluation. One of my colleagues, who identifies himself as "a purist," suggested a compromise as we were auditioning for *Guys and Dolls*. "How about we post a cast list by student number," he proposed, rationalizing, "It eliminates anyone having to see anyone else's name, and they can pick up their casting letters at the same time." I agreed to the idea because it was at least a step in the right direction; change happens slowly in a democracy because compromise limits the speed of change.

Students told me later that it was a fiasco. Kids who did not know their student numbers rushed to the guidance office to look them up. In the meantime, some students had already figured out not only whether or not they had been cast, but other students' roles as well. By the time actors returned from the guidance office, other students announced their roles to them. One student ecstatically screamed that she got the lead of Sarah Brown. Another student who received the understudy role for Adelaide was blurred by the chaos, thought she hadn't been cast at all, and headed to the bathroom to cry. Several students forgot about the evaluation forms entirely, so I had to put their envelopes in the mail.

The next year, when auditions approached for *West Side Story*, the adult collaborative production team discussed the issue again. I promoted the concept of individual notification, emphatically listing its educational values. The concerns expressed by the team were essentially about the time required to complete evaluation forms for the large number of auditioning students. We decided that after each audition, the vocal and stage directors and the choreographer would fill out half-sheet critiques related to their areas of performance. I agreed to compile them and complete the personal letters. The choreographer found it easier to videotape the auditions and review them later to complete the critiques, and it still took me almost three hours to prepare the envelopes for our 65 auditionees.

But in general, the process was smooth. Students nervously picked up their announcements: some opened their envelopes in bathroom stalls and hallway corners, some opened them on the spot, and others took them home to open. The public drama that adolescents are prone to when cast lists are posted was eliminated. Yet the letters cannot, nor should they, eliminate either the anticipation or the thrills and disappointments that come with casting notification. Two girls who received the roles of Maria and Anita in *West Side Story*, for example, each had pined to play the other girl's role: after opening their envelopes, one actress held back tears while the other (she later reported) went to the bathroom to throw up.

Students enter the rehearsal process tuned to the audition feedback from the director(s), and aware that no student is above receiving constructive criticism.

As with any method of cast announcements, after initial emotional reactions wear off, students accept their roles, jump enthusiastically into rehearsals, and come to love the roles they get to create. The difference is that students enter the rehearsal process tuned to the audition feedback from the director(s), and aware that no student is above receiving constructive criticism.

My students have become fond of this method. Student directors of the one-act play festival have taken on the responsibility of devising evaluation forms for their peers, discovering for themselves the demands on their time that this method entails. But they do it because they have already learned first-hand the value of receiving feedback alongside their casting notice. Especially interesting is discovering how much the actors cast in larger roles appreciate the feedback. Everyone recognizes that they have strengths, but everyone also recognizes that they have much to improve. While the audition is competitive, students learn that casting is difficult, and directors make decisions for multiple reasons, none of which is "You're no good." Drama Club members await with anticipation for the day they have fondly dubbed "Envelope Day." A friend of mine teaches technical theatre, and has adapted the method not only for his cast, but as part of the process of interviewing and announcing students for technical crews, as well.

But what does a teacher-director do when a parent complains, like one did after the *West Side Story* auditions:

> Last year you said my daughter should work on singing, so she spent a year taking voice lessons. This year you said she didn't get the part because her dancing is weak. If I spend money on dance lessons this year, what guarantee can you give me that she'll get a lead next year—her senior year?"

A theatre teacher at an EdTA conference asked that same question in a session I was leading when the topic of alternative casting strategies came up. When I admitted I hadn't had to worry about that (yet), he wisely suggested that one response might be, "Every show is different; each role requires unique sets of skills. And each year new combinations of students audition. There are no guarantees in the theatre, but the more skills your son/daughter gains, the more competitive s/he will be."

A parent query like this would never have even taken place under the old casting regime. This current practice might not be perfect and it is certainly more time-consuming than pinning up a cast last. But for me, my students, and even their parents, the educational advantages of written feedback and personalized envelopes outweigh the ease of a pushpin.

## NOTE

1 A portion of this chapter is reprinted with permission from the Educational Theatre Association. See Gonzalez (2009) for publication details.

# Chapter 7

## Shaping an Ensemble Approach to Casting Understudies with a Mindset for CODE[1]

When our school staged *Guys and Dolls*, we cast a few actors from the chorus to serve as understudies to the principal leads. We planned to feature understudies in the Sunday matinee performance. As the matinee date drew closer, the understudies' nerves increased, and during tech week we decided to call an additional rehearsal on Sunday morning just so that understudies could muster the confidence to perform their show. As the matinee performance drew close, the principal actors asked if they could watch the show from the house, since their roles were going to be performed by the understudies.

This experience left both me and many students unsettled. Though the understudy performance was ultimately strong, and nuances of stylistic difference added freshness to the third of five performances, the approach we took was not in the best interest of the students because it, one, provoked undue anxiety since the understudies did not feel prepared, and two, promoted a division between understudies and principals. I was compelled to discover an approach to using understudies that was more equitable and more educationally rich.

## CRITICAL PARTNERSHIP VERSUS CONVENTIONAL SUBSTITUTION

A couple of years later when we staged Shakespeare's *Twelfth Night*, I experimented with the framework for using understudies by integrating them more solidly into rehearsals and strengthening the partnership between understudy and principal actors. Forty-five students auditioned. I wanted to cast them all because I did not want to turn away any teen who was enthused about Shakespeare. Actors with little or no experience garnered roles in one of five ensembles as lords, ladies, sailors, servants, or musicians. Twenty-two other students received either principal or understudy roles. Both principals and understudies were also cast in one of the five ensembles. The understudies were to be featured in Friday night's performance, the third of four.

Using this method, I realized that actors develop a strong awareness of social responsibility when understudy, ensemble, and principal roles are mixed. Traditional double-casting reinforces power and competition. Traditional use of understudies underutilizes actors and can breed resentment. Thus, I believe it is crucial in educational theatre that understudies work toward a scheduled performance that features them in the principal roles. Guaranteeing my understudies this opportunity provided a motivation during rehearsals that was absent when these students were unsure if or when they would perform. The understudy actors worked hard, encouraged by the reward of a featured performance, and the principal actors were motivated to nurture their partners. Buoyed by achieving the principal roles, and knowing they would be responsible for a majority of performances, the principal actors comfortably observed, shared with, and culled ideas from their understudies. Likewise, understudies discovered that any competitive aspects of their relationship with the principals were tempered by the spirit of collaboration. What emerged from this cooperative learning method were enriched characters, diminished egos, and expanded perspectives.

Actors develop a strong awareness of social responsibility when understudy, ensemble, and principal roles are mixed.

Scheduled performances for understudies are one way to strengthen responsibility to the whole. Another way to broaden students' awareness of others is to give each principal and understudy actor a second role in an ensemble. Often considered the "majority minority" of a cast, ensemble actors contribute texture and can give clarity to a show. Yet, because they are not supposed to stand out like lead characters, they receive less attention from the playwright, audience, director, and even other cast members. This "attention-deficit" can create status demarcations among cast and crew. To counteract the potential for lowered self-esteem or inflated egos, and to capitalize on an opportunity to teach students about the values associated with performing in an ensemble, each principal understudy actor in our cast was also cast in an ensemble. While half of the cast shared key roles, 100 percent of the cast developed an ensemble role.

Because the stronger and more experienced actors earned principal and understudy roles (most having performed in ensembles of previous productions), they could reflect with maturity on the skills and effort required to play an ensemble character with strength and commitment. Additionally, when principals transitioned into ensembles, they often led staged moments of focused attention and bold reaction, and became role models for concentration onstage and theatre etiquette backstage. Finally, double-casting principals and understudies as ensemble characters led to student ownership, because actors needed to take charge of developing creative distinctions between their lead character and the character in the ensemble.

## CONDITIONS FOR UNDERSTUDY/PRINCIPAL CRITICAL PARTNERSHIP

Successfully casting understudies relies upon implementing three important conditions. The first is to allocate a primary performance that features understudies in the principal roles; the second is to cast understudies in ensemble roles; and the third is to double-cast the principals in ensemble roles so that they perform the ensemble roles during the performance that features the understudies in principal roles. With these conditions, I strive to develop a casting atmosphere in which students can practice what I call the three As of casting: Admit, Accept, and Advance. When actors learn what roles they have, they *admit* to their strengths and weakness, *accept* their roles with grace (in public, anyway), and *advance* into the rehearsal process.

"I think there's something to be said about knowing that one of you is more experienced, or received the principal role by virtue of another reason—maybe he or she is a senior, or is a stronger singer, or had a better audition, or just looks the part more."

To foster this atmosphere for *Twelfth Night,* I held three open workshops prior to auditions. The workshops introduced students to the play, the language, and the physical challenges of playing Shakespearean comedy. These fun and relaxed, informative, and confidence-building workshops helped students see others' strengths and allowed them to think about their own weaknesses. I believe students respect casting outcomes when they see that fairness and feedback is provided. As one student told me:

> I think there's something to be said about knowing that one of you is more experienced, or received the principal role by virtue of another reason—maybe he or she is a senior, or is a stronger singer, or had a better audition, or just looks the part more.

After casting, I encouraged the cast and crew to think of a time period in which to set their music-laden Shakespeare comedy so that they could incorporate melodies that were in their (and the audiences') collective consciousness. They decided the play would be set on a California beach in the 1960s. To accommodate the modern time period and the large cast, we characterized the five ensembles which comprised the background texture for the play. Orsino's lords became philosophy students, Olivia's ladies sorority girls, the sailors Coast Guard members and marketplace vendors, the servants groupies of a rock 'n' roll garage band called The Sir Toby Experience, and Feste and her musicians beatnik poet folk-singers.

Before rehearsals began, I had made a commitment to actively involve the understudies during rehearsals rather than, like our *Guys and Dolls* experience, have them observe and step in only when the principal actor was absent. As this inclusive effort unfolded, I became aware that the methods we employed bred collaboration, fostered mutual respect, and increased commitment. While I was excited to discover the potential advantages of an ensemble approach to understudies, I wanted to temper my enthusiasm with the perspectives of the students, and also reflect on ways to strengthen the method. So, I held a focus-group discussion with several principal and understudy actors in May, 2010, two months after their fifth performance. Students' observations are included in the following discussion of seven techniques that formed this ensemble approach to integrating understudies.

As this inclusive effort unfolded, I became aware that the methods we employed bred collaboration, fostered mutual respect, and increased commitment.

## Technique #1: Play Selection

*Select a play that will offer a place for each principal and understudy to develop a role in an ensemble when they are not performing the principal role.*

Shakespeare is an excellent genre for the integrated understudy approach because the difficult language poses many opportunities for students to confer. Shakespeare is also very adaptable, allowing the director and cast to expand the ensembles. However, any play that poses challenges to the cast would be suitable. Three years after staging *Twelfth Night*, we tackled Jim Leonard's *Anatomy of Gray* which features nine principal characters. The play also calls for townspeople who pepper various scenes. Therefore, nine actors were cast as townspeople, each matched to understudy a principal character. Understudies were featured in the first of three performances, during which the principal actors played townspeople. The principals were featured in the other two.

## Technique #2: Terminology

*Make a clear distinction between the terms "double-casting" and "understudying," and avoid language that implies that principal actors are superior to understudies.*

Double-casting implies two separate casts as opposed to integrating understudies and principals in the manner discussed here. The integrated ensemble approach prepares students to give full attention to both of the characters they portray, principal and ensemble. One *Twelfth Night* actor said:

> I don't think that double-casting would have developed the background roles as well. If I had just been thinking, "Okay, you're going to be Fabian B," I would've put all my attention in that and thought while acting in the ensemble, "Okay, I'm still Fabian."

It also encourages principals to look out for their understudy partners. The principal Olivia revealed an especially caring attitude during the understudy performance when she explained:

> I made it my goal to make Sheila as comfortable as possible. When the strap on the hat broke and she had to go on in the next scene, she didn't know what to do. I said, "Sheila, don't worry about it. Look over your lines. Get in place for your next cue. I will sew your hat."

The principal Viola contrasted the atmosphere in a double-cast production rehearsal with that of the integrated understudy method this way:

> I did a double-cast show once and the understudies spent most of rehearsal sitting in the audience watching what was going on. That kind of helped, because we could see what the staging was supposed to look like. But watching didn't help us develop the muscle memory we needed to really learn the role. And it also gave the understudies the feeling that we weren't as qualified. I always felt like whatever I was doing wasn't quite as good as the principal. But when Teresa and I played Viola, we worked off of each other. I learned by watching her, but I didn't feel like I had to match exactly what she was doing because we were doing it together.

Another actor observed, "Our production had such a sense of equality about it." I find it ironic that our principal-and-understudy approach fostered more equality than if we had double-cast the show.

In rehearsal, I try to avoid language that distinguishes the principals from the understudies. I refer to actors in other terms such as "partner characters," and when I give notes, I make sure it is clear as to whether the note pertains to the principal or the understudy or both. Another *Twelfth Night* principal actor commented, "It felt equal. When you gave notes, you gave them to both of us, regardless if only one of us had been acting that day." Another added,

"Every time you gave Carrie a note it went in my head and I started thinking about it." An understudy noted that the dual address kept him attentive.

Maintaining leveling language worked to form one cohesive cast. An audience member commented after the understudy performance that it didn't seem like a second-string show. One actor reflected, "At times I did feel like a second string, but when it came to understudy night, it felt like our show. Besides, I don't think second string is bad because it's another step in learning."

## Technique #3: Shadowing

*Formulate a rehearsal strategy whereby one actor literally stands behind the other and mouths the words during scenes.*

During blocking rehearsals, I stage each scene with the principal actor standing in front of the understudy. Next, we run the scene through, with the understudies mouthing the words while acting out the movements a few feet behind the principals. Then we run the scene again, reversing understudies and principals. Building muscle memory for actors and fostering collaborative character development are advantages to this tactic.

With a large cast, these blocking sessions and scene run-throughs need to be held in a space large enough to accommodate everyone. (During *Twelfth Night* rehearsals, we were stuck in a small studio, where the students later admitted they felt claustrophobic and struggled to focus from one scene to the next.)

Shadowing helps student actors become comfortable onstage and with other cast members as well. It also affords them more opportunity to practice. One principal noted that when they were at the point in rehearsal where they had to commit lines and actions to memory, "the process of doing it over with a different person speaking the lines while I mouthed them at the same time was like complete immersion." Another explained:

> It's like wearing a drag suit when you're swimming. Shadowing really slows you down at first and makes you go through the lines and blocking piece by piece and you feel like you're trudging through mud. Then you take the drag suit off and you're by yourself on stage, wearing your regular suit, and then you're kind of free. But you have the muscle memory.

Shadowing also makes students attentive to different interpretation choices, especially in terms of inflection and reaction. The principal Viola commented, "Because we were shadowing, I could hear Teresa recite lines differently from the way I said them. This gave me a whole other perspective that I wouldn't have had if I'd just done it the way I thought it should be." She explained:

> There was one time when you said to Teresa, "I like how you're being so genuine but try to have more fun with it." I realized that actually *I* was having a little too much fun, and was almost on the verge of making fun of Viola. And Teresa always reminded me that Viola has real feelings. So I think because Teresa was so serious with Viola at first, it got me thinking.

Her understudy added, "And I would consider the way Pam said things and then make them my own." The process of shadowing establishes conditions for students to listen to and observe another actor's choices, and gives actors a discussion partner. These conditions enhance actors' character development. Having a featured performance to look forward to also increases understudies' motivation and commitment throughout the shadowing process. The Sir Andrew understudy said, "I gave it everything I had because I have one shot at this!"

As principals and understudies worked like teammates to create characters, I was prepared to intervene if I noticed the development of dysfunctional rivalries. I didn't have to. The understudy Orsino described the tone of competition as friendly. He explained:

> It wasn't like Bob (the principal) would say, "I'm going to do something that will blow you out of the water," but more like, "I'm going to do something really cool." And I'd be like, "I'm going to try to do something like that, too—only *not* the same. You know—different … but better!"

The principal Viola added, "It was like an admirable competition, like, 'Oh I wanna be like that!'" An atmosphere of "admirable competition" stimulates actors to recognize personal sloppy habits and drives them to improve. Olivia's principal remarked, "Sheila (Olivia understudy) is so professional! She had her lines down way before I did, and that really challenged me. She was on the ball and I thought, 'Sandi, you should stay on the ball too.'"

Shadowing allows a director to harness the competition that arises naturally when roles are understudied or doubled and direct it to key areas that need work. As *Twelfth Night* rehearsals evolved, the understudy to Maria was developing a sense of fun much earlier than the principal. One time I challenged the principal to match her understudy's characterization. When she did, her character finally came to life.

Shadowing also gives students a person to consult with when puzzled by lines or other scripted elements. Students would often go over lines together and confer, one saying, "I thought it meant *this*," and the other, "I thought it meant *that*," or even, "Oh, *that's* what that means!" Eventually they find a middle ground or, if they don't agree, accept saying the line differently.

No matter the difference in age or experience between each principal and understudy, shadowing invites students to find the advantages in their relationship. The principal Olivia reflected:

> I think it was really helpful to have someone as strong as Sheila as my understudy. We're both seniors and have been really active Drama Club members, so it was a level playing field to begin with. Having her to play off of was really cool. But if my understudy was an incoming freshman we would make a strong match in a different way.

As Maria's principal noted, "Shadowing reinforced the idea that no one is too good to be learning."

## Technique #4: Ensemble Roles

*Give each principal-understudy team a role in the show's ensemble to rehearse and perform when not playing the character.*

Besides shadowing, in our production of *Twelfth Night* each principal and understudy was responsible for playing an ensemble role. This helped students gain perspectives on the scenes that featured their primary character. After rehearsing as a member of the ensemble in a scene where the sorority girls eagerly eavesdrop on Olivia and Viola's conversation, the Viola principal finally understood the scene's humor. The principal Maria reflected:

> I never realized how much I overheard. When I was a garage band groupie and Maria is plotting with Sir Toby to trick Malvolio, I wondered, "Am I hearing this or am I talking to somebody else?" I had to make that decision—to be totally into, or totally out of, hearing the conversation.

Actors also discover that it is much harder to keep focus when playing an ensemble role because background characters must constantly react. "I didn't feel like I had to think as much when I played Orsino," an understudy said. Principal role actors rely on the script to answer many questions in terms of character motivation. When the principal and understudy actors develop characters for the ensemble, they are struck by the amount of creative thought required. One principal actor believed that the doubling increased their respect for each other more, comparing the dual perspective to actors who work on tech crew and techies who act. Another principal actor noted a final advantage to the doubling. Meeting the challenges of developing and playing an ensemble role, she asserted, "Never [allowed] the principals to get a big head." Another principal said, "I like the 180-degree turn we had to do because it helped me grow."

## Technique #5: Ensemble Improvisations and Workshops

*Devise script-based improvisations into warm-ups and rehearsals that require actors within ensembles to work together. Devise improv scenarios that also require actors from different ensembles to work together. Hold workshops to help students hone in on the challenges specific to the play.*

Improvised scenes that help principal actors explore the text and develop character are valuable for building chemistry within each ensemble. Additionally, improvised group scenes between actors from different ensembles help actors adapt to one another when switching out (explained in the next section), or when an understudy is required for traditional reasons. A teacher might worry that inviting understudies and principals to invent background anecdotes for character development individually risks the creation of two competing stories. In my experience, understudies and principals who wrestle with the play's themes as character-teams early in the process establish a common background that guides them toward backstories that differ in detail but clearly stem from the same vision of the play.

During rehearsals for *Anatomy of Gray*, for instance, I asked the actors who played Crutch to create a story about a meaningful anniversary gift Crutch once gave his wife, Belva. The principal Crutch made up a story about the time he tinsmithed a bouquet of metal roses as an anniversary gift because the rose was Belva's favorite flower. During the marital spats in the years that followed, the principal Crutch invented, Belva would pointedly extract one, or two, or three roses, depending upon the level of her irritation. After they made up, she always put them back into the bouquet. The understudy Crutch invented his backstory around a blue dress he had secretly chosen and mail-ordered. The understudy Crutch was disappointed when Belva didn't wear the dress. But when their anniversary arrived, Belva put it on and Crutch recalled that she was as beautiful wearing it as he'd imagined she would be. The actor added that Belva wore the dress on their anniversary every year after. The details in the two stories differed, but the most important element—Crutch's deep love for his wife and her returned affection demonstrated by the meaning of the gift—dominated both stories.

I make sure to include both principals and understudies when planning warm-ups and rehearsal exercises. This provides another opportunity for principals to learn from understudies, and for understudies to work at the same level as principals. One such exercise was intended for students to analyze and practice expressing the language of Shakespeare. All the character teams stood, intermixed, in a huge circle. It was not obvious who was an understudy and who was a principal. After each actor recited a portion of his or her text in the center of the circle, I offered specific tips and the actor recited the text a second, and sometimes a third, time. When students experienced breakthroughs, the whole group cheered for them. I aimed my critiques to principals and understudies alike, and all students took part, the goal being to improve their individual abilities to interpret Shakespeare with increased understanding and confidence.

Warm-up and rehearsal exercises can easily turn into competition matches between understudies and principals, and I am cautious to avoid that. Seeds of comparison must be tilled with care to avoid reducing self-esteem and fostering doubt or resentment. During rehearsals for *Anatomy of Gray*, for instance, I instructed the cast to form two groups for a warm-up game that is better played with smaller teams. One actress shouted, "Understudies versus principles!" I intervened and mixed the groups. Later, three principal actors needed a speed-run of a scene to tighten cues. I decided to capitalize on the adrenalin produced by competition, and announced that the principal actors and understudy actors would have a contest to see which team could run the speed-through the fastest. The exercise served to tighten the principals' cues, and it was fun. But during the speed-through contest—which the understudy cast won—other cast members began to take sides. I reminded them that the purpose of the exercise was to tighten cues in a fun way, not to compare skills.

## Technique #6: Switching Out

*Allow partnered actors to discover for themselves the right time in rehearsal to transition from shadowing each other to taking turns onstage during scene rehearsals.*

Without my prompting, the week before tech week, *Twelfth Night* principals began to trade places with their partners so that understudies could gain practice running through the scenes. Actors alternated scenes over the course of about four rehearsals. Once tech week started, principals and understudies stuck to their assigned parts.

Not everyone switched out at the same time. While it does need to happen prior to tech week, I have found it better to let students find the right time to switch out on their own. Once one team does so, others begin to realize what aspects of the show they have confidence over (lines, blocking, dances) and what aspects they still need to rehearse.

Switching out becomes the next logical step in the process of preparing both actors for performance. One of the first *Twelfth Night* principals to make a switch recalled:

> We were getting really close to opening, and for a while you'd spent a lot of time with the principals without understudies shadowing. I knew the lines, and I felt like I was reaching that point that if we do this too many times it's going to get boring. So I thought, "My understudy should do this! I need to figure out what I have to do when I'm a sorority girl."

From that point, they alternated scenes. Switching out also provides actors with needed time to develop their ensemble characters.

Directors could argue that actor chemistry is special and actors need to work together to create and build it. They might question the value of switching actors in and out all the time because they fear it will weaken the show. However, I have found that alternating scenes keeps students on their toes. Because actors choose for themselves which scenes to trade, principals occasionally play opposite understudies unexpectedly. For example, the principal Olivia remembered one time she went onstage "expecting to marry Joe (principal actor for Sebastian), and I married Foster (Sebastian understudy)! That's when I realized, 'I'm not marrying Joe, Olivia is marrying Sebastian.'" The random switches help actors stay in character.

The surprises also keep their acting fresh. A principal actor noted, "Sometimes when you're playing a role as substantial as Olivia and Viola, with so many lines and specific blocking, it gets robotic." When an understudy appeared who was much taller than the actor she was used to playing opposite, she was taken aback at first. Yet she found the new angles fun, thinking, "Oh, now I have to be fluid. [...] My character would still be my character, but she wouldn't do exactly this motion because that doesn't work anymore." Rehearsing staged movements with unexpected scene partners also makes obvious those staged movements that actors need to refine with their regular partners. Another advantage to switching out is that it better prepares understudies for the shows in which they must perform because the principal becomes ill—a situation that can befall every theatrical cast.

## Technique #7: Added Time

*Build enough time into each rehearsal to accommodate the shadowing process. Also, incorporate a few rehearsals into the master schedule that are devoted solely to the understudy cast to help them gain confidence.*

Another advantage to this method was being able to accomplish as much as possible in each rehearsal because there was rarely an actor missing in a scene since a principal and understudy back each other up. However, the ensemble approach to understudies requires additional rehearsal time. Our original *Twelfth Night* schedule included one rehearsal for understudies the afternoon of their featured performance. But as rehearsals unfolded, it became increasingly clear that the understudies needed additional attention from me, both for skill development and self-confidence. I added one rehearsal over winter break, and the understudies later organized another rehearsal which they ran without me. On their own, partners often find pockets of time during rehearsals to build relationships, analyze scenes, or review lines. Through this process, principal actors discover that they have the additional responsibility of sharing with, learning from, and possibly nurturing their understudy.

Announcing cast lists by envelopes that include feedback and implementing an ensemble approach to using understudies are critically conscious strategies that can take place in any high school theatre program, no matter the size and age of one's performance facility. Both methods respect students by meeting them as emerging young adult artists at individual levels, and broadening their experiences from there. Both methods encourage teens to learn from one another and compare their personal strengths and weaknesses to their peers. As a critical educator, I believe these practices establish conditions that privilege students more equitably, strengthen ensemble, and fortify teamwork in an art form that too easily can spotlight a few at the expense of many.

## NOTE

1 This chapter is reprinted with permission from the Educational Theatre Association. See Gonzalez (2010).

# Chapter 8

## Adjusting to a New Theatre with Critical Awareness

The annual budget for the drama program at my school while I culled material for the first edition of *Temporary Stages* was $10,000. It is now $40,000, a spike directly related to the Performing Arts Center. I attribute this increase to expanded efforts such as staging Broadway musicals, hiring more guest artists, involving more students, presenting more awards, constructing bigger sets, purchasing materials and tools for the scene shop, and broadening publicity. The move to the "Taj Mahal" of school sites has produced tangible changes to the drama program. Incomplete understandings complicate learning in this privileged space, and alterations in power and authority impact student artistry.

Working in the new location prompts me to contemplate the influence the new theatre has on my pedagogy. The critically conscious high school theatre pedagogy I practice has grown out of an environment that operated on outdated equipment, crumbling and cramped storage spaces, uncomfortable seating, and a host of other hand-me-downs and leftovers from theatre programs past. Therefore, I wonder:

- What aspects of a critically conscious pedagogy in a high school theatre program thrive when the program's status is upgraded by a new state-of-the-art facility?
- What new cautions arise?
- Where do shifts in control, management, authority, and power occur?
- How does the new facility become a site for employing new strategies that promote social justice?
- How does the new facility limit, restrict, and marginalize in other ways? What forces counteract negative pressures?
- What is the transformative potential of a new facility to equitize members of a public high school student body?
- In what ways does the new facility reinforce entrenched hegemony?

## ADJUSTING WITH UNEASE TO A PLACE OF PRIVILEGE

Critical pedagogy is:

> an effort to work within educational institutions and other media to raise questions about inequalities of power, about the false myths of opportunity and merit for many students, and about the way belief systems become internalized to the point where individuals and groups abandon the very aspiration to question or change their lot in life.
>
> (Barbules and Berk 1999, 50)

Acquisition of a state-of-the-art theatre highlights a contradiction between place and oppression in high school theatre. Teachers with whom I've spoken who reminisce about their outdated theatres refer to their former sparse and dilapidated conditions as "impossible," "nightmarish," "insane," "unsafe," "with next to nothing wing space," and "it's either 110 degrees or an icebox."

My previous theatre home was the original high school-turned-junior high, circa 1920. The dressing rooms, under the stage, flooded after most heavy rains. Students nicknamed our costume and properties storage space the "dungeon;" to access it, one had to cross through a custodial storage room, and cautiously step down a crooked set of crumbling stairs that led to small cement rooms under a boys' bathroom. The area stunk, literally. When I once requested a better storage location for costumes, the custodians obliged by mounting bars from wall to wall in the same small cement room. Stored items were in constant danger of floods and always susceptible to ruin from dank humidity.

It was while working in these surroundings that the mother of a student wrestling with self-injury issues (and whose original scenario I describe in Chapter 10) expressed appreciation for theatre education. She mentioned the positive impact that drama classes and production experience had on her daughter, and called the drama program, even as it operated within the seriously deteriorating facilities, "the best kept secret in the high school." It is revitalizing to remember the impact that theatre experience makes on our students, regardless of the quality of our facilities.

It is revitalizing to remember the impact that theatre experience makes on our students, regardless of the quality of our facilities.

Our theatre program is invisible no more. The LEED-certified facility in which I now work is equipped with a tracked set of twelve acoustic curtains above a 738-seat house; hydraulic lift orchestra pit; director/stage manager's loft; three acoustic shells permanently secured to pipelines above the stage; 34 line sets including four electrics; five separate storage rooms upstage for lighting equipment, sound equipment, platforms, chairs, and a grand Steinway piano; two new spotlights; nine acoustical curtains in the grid above the house, pulled open or closed to enhance the musical and spoken sound emitted from the stage; 42-channel lighting console; sound system complete with dozens of various microphones, monitors, and cables; sprung stage floor; scene shop; storage room half the size of the scene shop; large properties loft above the scene shop; wood-floored, mirror-walled rehearsal room equal to the size of the proscenium stage with dance bar and director's loft; men's and women's dressing rooms equipped with 42 lockers and shower; and large make-up room with 20 hydraulic swivel chairs.

Privileges like these notwithstanding, some teachers enter their new theatre homes reluctantly. Students and teachers attached to former structures feel personally connected and may resent diminished control. Mary Lenning, drama teacher at Cincinnati School for the Creative and Performing Arts, missed the historic architecture of her previous school after a beautifully designed new building was constructed, sighing, "I can't say it's my favorite, because I'm still in love with the old school" (Lenning, personal interview, June 27, 2011). Theatre teacher Pam Christian explained why students felt disenfranchised after the new theatre opened in her school:

> Our facility was falling down around us and yet the students loved it. They worked, played, relaxed, even slept there. The green room was their club house and the theatre was their own private world of arts, community, society, and refuge. In the new facility there is no struggle for them to overcome—no leaky plumbing, unreliable fly system, mice discovered in woodpiles, or graffiti on the walls to provoke memories and legends. The new place is sterile and the PAC Manager, who must approve our presence through a system of building permits and negotiations, is a benevolent interloper. [...] [whom] the students resented because he was there to do something that they were not—taking care of the auditorium.
>
> (Christian, e-mail correspondence, 12 July, 2012)

Christian's students had *dwelled* in their old theatre. Students fond of their theatre homes linger there; they do homework, have one-to-one chats with the drama teacher, and step into the other world of their plays. For some, hanging out in the theatre diverts attention from the realities of family problems. The theatre home becomes a healthy respite, and dwelling there moves students to experience "an intimate, organic, and mutually nurturing relationship with a place" (Orr 1992, 130). When Christian's program shifted to the new theatre, her students felt uprooted. A new theatre grants privilege with consequences.

When a theatre community transitions from old to new, its operations change: opportunities for growth guide play selection, casting decisions, and technical choices. While new spotlights shine on my drama students, illuminating them literally and figuratively, in fresh light, I notice more than before those students who are *not* in the spotlight, *not* onstage, *not* backstage, and *not* in the audience. As my students and I adapt to the change in locale, I wonder how the drama program can change so our expensive theatrical lighting illuminates the marginalized students as well.

A high school theatre community, for all its virtues, is by its very nature exclusionary. Ruitenberg forwards the notion that "identity and coherence of the community are structurally incomplete and imperfect," explaining that "the sense of belonging together is possible only because there are others who do not belong, who are outside of the community" (2005, 218). Some, lacking confidence, need personal encouragement to participate; others, lacking examples of themselves on and backstage, need assurance that the theatre community provides comfort.

The motto of our Drama Club is "Take Your Mask Off and Stay Awhile," inviting all who want to be "themselves" to join.

No place is uncontaminated by hurtful language and other behaviors that classify, sideline, and ultimately divide. Thus, any theatre, new or old, is a site as potentially able to inflict emotional harm as it is to nurture the soul. I am aware that marginalized students in my school may desire but are hesitant to take advantage of our new theatre's remarkable opportunities. The motto of our Drama Club is "Take Your Mask Off and Stay Awhile," inviting all who want to be "themselves" to join. But many students of color do not yet feel that the club is "for them;" although participants represent diversity through socio-economic class, gender orientation, and academic performance, the club, like the high school, remains dominantly white. By prescribing to a radical pedagogy of place, I contemplate the "liminal border-zones [of my theatre program] [...] and the exclusions on which its communal identity relies" (Ruitenberg 2005, 219). Those of us granted the privilege of working in state-of-the-art theatres are more responsible than ever for broadening our theatre communities and breaking traditional societal rules that reinforce behaviors and expectations that marginalize students (Redmond 2010, 7). Christian acknowledged that soon no students will be left who have first-hand knowledge of her old theatre, and that new students, adjusting to new rules, will operate under the new normal. Our new normal should reflect ever-constant awareness of privilege, and commitment to sharing that privilege with all.

## EFFECTIVE POWER DYNAMICS MANAGE TRANSITION INTO A PERFORMING ARTS CENTER

When preparing for the transition into the new theatre, I pondered how my theatre/program would fit in the new space. I feared losing the creative energy that the lack of facilities sparked in our script interpretations, and I lacked confidence in my technical theatre skills. I also was reluctant to accept the diminished autonomy and control that surely would accompany the change, because the complexities of the new theatre required strong oversight. What if the individual selected to manage the transition did not understand or care about the needs of our arts programs? What if that individual adhered to our society's dominant *power*-driven model of leadership, and our voices were silenced? Lenning suggests conducting a strategic plan to figure out what is going to be different in the new building, explaining:

> You really have to look at how the heart and soul of your program changes and if you're not willing to go there and do that surgery, you're shooting yourself in the foot. You've got to let go of what was [because] there's no way it's going to fit. That's a difficult task and you have to have a very strong leader and someone who's willing to let people be mad at them [to make the transition work].
>
> (personal interview, 27 June, 2011)

Fortunately, the administrator appointed to oversee our transition was the kind of leader Lenning describes, and she wielded power with a blend of feminist and old-style leadership. Her approach closely represented a model of leadership coined "servant-leadership" by Robert Greenleaf, former AT&T Director of Management Research. Servant-leadership constructs a power dynamic that decenters hierarchy. While all leaders must exercise power, engage in heated discussions, and strategize to win, the difference between a servant-leader and a power-leader is that power becomes just one of many tools that a servant-leader utilizes to work on behalf of others, not of him or herself. Servant-leaders establish environments of freedom that enable colleagues to apply their energy and intellect for the long-term benefit of the organization (Keith 2009, 3–4). When prioritizing the needs of others, Greenleaf encourages the servant-leader to ask:

> Do those served grow as persons? Do they, while being served, become healthier, wiser, freer, more autonomous, more likely themselves to become

servants? And, what is the effect on the least privileged in society? Will they benefit or at least not be further deprived?

(Greenleaf, quoted in Keith 2009, 4).

Referring to Paulo Freire's claim that dialogue cannot exist in the absence of profound love for the world, bell hooks criticizes past feminist self-appointed leaders who pushed their own agendas rather than listened to people with various backgrounds and political experiences. hooks advocates for leaders of the feminist movement who "acknowledge their relationship to the group and who are accountable to it. They should have the ability to show love and compassion, show this love through their actions, and be able to engage in successful dialogue" (hooks 2000, 163). Establishing a new approach to scheduling activities in the Performing Arts Center that would calmly satisfy the many art teachers who held vested interests in the facility required our leader to express compassion, build relationships, and promote dialogue.

## SCHEDULING ACTIVITIES IN THE NEW PERFORMING ARTS CENTER: FEMINIST LEADERSHIP INVOLVES ALL

When scheduling activities in the new Performing Arts Center, our administrator understood that limited availability coupled with maximum interest breeds territoriality. To minimize tensions associated with the complicated scheduling of concerts, performances, school functions, and outside renters, our administrator introduced a three-step process for scheduling activities in the Performing Arts Center: 1) teachers and administrators submit event dates, 2) the administrator compiles and returns calendar drafts with all conflicts identified, and 3) the parties gather for a 90-minute face-to-face meeting to negotiate compromises. My administrator declared, "I wasn't hired to be the friend of everybody; I was hired to make hard decisions." She believed the time she took to identify conflicts prior to personal interaction paid off by breeding collaboration, support, and trust. This strategy, she asserted, "keeps teachers from having to be mad at only one person instead of each other." With the acumen of a seasoned administrator, she acknowledged that she had to make decisions that were not always in someone's best interest, but by following two premises—What is best for kids? and Does it work for teachers?—problems were resolved (Tache, personal interview, June 29, 2010).

The cursory, fast-paced instruction we received from the industry representatives who installed our theatre's rigging, lighting, sound, and the hydraulic lift primarily taught us that hours of hands-on practice would be necessary before we felt comfortable with the technology. Aware of our needs, our administrator guided our professional development with commitment to a learner-driven curriculum. She explained:

> By the end of that first year, you guys were starting to say, "OK, we need time to *do*, or we need time to *see*, or can you get ..." And that's what's supposed to happen with adult learning. We start you off with little baby steps, and then eventually you take on that role to determine what you need. I hope that momentum continues, so I can ask "What kind of things do you need?", "Do we need to bring an expert in to show you some more?", "Do we need a brush up on anything?" Keeping that ongoing learning in place is the most effective professional development model. And when we come together, one of us will say "I remember this," while another says, "I remember that ..." or "I understand this ..." Pulling together to learn together is essential to adult learning.
>
> (Tache, personal interview, June 29, 2010)

While our transition into the theatre was far from democratic, frequent open dialogue helped us negotiate responsibilities, hire theatre technology experts, establish rules, and continue our education in the Performing Arts Center with enthusiasm, not animosity.

## TOP-DOWN MANAGEMENT SEEPS IN

Traditional leadership methods establish policies for other circumstances. For instance, distribution of devices that provide entry keys to the Performing Arts Center on weekends is limited to a few select administrators and custodians. Other restrictions are fueled by insecurities based on unfamiliarity with theatre technology and theatre in general. For example, even though our stage floor is comprised of 4 × 8' black platforms and we have permission to drill scenery into the floor, we are not allowed to paint on the stage, even with thick covering. Nor are students permitted to focus lights in the catwalk, even if safety harnesses attach them to the grid. Acute awareness of the potential for serious accidents absolutely should dominate all decisions in a theatre. Over time, I believe that if we consistently demonstrate that our primary concern is safety, these restrictions will relax to allow us to augment students' scenic and lighting education. While conservatively conscientious, our administrator was effective because she fostered cooperation and communication, keys to guiding policy-making that result in what is "best for kids and works for teachers."

## THE POLITICS OF DANGER: TECHNOLOGY PRESENTS NEW CAUTIONS

Frequently, constraints on our time as teacher-directors place us in potentially dangerous situations. Of all the new technologies in the theatre, my favorite is the rigging system. I love climbing the corridor stairs into the dark and foreboding aerie of the theatre and angling the heavy, cool metal bricks off the arbor. The complete concentration needed to grab, hold, lift, and pull excites me; the sharp clang of metal on metal sharpens me; the sequence of safety calls controls me. But the bricks on the arbor can kill, and that potential exists every time we load and unload weight. (Faculty and administrators are aware that, in 2008, a young woman performing an aerial act during a Christmas pageant in Cincinnati, Ohio, fell to her death. A problem with the performer's safety harness was determined to cause the fall.)

Ten minutes before beginning a tech rehearsal for *The Music Man*, a scenery piece that had just been added to a pipeline required the counter-balance of additional bricks. It was my responsibility to load the weight. My heart began racing: I'd taught classes all day, four hours of intense rehearsal with full orchestra was imminent, and pre-run warm-ups hadn't yet calmed and centered me. I told myself to slow down and breathe deeply. I trotted up to the pin rail, then climbed the circular stairway to the loading deck. Looking down the narrow, shadowy deck lined with metal bricks, I reminded myself to concentrate only on the load. I stepped onto the arbor, bellowed the safety calls, loaded the weight, paused for the weight test, then beamed at the pipeline's perfect balance. I descended both flights back to the stage with two minutes to spare. If I hadn't put my physical and mental state in check prior to climbing to the load deck, I could have easily tripped, slammed a brick on my finger, or worse, slipped a brick from my hands.

None of us knew going in how steep the learning curve would be when acquiring the skills and knowledge to operate theatre technology efficiently and safely. Limited access to training increases the challenge to learn and practice. Dana Taylor, technical theatre teacher and technical theatre editor of *Teaching Theatre*, identifies two ways that students typically gain technical theatre experience in high school: 1) participation on crews of extracurricular productions or 2) a technical theatre class. Rarely, he assesses, does a school provide both, and ascertains, "The ones that are focused on production seldom even identify what students need to know beyond the requirements of the next show" (Taylor 2011, 30). Only five states offer vocational training in technical theatre: Arizona, Washington, New Jersey, Florida, and New York; the exit exams of Arizona and New York are the most comprehensive. It may not be surprising that technical theatre education for adults and students is limited, for only in the past decade has any attempt been made to formally identify what professional technicians in the entertainment-technology field should know (33).

When we first moved in to our new facility, I questioned administrators about who would be responsible for focusing lights for various events scheduled to take place in the spacious venue. "Well," one pondered, "you could ask Mike—he's the head custodian." I swallowed an internal gasp. Did they not know that theatrical light design, including the skills to hang and focus them, is a profession for which technicians receive college and graduate degrees? Perhaps I should have offered to troubleshoot the next time the boiler malfunctioned. It is not uncommon in school theatres that lack a technical director for a custodian to take on technical theatre responsibilities. Sometimes school administrators must be persuaded that the salary expended to hire a knowledgeable and skilled technical theatre professional will pay off in safety, protection, and maintenance of the new theatre, and maximize the facility's technology to benefit students and the community at large.[1]

I swallowed an internal gasp. Did they not know that theatrical light design, including the skills to hang and focus them, is a profession for which technicians receive college and graduate degrees? Perhaps I should have offered to troubleshoot the next time the boiler malfunctioned.

Potential political ramifications of public attention can also sway administrators. A few weeks prior to the musical, the orchestra pit broke. The sump pump under the theatre had malfunctioned, and water seeped into the pit, causing a breakdown that made us unable to raise and lower the hydraulic lift. We weighed two options for performance: place the orchestra onstage, which we had done in the aged auditorium we'd just moved out of, or extract a row of seats to fit the orchestra in front of the pit. The orchestra director pressured the administration to recognize that either choice would make a negative impression on the public, who were to vote on a school levy a few days after the musical. While the superintendent agreed it was disadvantageous to focus attention on the broken pit during the inaugural musical at this crucial time, he was also keenly aware that a permanently lowered pit would increase the chance for serious accident.

He considered the drawbacks to both options. With a school levy pending, could the school district risk making a negative impression on the public? Which negative impression was more likely to happen? Which risk could be protected against more successfully? He gave the go-ahead for custodians to link six unfixed light poles along the pit edge with thick yellow rope to serve as a barrier. In front of those, we ran a length of

With a school levy pending, could the school district risk making a negative impression on the public?

glo-tape to serve as a warning after the barrier was removed for performances that students named “the line of death.” (We continue this safety measure during rehearsals whenever the pit is lowered.) Pressure of the impending levy motivated our superintendent to face danger with us, a risk that avoided embarrassment to the school district. Despite the temporary failure of its technology, the performing arts center helped our community applaud arts education. The levy passed.

## EVALUATING CO-GOVERNANCE IN A TECHNOLOGICAL ENVIRONMENT

Teaching the Theatre Design class with access to the new Performing Arts Center complicates a complex pedagogy. The critical approach to theatre design and construction that I describe in Chapters 5 and 6 helps students practice compromise, collaboration, voicing, listening, productive confrontation, and other skills that prepare them to grow into adults aware of the dynamic presence of others. The course philosophy evolved as I practiced teaching the class with minimal resources, no technical theatre director, and very limited knowledge. Displacing my authority was key to these outcomes. But because the facility poses physical dangers and misused equipment is time-consuming and expensive to repair, I can no longer displace my authority in the new theatre in the same ways. What revised approach to critical teaching addresses the concern of a student who, reflecting on his experience in the first theatre design and construction class held in the Performing Arts Center, offered, “I think the course should give more focus to technical theatre. We have the equipment—I'd like to learn more about its fuller potential.” Is it possible to co-govern a theatre design class in a state-of-the-art facility?

I was participating with a group of theatre educators assembled to revise Ohio's standards for arts education when the sequence in which students need to learn skills for constructing and designing sets arose for discussion. Based on past experiences in the Theatre Design CODE classes, I opined that students should learn to conceptualize first, and practice the skills they need to put their ideas in place second. Two teachers who have long taught in well-equipped theatres, one as technical director and the other alongside a full-time tech director, vehemently disagreed. “You give them a hammer, you show them what to do, they practice, they do it. They follow your plans. When they prove they can do that, then they are ready to design,” they affirmed to one another and added emphatically, “Designing is a solo project. Construct first. Design second.” We were drafting standards, so I deferred to the teachers in the group with far more theatre technology experience.

Ironically, a majority of teens have little hope of achieving some of the technical theatre standards because resources required to achieve them are unavailable. The National Center for Education Statistics reports:

> Of the secondary schools that provided drama/theatre instruction in 2009–10, about half (52 percent) reported dedicated rooms with special equipment as the primary space for instruction in the subject. Smaller percentages reported the use of dedicated rooms with no special equipment (22 percent) and gymnasiums (22 percent).
>
> (National Center for Education Statistics 2012, 50)

Far fewer high school theatre teachers and their students in the United States are fortunate to work in fully equipped, state-of-the-art theatres. National inequities in public education result in minimal opportunities for the majority of teens to study and practice technical theatre with equipment that prepares them for college programs. Therefore, a critical approach to theatre design remains appropriate for theatre classes, and I contend that a critical approach to theatre design can underscore the curriculum even when advanced technology is available.

In the new Performing Arts Center, our students have the opportunity to stage full-scale family theatre productions. *James and the Giant Peach* (adapted for the stage by David Woods, 2004) challenged us to make theatre magic: perspective changed when an orange spotlight on a scrim that increased in size suggested the giant peach approaching the doomed aunts as they ran—in place—away; another peach, stuffed and mounted on a dowel rod and topped with pipe-cleaner figures, floated through the audience surrounded by puppet seagulls; flats designed and painted by students showing the interior and exterior of the peach flew in and out; blacklights evoked a world under the sea, and a strobe light intensified slow-motion fighting under water; the giant peach, 20 feet in diameter, flew from a pipeline; fog through which actors on stilts entered as Cloudmen created spectacle; and audience members were invited onto the large stage in one scene when the aunts put the Giant Peach on public display. All of these ideas were democratically processed with acute attention to hesitations, fissures, sidesteps, and other challenges of a CODE classroom, similar to those described in Chapters 5 and 6.

Throughout the course, a freelance technical director taught students techniques for scene painting, crafting set pieces with foam, rigging hardware, shaping metal conduits, analyzing gravity's effect on size, applying math skills to the construction process, and operating the light and sound boards and spotlights. An advantage to this process is that students are responsible for figuring out the practicalities of what they need to know in order to bring the concept to fruition. Students are asked to consider what can work safely, within budget and time restraints, and with the skill levels that they have or can develop. Students are required to evaluate their concepts in light of these factors, and seek means to learn the necessary skills. The following comments indicate that students experienced self-agency in a culture that fostered the possibility of transformative change, paralleling previous semesters where Theatre Design students had no access to a high-tech theatre:

- You can truly say that *James and the Giant Peach* was produced by the students. It's just cool to be able to say that WE built the props and WE made the costumes and WE worked hard on everything.
- I learned to make my voice heard without overpowering everyone.
- I had fun creating the peach "butt." I had never worked with foam, so it was a brand new experience. [Our tech director] let me be as creative as I wanted to, but she gave me guidelines and suggestions. I'll always remember what a joy it was to come in day after day and see the butt take shape.
- I learned a lot about compromise.
- With the environment in the scene shop, we could all be creative. Ideas were only ideas and they were all thought about and considered and weighed.

## A STATE-OF-THE-ART SPACE: THE CREATIVITY/ TECHNOLOGY BINARY

Decades ago, Peter Brook described in *The Empty Space* "a hush that settled into a deep and true theatrical silence. An image was being made real, in answer to the need for something that was not there" (1984, 43–44). The hush that Brook describes comes from a creative spirit, the same spirit that compels me to guide teens into the joyful giving of theatre arts. This spirit manifests in an *empty* space, and I believe in this spirit. So when voters passed the levy to build a performing arts center laden with some of the most current innovations in technical theatre, I mulled disconcerting thoughts. What if we become so immersed in our new theatre's technology that we lose contact with our childlike imaginations, the heartbeat of the theatre? Brook declared, "If the need for a true contact with a sacred invisibility through the theatre still exists, then all possible vehicles must be re-examined" (48). Could theatre technology be one of the vehicles that blocks contact with "sacred invisibility"? How do we teach students to use theatre technology in service *to* the imagination, not in place of it?

Learning to use theatre technology broadens students' education, multiplies avenues for entry into a theatre program, and inspires creativity that, when applied proficiently, enhances a theatrical work. Though inadequate spaces force student artists to think outside the box, Lenning considers that artists using technology need to be creative in a different way. She asserts, "The creativity of the twentieth century is not the creativity of the twenty-first century. Teachers need to realize how kids look at creativity, meet students where they are, and draw them back to what we know" (personal interview, June 27, 2011). She explains that while students may have mastered the operation of sound systems and computers better than their teachers, they need teachers to demonstrate how technology can help them see and analyze their own place in the world.

What if we become so immersed in our new theatre's technology that we lose contact with our childlike imaginations, the heartbeat of the theatre?

## TECHNOLOGY AND THE SPIRIT OF THEATRE

Regardless of a program's resources, high school theatre nourishes teens' collective souls, and connection among souls creates community. Elite drama programs that operate on budgets upward of $150,000 nonetheless can retain "the sweet, seat-of-the-pants quality that can make even the humblest high school production lastingly meaningful" (Green 2005). Though upscale productions might teach students the wrong lessons from Broadway, journalist Jesse Green points out that "[I]n terms of pure devotion and uncritical support [in high school theatre], the theatrical life never gets much better" (2005).

Regardless of a program's resources, high school theatre nourishes teens' collective souls, and connection among souls creates community.

Theatre technology requires increased budgets; larger budgets increase status. The Educational Theatre Association's 2012 Survey of Theatre Programs in United States High Schools informs that responding teachers reported spending an average of $2,701 on full-length non-musicals and $7,510 on musicals. By contrast, the drama program at New Albany High School in New Albany, Indiana, produced Disney's *Beauty and the Beast* (lyrics by Howard Ashman and Tim Rice; music by Alan Menken; book by Linda Woolverton, 1994) with a budget of $165,000. Students performed the show in the school district's $17 million performing arts annex that was financed by property taxes. Over the years the arts had brought to New Albany (a community struggling to combat local poverty), "a measure of pride, comparable only to that generated by the sports teams" (Green 2005). But bigger budgets that provide kids access to theatre technology create the risk of limiting as well as expanding innovation. Furthermore, technology can redirect teens from learning basic theatrical skills when, for example, the amplification system reduces students' need to practice stage projection. Yet even massively scaled musicals like New Albany's can generate pride in students' work, build peer cohesion, and demand the hard work that shapes positive self-image. "This is really a magical time, when they're still doing it for the joy of it," reflects Guy Tedesco, a professional who had designed the costumes for New Albany's *Beauty and the Beast.* Once they get to college, he wryly added, "From here on out, it's prostitution" (Green 2005).

## TECHNOLOGY: THE SCIENCE/THEATRE BINARY

Prior to my school's new theatre opening, the arts faculty met the architect who designed the configuration of the house for optimum acoustical quality. His talk introduced me to the complex physics involved in the shape and transmission of sound. That experience planted a seed of thought that evolved into a collaborative project between the theatre and science departments. I seriously considered the intrinsically scientific nature of theatre technology, and contemplated how the Performing Arts Center provides opportunities to make this quality of the art form visible and tangible. Most significantly, I pondered how the arts might exploit the dominant core curricular subject of science in order to advocate on behalf of theatre arts in the public schools.

Arts programs jockey for attention in the public school while state and national mandates prioritize needs by funneling money to increase math and science skills. Yet science and mathematics are typically taught in lecture-centered classrooms that marginalize interest among diverse populations of students. One factor that marginalizes students is the competitive climate that permeates many science classrooms; another is teachers' low expectations about the ability of women and students of color to participate in scientific inquiry. During the second year that we had access to the Performing Arts Center, a science colleague and I wrote a grant shaped within a feminist framework. A feminist approach to teaching science strives to "empower marginalized students, acknowledge different ways of knowing, and provide a safer environment in which students' experiences and concerns will become central to the learning process" (Mayberry and Rees, 195). Awarded for two years, the project gave us the chance to address the inequities of science education cited by feminist science scholars.

## PERFORMING ARTS CENTER-TURNED-CLASSROOM ENGAGES SCIENCE STUDENTS IN A FRESH WAY

The arts are official components of the core curriculum in the United States, but in our public school (like most) English, math, science, and social studies are the focus of administrative concern because students take state-mandated standardized tests in those subjects. One way that theatre gained attention in our school was through a grant that promoted twenty-first century skill-based science education. Since science is a dominant department in our school, might connecting theatre to that centralized subject raise the profile of theatre? I invited a physics teacher to join me in drafting a grant proposal to teach science lessons for ninth graders in the Performing Arts Center that combined drama, theatre technology, and science.[2] We agreed that while students learn about the science of sound and light in classrooms, applying the concepts hands-on in a real-life environment intensifies learning. The two-year grant would accomplish three goals: 1) use dramatic metaphor as a technique for introducing science concepts to alternative learners, 2) ensure correct presentation of science concepts, and 3) introduce students to the technologies of the auditorium and how they contribute to a theatrical production.[3]

Collaboration underscored the development of our lessons, and one situation in particular demonstrated our commitment to process learning. The physics teacher was flummoxed by the rigging system's operation, which did not adhere to the scientific principles of vertical force that we were preparing to teach. After showing him the rigging system in the theatre, he sauntered pensively out of the auditorium. The next morning, he bounded into the Theatre Studio with a model pulley system, eager to share an "a-ha!" moment. He explained that he'd gone home to explore the model pulley and introduced the small system as a toy to his own young sons. While playing, he figured out that the difference between the science concept and the reality of the rigging system was the additional weight of the cables, which we hadn't factored in. When it came time to present the vertical force lesson to the Science 9 students, he was quick to point out how he had made a discovery himself, and challenged the students to make that discovery as well.

Follow-up surveys revealed that three-fourths of the 240 participating freshmen believed that exploring science concepts in the Performing Arts Center gave them a greater appreciation of science concepts. Realistically, it is unlikely that disinterested students were inspired to study science further because they experienced a hands-on lesson in the theatre. However, this grant project augmented my science colleague's respect for theatre. Through the course of devising and teaching lessons that connected science to theatre technology, he came to value theatre education for its significant abilities to prepare students for life. He surmised:

> We talk a lot about 21st century skills and authentic learning. As I spend more time in the theatre and see all the behind-the-scenes work that goes into it, I realize it is one of the best avenues we have to teach students about a complex project, especially all the problem solving and different skills that go into a production. I can't think of another thing our students do that is this complex; [theatre experience] will prepare them for any job that involves project-oriented work.
>
> ("The Science of Theatre" 2012)

Despite misgivings about decreased creative inspiration, technology overload, diminished autonomy, and commitment to directing annual musicals, I am gratified by opportunities that have raised the profile of theatre arts in our school district because of the Performing Arts Center. Additional challenges such as school levies and staff changes loom in the wings. This new theatre remains a temporary stage.

## NOTES

1 The road to a full-time theatre manager hire was long, but I kept the squeaky wheel in motion. Continual reminders about safety and protection paid off. The first two years that the Performing Arts Center was in use, I hired a former student with a college degree and professional experience in technical theatre to work with the Drama Club as a freelance artist. During those two years, I advocated tirelessly for the full-time hire of a theatre manager/technical director. At the beginning of the third year, the school board approved the hire of a half-time business manager and a half-time technical director. At the beginning of the fourth year, when the part-time business manager quit to gain full-time employment, the technical director embraced both positions and was employed full-time as Theatre Manager.

2 The grant, awarded by the Martha Holden Jennings Foundation in Ohio, enabled us to hire the freelance technical director whom the school board employed as half-time technical director.

3 For a deeper reflection on this project from an artistic perspective, see Gonzalez (2014).

# SECTION THREE

## Critically Oriented Drama Education Examines Controversy and Oppression

# Chapter 9

## Establishing a Foundation for Examining Tough Issues

A circus came to town the summer before I launched the first Play Production CODE course. I took my two young daughters. We sat on the bleachers eating popcorn and watching the acrobatic act.

Mexican concessionaires wearing caps that sport the Coca-Cola insignia hawk American flags. Mexican performers with names like Mikaela perform aerial tricks to instrumentals of songs such as "The Shadow of Your Smile." Six Appaloosa horses adorned with fluffy, pink, feathered accouterments trot in a small ring. The music? The children's song "Ten Little Indians" and "Colors of the Wind" from Disney's animated film *Pocahontas* (1995) rise above the steady rhythmic beat of a kettle drum.

The ring master announces two young Mexican girls as the fifth generation of a family of circus performers. The girls, about six years old, are dressed in black halter tops and spandex shorts with gold trim. They climb onto two low-hung half-ladders suspended from the Big Top. The ladders are attached so they will swing in sync; each ladder is equipped with foot straps for safety. This is clearly an act in training, for looming tall and suspended high above the two half-ladders is the ladder that "Stephanie" will use.

Stephanie—one of the few white performers in the circus besides the ringmaster and the clowns—is clad in a bikini. She enters from behind the two little girls wearing a long, sheer, pink-ruffled robe and plastic heels. After the girls are introduced, Stephanie glides to the ladder and the performance begins.

The music is slow and sensual as Stephanie stretches her legs apart in an upside-down split, curves her muscular thighs around the bar, and then arches her back, touching her head to her foot. As these sinewy contortions continue, slowly and gracefully, more than one man whistles and shouts. The little girls swing back and forth on their ladders on either side of Stephanie. Smiling, they stretch their arms outward to recognize the audience. Then they slip their feet into the protective sheaths and drop themselves quickly upside down, as their ladders swing double-time to the languid, erotic movements of Stephanie's muscular body.

Then the music ceases and the drum roll begins: Stephanie is going to spin around and around underneath the ladder, holding on with nothing but her teeth, her jaw clamped tightly to a leather strap suspended from the bottom of the ladder.

Ta-da! The act is over! The young girls drop off their ladders and bow as a man on stilts assists Stephanie off her ladder. Stephanie bows to the audience, then gestures to a clown who kneels and hands her a red rose. The performers exit.

The legacy passes on. The simplicity of a young girl's act will evolve, in parallel with the maturation of her body, into a sultry series of coils and twirls that will beckon the interest of men. The circus ushers her into womanhood. She'll become tough, deft, and strong; she will discover ways to make men and women alike hold their breaths in anticipation.

In the circus, identity performs on the high wire. Girls practice on the "daring trapeze" so that it appears both easy and enticing. But there is other danger in this act. Two young Mexican girls, exotic in their otherness, watch a beautiful white woman on the bar above. The girls gaze upon an unattainable ideal as the white audience, their assumptions of gender and ethnicity affirmed by the circus, gazes upon them.

## EVOLUTION OF ORIGINAL SCRIPTS WITH CONTROVERSIAL THEMES

Like high-wire circus performers, students onstage perform acts of risk, too. In two courses, Play Production and Social Issues Theatre, students have freedom to write, stage, and perform stories that reveal truths about their lived experiences. In rehearsal for co-curricular published productions, they explore the oppressions of others, real and fictional, and relate their stories to aspects of their own lives. All of these stories, original and professionally written, can motivate students to rethink accepted notions of marginalized ideologies. I, like a harness, support them as they gain insight and confidence to exert control over oppressive forces that pressure their daily routines.

Both CODE courses are divided into two nine-week sections. During the first half, students research, practice theatre skills, and write; during the second, they cast, rehearse, refine, and perform. The goal of students in Play Production is to gain complete ownership of one scene. Elements include writing, casting, directing, and establishing lighting and sound cues. Additionally, students serve as peer editors and actors for one another. Initial free-writings prompted by thought-provoking questions such as, "A discovery I made about someone whom I once ignored was ..." evolve into scenes three–eight minutes in length with themes such as teen incarceration, suicide, agnosticism, sexual orientation, death, greed, and war. I encourage students to explore controversial topics as they shape drafts; those with gentler content portray characters in classmates' edgier scenes. Before the Performing Arts Center was available, students performed in the intimate make-shift 40-seat Theatre Studio.

Subjects that have become the focus of study and scene development in Social Issues Theatre include abusing prescription pills, homophobia, technology's influence on humanity, human trafficking, stereotyping, self-injury, dating abuse, domestic violence, and driving while intoxicated. The overriding goal of the class is for students to recognize everyday acts of sexism, racism, classism, ageism, and other forms of oppression that are hidden by the accepted ideologies of their school, communities, and nation. Toward the end of the semester, students invite peers to an all-day workshop that includes trust-building activities, information about the topic, satire, theatre exercises used to explore the subjects adapted from Augusto Boal's Theatre of the Oppressed techniques, and presentation of an original activating scene.

In the workshop, attendees engage with the activating scene, which stops when the protagonist is stuck in a moment of crisis. At that point, students are invited to explore the unscripted conclusion together. This strategy helps students find multiple ways for the protagonist to extract him/herself from the situation. In an activating scene, each option the protagonist seeks must be denied by fellow actors to stimulate as many safe alternatives as possible.

Teaching students to be cognizant of conditions that they can change, and modeling for them how to change are keys to their developing self-agency. In Section Three, I describe and analyze factors in the CODE Play Production and Social Issues Theatre classes that cultivate critical inquiry. I augment this inquiry of classroom practice with examples from rehearsals and performances of co-curricular productions to examine the limitations of critically conscious teaching and directing when edgy topics are investigated and shaped for performance. Illustrations from the courses and co-curricular productions alternate as I scrutinize challenges induced by critical theatre teaching at the high school level.

## LEADING DISCUSSIONS OF CONTROVERSIAL SUBJECT MATTER

In a traditional educational setting, institutionalized knowledge protects the status quo. When teachers expect students to consume knowledge, "[their] work becomes confined to controlling classroom life and exerting institutional authority" (Britzman 1991, 225). Teaching for critical consciousness requires theatre teachers to recognize that the knowledge they bring to the classroom and rehearsal is partial and biased. Also, even the most liberated of teachers work within oppressive systems. Britzman contends that "the context of teaching is political, it is an ideological context that privileges the interest, values and practices necessary to maintain the status quo, and ironically, the powerlessness of teachers" (11). Britzman refers to the education students attain in this setting as "artificial school knowledge" (45). When students engage in the process of knowing in a way that is visceral and real, they weaken the power that artificial school knowledge has to normalize (45).

In CODE classrooms and rehearsals, students add knowledge about themselves and the world by learning from each other. Multiple voices and realities clash when students listen to a cascade of peers' stories in a moderated classroom setting. This dissonance energizes them to consider and evaluate, and then ultimately begin the self-actualizing process of forming, and then clarifying, personal perspective on potentially controversial subjects. Under these conditions, inviting discussion on controversial topics to promote responsible citizenship can seem not only surreptitious, but subversive. This is because, unlike the clear resolutions of decision-making, controversy is "always emotive, threatening to disorganize social convention and individual preconceptions" (Britzman 1991, 187).

Some teachers may steer teens away from class discussions on controversial topics because these talks can consume time, thwart control techniques, border on subversion, and require teachers and students to question together. More conducive to school schedules are character-building programs that teach good decision-making skills. These programs are often limited to guest speakers at assemblies centered on adult-authored stories. In such instances, students are receptors of knowledge. For example, the dangers of sexting was the subject of one recent presentation by a guest speaker for our middle and high school students. The information was delivered clearly and energetically, but students engaged in no teacher-moderated small-group conversations after the assembly.

Some teachers may steer teens away from class discussions on controversial topics because these talks can consume time, thwart control techniques, border on subversion, and require teachers and students to question together.

The following year, administrators launched a program wherein teachers would lead workshops in their individual classrooms on the national hot topic of bullying. Using the Olweus method as a template, once each month every student participated in a prescribed, teacher-led mini-lesson.[1] The classroom/discussion concept aimed to impact students more effectively than an all-school assembly might; the goal was that students would acquire insight and build confidence to speak out when bullying situations arose in hallways, classrooms, the cafeteria, and other places identified as common sites for harassment.

While many teachers reported positive interactions with their classes, some students said their teachers led the lessons perfunctorily. Perhaps they viewed the mini-lessons as an intrusion on class time, or they were not comfortable stepping away from the power-center to make room for student authority. Teacher buy-in is essential for meaningful conversations about a controversial topic, especially when the topic is not directly related to class curriculum. With teacher buy-in, seemingly disjointed content finds meaning.

Political science professor Andrew Hacker believes that mandates to increase the rigor of mathematics requirements aim at the wrong objective. Claiming that the majority of students will not apply abstract calculations such as quadratic equations in routine work as adults, he proposes that mathematics be introduced in conjunction with art, music, and even poetry. "The aim," he rationalizes, "would be to treat mathematics as a liberal art, making it as accessible and welcoming as sculpture or ballet" (Hacker 2012, 7). In traditional classes, topics that invite dialogue about challenging social issues are an intrusion if not integrated creatively into the course curriculum. Meaningful exploration of controversial topics takes commitment on the part of the teacher and the students; it requires time, as well as creativity, to find connections between the social issue and the state-mandated course content. The CODE classes that I teach may be highly tuned for student self-agency, but all teachers can look for and open the pockets—the potential moments that arise in their classrooms—for student self-agency.

Meaningful exploration of controversial topics takes commitment on the part of the teacher and the students; it requires time, as well as creativity, to find connections between the social issue and the state-mandated course content.

Admitting discussion of controversial topics into our classrooms allows students to engage responsibly in conversations about contemporary, real issues that increase students' respect for, and ability to listen to, each other. Commitment increases when students recognize that discussions create the foundation for *performance*, for performance illuminates self-image, a powerful motivator for adolescents. From the thicket of dialogue emerge students with greater understanding of other perspectives and a clearer sense of their own opinions. Together, these new perceptions inform wiser decision-making.

The knowledge that students gain by participating in moderated dialogue with their peers about controversial topics is grounded in interpretation because everyone brings a different context to the experience (Scholnick 2000, 39). In Social Issues Theatre, individuals' good decisions are informed by group-developed understandings that lead to fresh ways of thinking.

Christopher Worthman (2004) describes these processes as "dialogue," explaining:

> Indeed, dialogic practice begins with students defining and reflecting on their own perspective and seeing those perspectives as multifaceted and influenced by others' perspectives. [...] Consciousness of one's perspective and the dialogism necessary to foster voice and perspective development are grounded in a growing awareness of the multiplicity of perspectives in the world.
>
> (366)

Ellsworth claims "it is precisely the imperfect fits and slippages in the space of difference between text and world, knowledge and the real" that makes it possible for our students to "recognize what counts as valuable in their lives" (1997, 161). Mutability makes working with issues-based theatre exciting and rewarding. Recognizing that teaching is, by nature, unstable can give us confidence, rather than doubt, to foray with our students into territory where difference, contradiction, and pools of "un-answers" mark the terrain.

## EXPLORING WHAT WORKS ... AND WHAT DOESN'T: SOMETIMES TRADITIONAL TEACHING METHODS ARE BEST

I did not learn to teach in ways that apply precepts of feminist pedagogy, wherein teachers accept notions of "unknowability," partial understandings, and shifting, multiple points of view. In classrooms and rehearsals, I often follow what Scholnick calls "masculinest" models of teaching, out of habit (2000, 32–34). Only later do I realize that I've made assumptions without realizing it because ingrained in my educational psyche is a model of teaching whereby I am the all-knowing "vessel" out of which pours knowledge.

Of course, there are times when teachers need to disseminate information, and effective critical educators recognize where masculinist teaching and directing methods are necessary. For years I envisioned my tenth-grade English classroom as a site for critical, feminist leadership. I would consciously step out of my authoritative stance, adapting drama-based activities into lessons as often as possible. I taught sophomore English in the Theatre Studio, an appropriate space for creative expression. But unlike the theatre courses I taught in this room, short attention-spans, unfocused conversations, inhibitions, and weak student self-discipline characterized my sophomore English students. Teaching sophomore English was frustrating.

A school counselor suggested that I rethink my approach to teaching tenth-grade English. After all, some students in a required course just want to pass the class and move on. Others are inculcated into a system of learning by rote from teachers they trust are always right; those students are discomforted when taught by a teacher whose authority they perceive is lax. Their feelings of awkwardness manifest in disruptive behavior. Ira Shor asserts that in a class without traditional discipline, "students can doubt the seriousness of the course, thinking that real education is not going on here because the teacher's authority is low-profile and nontraditional." He explains that in the whole of their experience, "students have not had much chance to practice mutual dialogue, co-governance, self-control, and cooperative learning" (157, 1992).

Taking the counselor's advice, I asked to teach the sophomore English class in a more traditional classroom. Bulletin boards displayed content pertaining to French literature, not sophomore English, but that didn't matter. What mattered was that students sat in rows of chairs facing me, where I stood front and center before them, flanked by a smart board. The change in student focus was immediate and consistent. They were comfortable, and I had less stress. Whenever I would introduce a drama-based lesson or invite their input, students valued the approaches for their uniqueness. For the most part, though, traditional routine was their favored learning companion. This experience reminded me that to effectively navigate the waters of tradition in a feminist ship, sometimes we must steer into, investigate, and use to our advantage channels of masculinist tributaries.

This experience reminded me that to effectively navigate the waters of tradition in a feminist ship, sometimes we must steer into, investigate, and use to our advantage channels of masculinist tributaries.

## TESTIMONIES CONTRIBUTE SUBSTANCE TO RESEARCH

Qualitative researchers are challenged by the accepted notion that hard results—quantified numbers—better communicate successful learning and growth than anecdotal evidence or interpretation of long-term effects. Cognizant of this comparison, McCammon and Saldaña describe their research on adults' perceptions of the impact theatre experience has made on their lives as a study centered on systematic research methods. The collective testimonies of over 200 interviewees holds much more value, they assert, than data compiled by a single academic (2011, 9).[2] I am always in the position of convincing administrators that what happens in the classroom and onstage, though difficult to quantify, richly impacts the lives of students far beyond high school. Omasta asserts that the field of theatre education would benefit significantly if more teachers would publish case studies of their individual program models (Omasta 2012, 26). Encouraging teachers to contribute qualitative research, Jim Palmarini, EdTA's Director of Advocacy, asserts:

> Without those stories, our allies—parents, decision makers, and arts advocates—have only half the evidence they need to make the case for a theatre program. Between research like that contained in this survey and the stories we all know, theatre education's champions can help shape methodology, training, public policy, and more.
>
> (Palmarini 2012, 30)

Thus, when I feel change is taking place but have difficulty quantifying the evidence, I am disconcerted and unsettled. I will always be learning how to teach from a critical perspective. In the next chapter, I analyze five strategies for CODE to unfold an ongoing reflexive practice that informs my ever-evolving insight into how and why I teach theatre in ways that aim to liberate rather than conform.

## NOTES

1 Our school utilized resources developed by the Olweus Bullying Prevention Program, Hazelden Foundation, 2007.

2 The complete monograph is unpublished, but a detailed summary of the study is published in *Youth Theatre Journal* 26 (1) (2012): 2–25.

# Chapter 10

## Unfolding Ongoing Reflective Practice Through Five CODE Strategies

In Play Production and Social Issues Theatre, content is open to student input and therefore highly flexible. While indoctrination has induced many students to feel most comfortable learning course content through teacher-fed methods, the continual practice of being told what is right and wrong has also tuned students out. By high school, information about safety, healthy relationships, and good decision-making falls on adolescents' deaf ears. Students view adult-delivered social messages as if they were bad-tasting medicine. CODE offers an alternative angle, one comprised of student-driven but teacher-guided strategies for student-crafted original scenes about serious, edgy topics.

## STUDENTS RESIST TEACHER-FED SCRIPT

Students in the first section of Social Issues Theatre reacted with misgivings about teacher-fed material on the topic that they had chosen to explore: driving while intoxicated. What resulted influenced the direction of the course syllabus for subsequent classes, for it led to the inclusion of original short satirical scenes that students annually perform in the culminating workshop. Additionally, the anecdote compares the connection students have to their own research with information imposed by an adult authority.

Community leaders interested in youth issues expressed concern about driving while intoxicated because prom time was approaching. These adults were planning a public forum to increase parent and teen awareness of underage alcohol consumption. One individual involved in this project provided me with two short scripts written by a professional adult playwright who explicitly depicted the dangers of driving while under the influence of alcohol. Because this adult was interested in teens putting on a short play for the community, and as students had yet to create an activating scene, I agreed to have the class rehearse the scripts.

The plays were didactic, simplistic, and very serious. One took place in a nondescript location where characters realize each has been killed in accidents involving drunken drivers; the other was narrated by a teenager who, having been killed in a drunken-driving accident, recalls the events that led up to the accident and her funeral. The discourse of the "announcer" was formatted as a droning lecture:

> The short play that you are about to see is based upon actual tragedies that have resulted from drunken driving. It is called *The Waiting Room*, and it carries a dramatic and important message for all of us. [...] Two out of every five Americans will be involved in an alcohol-related crash during their lifetime. On an average weekend night, one out of every ten drivers who pass you on the road is legally impaired or drunk. [...] Each year, about 500,000 people suffer injuries in alcohol-related traffic crashes. [...] With the help of tougher laws, and with better public awareness through programs such as this, we pray that the wholesale slaughter on our highways will soon become only a memory of a hard lesson learned.
>
> (Roberts 1997, 5; 20–21)

While students obliged me in the process of rehearsing these teacher-fed scripts for four days, their politeness verged on apathy. The premise wasn't new to them, although they considered the statistics suspect because they'd not done the research themselves. The scripts explicitly communicated a single interpretation, closed to dialogue: "If you drink and drive, you will die." After four days of reading, casting, and staging, I asked the class if they thought the play would work for their peers. They opined that the play could be valuable for a team of fifth-grade performers and an elementary school audience, but it was much too "preachy" to maintain the interest of teens. I told them I understood their point of view, and they exhaled a palpable, collective sigh of relief. Then a senior, Jake, suggested that the class could write a better play; the students in the class with experience of writing original scripts became vocal proponents of the idea and swayed those with less experience.

The scripts I had given students held little potential for student ownership, but because they had the freedom to dismiss the idea, students now shared an experience to which they could compare their own creative, collaborative efforts. When I responded positively to Jake's suggestion, the class recognized that they could disagree with my authority-offered script and also conduct research to point out the dangers of drinking and driving.

## CODE CONDITIONS IN A CLASSROOM SUPPORT STUDENT-WRITTEN SCENES ON HOT TOPICS

Students must gain a degree of depth in order to craft original scenes realistically about sensitive social issues. Conducting research and holding conversations with guest experts on the subject enables students to learn facts, gain statistics, and understand bases for conflicting points of view that create convincing scenarios. In addition to research, teacher-moderated student discussions about topics build trust and community, factors essential to forming a positive, creative atmosphere for building original scenes. Because students can feel exposed if classroom conversations hit close to home, teachers can model the appropriate tone for sharing personal anecdotes by telling a story themselves. Remaining sensitive to the pulse of the group, teachers also should be willing to allow students to explore non-realistic and even comical approaches to capturing the essence of the topic when crafting scenes. Finally, teachers should sense those moments when students need traditional teacher-presence for maintaining commitment and meeting deadlines, and step in as the authority when necessary.

## Strategy #1: The Spoonful of Sugar—Incorporate Satire to Advance Serious Work

Though teens can be quick to use ridicule as a defense mechanism, teens simultaneously understand that well-shaped ridicule makes points worth considering. In Social Issues Theatre, satire provides more than comic relief.

In the process of writing the realistic, serious scene about driving while intoxicated, students became bogged down early in the process. Some didn't understand how their ideas would transform into a polished script; others felt the script would lack the kind of energy that made it fun to perform. Once again, Jake had an idea. He suggested that we look at the subject from a satirical perspective. Students discussed the implications of this: Would they be making fun of the issue? Would they be laughed *at* rather than laughed *with*? What point would the satire make?

The majority of students were enthusiastic about giving satire a try, and they immediately brainstormed conflicts. The procedure I devised with them remains the model students follow to develop satirical scene work in Social Issues Theatre. I divide the class into teams of three. This marks the first time students less familiar with one another strive to accomplish a goal related to the workshop that their individual cliques of friends will attend. Fifteen minutes is all they need to create satirical scenes about social issues, because teens relate to satire; it pushes boundaries, it's fun, and the points are important. Simple, direct, short, and clear, the scenes remain for the workshop almost exactly as they were staged in the original improvisation. Two scenes are presented below. The first evolved out of the class that explored driving while intoxicated; the second was devised by a class that studied homophobia.

## Scene 1: "The Best Drunk Driver"

*(Brenda, Emily, Kayla, Steve, and Deb are gathered on the floor, playing cards, drinking, and munching on snacks.)*

BRENDA: Oh man, it's getting late. I really gotta get goin'.

EMILY: All right, man. Have a good one. (*Brenda pulls out her keys to leave.*) Wait a minute! How much have you had to drink?

BRENDA: Nothing.

EMILY: Dude, you can't drive like that, you're sober! (*Emily takes keys from Brenda.*)

BRENDA: Man, I can't believe I tried to do that. What was I thinking? Good call! (*Emily prepares to leave with Brenda.*)

KAYLA: Ha, ha! Emily, you are almost as sober as she is. You are in no condition to drive. I'll drive. (*Kayla, obviously drunk, takes the keys from Emily.*)

EMILY: You're right, man. What was I trying to do? Thanks, girlfriend! (*Kayla gets ready to leave with Brenda.)*

STEVE: Wait. What? You think you can drive? I am a much better drunk driver than you are!

KAYLA: Oh, you're right. Here. (*Hands him the keys, and Steve and Brenda prepare to leave. Deb falls over drunk on Steve.*)

STEVE: I think we found a better drunk driver than me! Take these. (*Steve hands the keys to Deb.*)

Deb: H-how many b-beers have you guys had? (*Everyone rattles off numbers.*) Man, if you guys can count, you're not drunk enough! Carry me to the car. I'll take her home. (*Deb and Brenda leave the scene, as everyone agrees that they found the best drunken driver among them.)*

## Scene 2: "Fagzilla"

A reporter describes to a friend a horrible beast he claimed he just saw, as two girls pick flowers in Central Park. An effeminately portrayed male asks for directions to a clothing store. The girls notice the male, shriek "Fagzilla!!" and run away.

Students discover on their own the value of research-based knowledge. They desire rather than disdain it, and want to share it with their peers. The year that a class chose dating violence as their topic, students wrote a 20-minute satire called "Sadtown Zombie Puppet Theatre." Fueled by individual and group research, and information delivered by a guest speaker, writers smoothly incorporated 85 facts about dating violence into the scene, scripted for delivery by various sock puppet characters.

When asked to reflect on the scenes, students offered comments indicating that, for the most part, satire achieves its intended effect. One student explained:

> Our friends saw that we have a sense of humor and, if nothing else, we can make fun of being too serious. This was a strong point, because the laughter unified the participants into knowing that we were an all-right bunch.

This student instinctively understood how comedy can level class facilitators with their peers. The satirical scenes communicate that course members are not trying to put on the guise of expert; they are learning with their peers, not "teaching at" them. Students also recognize that satire lightens the mood and thus becomes a gateway into the serious work. As one student commented, "It's easier to open doors and let people choose to enter than to push people through."

Humor was not a path I had originally thought students would or should tread in Social Issues Theatre. In fact, had I suggested satire, they might have dismissed the idea. Satire scenes, written alongside the serious scene, add to students' sense of ownership. Furthermore, more successfully than any message play or teacher-fed acts, student-written and performed satire scenes can point out the ridiculous extent to which human beings divide, marginalize, and inflict emotional and physical harm.

## Strategy #2: Invite Self-Disclosure

Building trust among students early in the semester of both courses is vital because the honesty and depth of their scripts involve self-disclosure. Self-disclosure is a powerful element in the process of transformation, which refers to the ongoing influence that a class can make on a student, even after the course is over. Occasionally, transformation leads toward students' increased self-esteem, a decrease in risky and unhealthy behavior, and reconsideration of embedded beliefs.

One student, Sue, wrote an autobiographical scene she called "Oppression," in which demon voices tell her she is worthless, ugly, and unloved. These voices represent failure in the form of friendships, school, and communication with parents. Sue tries to block out the voices but is successful only after cutting her wrist with the sharp point of a compass until she bleeds. The stage lights pulsate red as Sue asks the audience, "Sometimes I wish this was over. Don't you?"

Three years later, when Sue was 19, she commented on the script she had written:

> Sharing what I did in my play opened so many floodgates of healing. [...] I often go back and reread my play. [...] I know that if I forget what happened to me, it will be so much easier for it to happen to me again.

The following year, Sue enrolled in a different drama class that required students to write, stage, and perform original monologues. The monologue that Sue wrote was a positive affirmation of how one can live through and out of darkness. Sue explained in retrospect:

> A part of me needed to prove [...] that I had overcome the depression and the demons. I wanted everyone to know how I came out, because [...] that oppression made me realize what can happen to a human soul. There are ways out of it, though. I wanted to share what mine was, and show that I had become strong and conquered the depression in my own way.

Sue's self-disclosure represents a nonhierarchical classroom "where all voices can be heard because all students are free to speak, knowing their presence will be recognized and valued" (hooks 1994, 186). Sue's scene increased her self-confidence because, through composing the words and shaping the structure of the piece, she faced her fears; she trounced on her fears by performing them.

She trounced on her fears by performing them.

Autobiographical dramatization is a powerful means for students to gain self-agency, but autobiography critic Wendy Hesford cautions teachers to beware of the coercive nature of self-disclosing accounts. She asserts that autobiographies reinforce prevailing assumptions embedded in educational structures. Because students learn to write scenes in ways that help them pass standardized tests, the style and discipline required for passing such tests normalize their writing techniques. This process, in turn, standardizes their self-narratives (1999, 35). Through this lens, Sue's publicly dramatized personal narratives were but a step toward a truly complex liberalizing pedagogy. The initial scene was progressive because it addressed factors that lead to self-injury, including thoughts of suicide. But it was also reactionary because it was shaped by the standards of the institution. When we equate individual voice with democratic pedagogy, we ignore the power relations within and outside the school "that continue to disadvantage members of oppressed groups and leave the language and terms of the discourse unchanged" (Maher and Tetreault 2001, 218). Sue's dramatized narrative represents a radical pedagogy with limitations. Remembering this keeps my expectations realistic, even as I teach with the hope that students are gaining liberatory experiences.

## Strategy #3: Build Trust to Raise Social Consciousness and Express Emotion Honestly

Despite implications that self-disclosure through personal narrative reinforces the privilege of institutionalized norms, the collaborative, cooperative, collective process of CODE builds trust among students and leads to discussions that raise student consciousness about issues that extend beyond their personal lives. Discussions spring up throughout the research and writing processes in Play Production and Social Issues Theatre. Some of these are formal, where we pull the chairs into a circle and discuss current newspaper and magazine articles that resonate with issues they are contemplating; many others are impromptu. The process of dialogue provides students the "opportunity to learn from and teach each other, collectively address problems of social injustice, and imagine and think through alternative responses" (Fisher 2001, 32). These discussions become a bonding element, raising students' self-awareness in relation to each other and to teens nationwide.

In a 1999 Play Production post-performance reflection, some students wrote about the shooting at Columbine High School in Littleton, Colorado, about which the class had held several discussions. Their references to Columbine demonstrate that the issues with which students were dealing raised their consciousness both of themselves and the nation at large.[1] One student, noting that the discussions we had about the school shooting were a memorable element of the class, recalled, "not only did [the discussions] help all of us deal with the whole ordeal, but it made us really think: what can we do to help prevent it from happening to us?"

Unfortunately, the Columbine shooting is no longer the landmark of contemporary U.S. gun massacres that it was when the first edition of this book was published; it was in the spotlight temporarily, serving now as a backdrop for conversations about subsequent mass killings that have terrorized the American public. Writing this second edition of *Temporary Stages* in the wake of the Aurora, Colorado movie theatre massacre in the summer of 2012, I anticipate stimulating dialogue in my upcoming Social Issues Theatre class about gun control, or how family members of killers react, or what students thought of the police officers who were unusually stationed outside the cinema in our own town's small mall in the aftermath of the shooting.

No doubt there will be conflicting viewpoints when this topic arises. Jakubowski and Visano opine that dissenting students stimulate discussions because the turbulence of controversy can aid students' ability to:

> ... look at what assumptions they are bringing to a discussion, and at where these seemingly fixed assumptions are coming from—leading them to recognize their own biases and, possibly, the origins of those biases. Ideally, it means encouraging them to get out of the frames they have been using and perhaps thinking more unconventional thoughts.
>
> (2002, 11)

In the class that chose the topic of driving while intoxicated, one student asserted that its strongest aspect was the expression of feelings when it came to "class talks" about the so-called Trench Coat Mafia and Marilyn Manson, images that figured prominently in the news after the Columbine High School shootings. She explained, "We all developed such powerful bonds that we were comfortable around each other at all times. We could give one another advice without hurting feelings." Fisher claims that bonding emerges when a classroom discussion raises students' consciousness of social issues because it invites emotional forthrightness (2001, 70). CODE classrooms provide a protective outlet for students to share their thoughts on significant social shocks like mass tragedies because discussions are guided by a responsible, caring adult. Educational psychologist Jan Hughes claims that building trusting relationships between teachers and students reduces violence in schools more effectively than surveillance cameras and metal detectors (Kalb 1999, 43).

The mass shootings of the past decade at Columbine High School, Virginia Technical University, the cinema in Aurora, Colorado, and—most recently—the massacre of 20 Sandy Hook Elementary School children and six educators in Newtown, Connecticut, were perpetrated by young men burdened by emotional problems. The teenage boys in my CODE classrooms talk about these actions with concern about their self-images as guys, gun-law protection, and appreciation for freedoms we generally take for granted. As a theatre teacher in a co-ed public school, I help boys express themselves, and I foster communication between boys, and between boys and girls. Boys need this support. Norah Vincent observes in her memoir *Self-Made Man*:

> So much of what happens emotionally between men isn't spoken aloud, and so the outsider, especially the female outsider who is used to emotional

> life being overt and spoken (often over-spoken), tends to assume that what isn't said isn't there. But it is there.
>
> (2006, 46)

Part of the process of girls establishing their social identity involves recognizing that boys' emotions exist, though often they appear buried. The feminist high school classroom can foster interactive communication and dialogue so that girls encourage boys, and boys encourage boys, to bring more of their emotions to the surface.

This was brought to life for me in the Play Production class during the rehearsal of their production titled *Seeing Eye-to-Eye: A Glimpse of Reality*. In one vignette, the male author, Tom, composed seven different reasons why a teenage boy would consider killing himself by driving suicidally fast down a flat, open country road. Confused, angry, depressed, sarcastic, each character was intent upon testing the limits of his control behind the wheel. Part way through the rehearsal process, Tom decided to add a laugh track to underscore the piece. My initial reaction, which I kept to myself, was, "That would destroy the poignancy of every moment Tom has created!" But I chose to remain silent, and let the class discuss the idea.

After the actors staged the scene in rehearsal, I asked, "What do you think of the addition?" Some students were unsure why it had been included, but others commented that it added humor to the scene. Near the end of the conversation, one senior girl, Jane, commented, "I think it's cool the way you guys show your emotions onstage relating to such a serious topic. I think the laugh track takes all the honesty away." Later, Tom reflected in his journal, "I didn't want my scene to come off looking stupid. What Jane said made me think, so I took the laugh track out. But I still think it would've been funny."[2]

How truly humorous he thought the laugh track was, or whether the laugh track was a cover-up for real thoughts of suicide, I can only guess. What I do know is that our high school was experiencing a rash of suicides at the time this class was held. Because class dialogue focused on topics that genuinely mattered to teens, Tom listened to the opinion of a female peer who wanted to see boys express emotions with sincerity and simplicity. Jane appreciated Tom's public expression of emotions, an observation that contrasts sharply with a parody once performed during an all-school pep rally in which a male teacher, acting like a newly crowned beauty queen, wiped away mock tears.

Carol Gilligan, attending to today's "boy crisis," asserts that the mental health of boys would increase if they gained comfort expressing themselves emotionally:

> Emotions and relationships, once associated with women and therefore with limitation, are now understood to enhance intelligence and the self,

> and have become desirable attributes of manhood. [...] An effective strategy for preventing boys' psychological difficulties and educational problems would involve recognizing their sensitivities, building honest relationships and strengthening a healthy capacity for resistance.
>
> (Gilligan 2006, 53)[3]

The consciousness-raising precept of feminist pedagogy that shapes CODE also provides an opportunity for boys and girls to challenge accepted notions of masculinity. In our culture, few spaces permit boys to show a variety of emotions. A feminist theatre classroom is one of them. In light of a decade's slate of mass killings, how the fight for male superiority festers into violence in our culture is a topic that simmers under the surface of discussions. While students don't explicitly describe "the fight for male superiority," student writers often wrestle with the "Tough Guise," a term Jackson Katz coined to refer to the gendered image of masculinity which links power, control, threats, violence, homophobia, and the glamorization of drugs and alcohol to "real" manhood (2000).

In our culture, few spaces permit boys to show a variety of emotions.

In Play Production, some male students choose to critique society's perceptions of teen boys. One student, Blake, wrote and delivered a monologue entitled "Guys Like Me." His monologue questioned whether or not men attract women more successfully through bravado rather than by demonstrating vulnerabilities, passion, and caring:

> I've been hearing all my life from the opposite sex that they're looking for [...] a guy who isn't selfish, who is in tune with what he's feeling, who isn't looking for "wham-bam-thank-you-ma'am," but rather a meaningful relationship. "I need a guy like that, but not you because" and here are the words which haunt my nightmares, "you're my best friend." Apparently I'm everyone's best friend these days. Apparently that nice guy crap goes out the window when the thinker clicks off and the simian instinct takes over. Apparently nice guys aren't chic. Apparently, Bad-to-the-Bone George Thorogoods are the real winners.
>
> (*Anything Else Would Be Substandard* 1999)

Blake's monologue made visible the connection between male image and brute force by suggesting an alternative construct of masculinity that celebrates intellect and sensitivity. His re-vision of masculinity became a consciousness-raising opportunity because it allowed Blake to present another construct of the male teen, although it remained safely within the boundaries of male/female pairing.[4]

## Strategy #4: Integrate Teacher Voice to Model Vulnerability as Strength

As students self-disclose and express emotions in CODE classrooms, they make themselves vulnerable to peer and teacher judgment. No human is invulnerable; it is inevitable that in sharing points of view about issues important to them, some teens will tell personal anecdotes which expose circumstances or feelings that compel group trust. This trust is essential for developing insight into controversial issues and experiences in which students feel oppressed.

In the Social Issues Theatre class, students spend one class period telling "It Made Me Think" stories. Limited to a one-minute story per student, this exercise asks students to depict incidents from their own experiences that relate to the topic. In the class that explored driving while intoxicated, for instance, the stories had to involve someone who drank and drove a motor vehicle. The storyteller concludes with the words, "It made me think." Storytellers do not tell what the story makes them think about, just that it made them think. After each story, students write a comment or question to the storyteller on a notecard that informs the storyteller about what the story makes the listener think about.[5]

Emotional tones range from serious to ludicrous, but no story is deemed trivial and all students participate. In the class that examined drunk driving, one student told of a traumatic car accident she had been in the previous summer when a motorcyclist, driving under the influence, had struck her car and lost his life in the crash. Another relayed that her four-year-old brother was run over in the driveway by a vehicle being backed out of by a drunken family member. Knowledge is fluid, introduced by the students, and engaging for every person in the class. In this activity, students construct knowledge about the pervasiveness of the problem as they listen and respond to one another's anecdotes.

I am highly conscious of if, when, and where my own voice should fit into the activity. Moderating the activity but not knowing in advance what each student's story will be, I operate in the state of unknowing. What if someone tells an inappropriate story? What if someone cries? Will these stories give us enough substance to lead us to the next step? These questions keep me both on edge and at bay, teaching from an altered position of power that centralizes students' voices.

Mandell and Wolf explain that in a class where students reveal emotion, personal information, and conflict (which occurs infrequently in their other classes during the school day), students need to be sure of the teacher's commitment to their agreement that, within the safe space, they will take risks together and that exploitation will not be a consequence of mutual risk-taking (2003, 40).[6] In other words, students need to feel that I am a member of the ensemble, too. Thus, for the class that explored DWI, I decided to tell a story myself. Yet, risk accompanied this choice, because teachers should consider carefully before sharing personal information. Fear of administrative reprimand might unsettle teachers who tell a particularly gruesome tale or one that makes them suspect of illegal activity. Students unaccustomed to personal engagement with teachers might be leery of teachers who reveal aspects of their personal lives. At the same time, sharing reveals a teacher's humanity, which can make the teacher more accessible. Nevertheless, teachers who choose to tell about troublesome situations from their personal lives make themselves vulnerable, and vulnerability can be lonely and unnerving.

CODE is designed to maximize student engagement and minimize authoritative answers. Thus, students and I were working together through the problem of driving under the influence, because I believe none of us—teacher/adult or student/minor—is immune to the problem. All humans are tempted by vices (food, alcohol, gambling, addictive behaviors to improve body image, and others), and we continually fight temptations that put us at risk. I posed my story to strengthen the ensemble commitment of the class and to deepen their thinking on the problem of driving while intoxicated.

I told of the time when I was in graduate school and had participated in a friend's wine-tasting party. Afterwards, I drove six miles on a highway to my apartment. Halfway there, I observed a police car behind me, no lights flashing. The police car followed my car off the exit ramp and along the street to the alley next to my garage. The policeman parked his car beside mine and sat with the motor running as I got out and walked toward my back door. Then he drove off. Recalling the anxiety, and subsequent relief, connected to that experience, I still speculate why the policeman followed me home.

In the back of my mind I wondered if students would think less of me or if they would tell their parent "my drama teacher drove while intoxicated," which could lead to a conversation with my principal. But there were no repercussions, perhaps because students were able to accept my story at face value, silently and individually, before they moved on to another peer's anecdote. Or perhaps there was no consequence because students discerned that we were members of the ensemble together, agreeing to takes risks in confidence. Like the students who received peer responses to their stories, I received responses from students to mine. Some of their feedback made *me* think, including, "Why did you have to be home right then? Couldn't you have just waited till you were completely sober?" Wise student. The answer is yes, of course I could have and should have. But I didn't.

> I was vulnerable because I made it clear to students that I have been in, and still find myself in, situations where I'm not sure I have done the right thing.

I was vulnerable because I made it clear to students that I have been in, and still find myself in, situations where I'm not sure I have done the right thing. Ruth Behar states, "When you write vulnerably, others respond vulnerably" (1986, 16). Is the vulnerable teacher responsible if actions by a student result in a harmful outcome? Theatre educator Abigail Doust, who has created plays with teens for junior high students on the topic of premature sexual activity, keeps in mind the fact that teachers are always the Adult (Authority). "If we tell our students a secret, they must keep it, so what you say becomes their burden," she cautions (Doust, telephone conversation, August 13, 2004). In CODE, we play at the boundaries of what constitutes traditional authority, crossing into one another's space and constructing knowledge in the zone between teacher and student. But even as I make myself vulnerable, my authority is present because it always is, by nature of my position as a teacher in the high school.

Teachers who allow themselves to be vulnerable for the applicable lesson at the appropriate time should remain cautious of the possible after-effects of sharing personal narratives.

Teachers who allow themselves to be vulnerable for the applicable lesson at the appropriate time should remain cautious of the possible after-effects of sharing personal narratives. A teacher should be prudent about what and how much to share, gauge the maturity levels of students, and understand clearly the intent of revealing a personal account. Stepping out of the confines of teacher-as-authority by showing vulnerability creates a classroom environment in which teacher/students work in tandem to compile and weigh new knowledge. In a context of collective education, students who hear their teacher reveal a transgression are emboldened, I believe, to share their experiences and perspectives with one another.

## Strategy #5: Involve Tempered Teacher Authority as Process Evolves into Product

The relaxed, casual ambiance that is conducive to supporting vulnerable self-disclosure related to edgy issues in CODE invariably shifts to an increasingly tense atmosphere driven by performance deadlines. As a result, my role as teacher modifies. In Social Issues Theatre, I don the cap of director because the majority of students who enroll in that course have little, if any, theatre experience. Conversely, the objective in Play Production is for students to take complete ownership of their scenes. Students know I am available at all times for advice and guidance, but I step aside so students can learn from each other.[7] In Play Production, the security fostered by incremental risk-taking and trust during the writing portion of class contributes to students' intrinsic motivation to take whatever steps they decide they need to perfect their pieces.

As students move their scenes from page to platform, they rehearse first in private groups and then in run-throughs before the class. I organize rehearsal sequences for them, but students are responsible for blocking the scenes, focusing on details, using time wisely in rehearsals, and providing notes to one another. It is during this process that students teach themselves. After directors have run through a scene, for example, I make it a point to give my notes only after they share theirs. As the production date approaches, I force myself not to intrude with suggestions, advice, or reprimands; my director's eye keenly observes, but my teacher's voice is silent. This is because I am convinced that students' learning will be longer lasting and their insights deeper if they take ownership. Because students' self-esteem is on the line when they perform for a public audience that includes their parents, this aspect of CODE intensifies their commitment to quality. More often than not, the performances connect to the audience through poignancy and humor, and their acting is sharp and clear.

During the last week of rehearsal for the production *Anything Else Would Be Substandard*, a student named Leslie revised a vignette she had originally scripted as a dramatic scene into a monologue. The monologue ruminates on a typical characterization of high school girls that is constructed in part by the widely accepted view that men are aggressive by nature. Entitled "The Cycle," the vignette was set at a weekend party in a friend's home and typified the perpetual "victimization" of freshmen girls by senior guys at high school parties. Leslie speaks to the audience:

> God, these parties get more and more disgusting each year. The same old people drinking the same old beer, having the same old drunken conversations. The only thing different about this year's upcoming parties are the new freshman girls. Poor things, after tonight, their reputations are gonna be shot to hell. There's nothing I hate more than watching people do things I know they'll regret later, and [having no] control over the situation.

At 9:15 on Thursday morning, the day of the performance, Leslie asked to restage her scene by incorporating nine classmates into nonspeaking roles What?! My director's brain screamed at her, or maybe at me, I'm not sure which. I looked at the clock. "Sure," I replied calmly. "You have until 9:34. You better get going." Her actors worked with keen attention for 14 minutes as she told them the kinds of characters they would each portray and their placements onstage. The changes made the scene one of the most memorable of the production. The next day, when the class discussed the last-minute staging of Leslie's scene, she

> I consciously refrain myself from exercising power during the "push-comes-to-shove" phase because it is during this last phase that students come into their own self-agency.

admitted to me, "I knew you would freak out at that." I infer from her comment that she recognized both the risk she was taking and that I was not going to stop her from taking that risk. Altering power relationships creates a dynamic tension between student and teacher that becomes an energizing force in student-produced work.

I consciously refrain myself from exercising power during the "push-comes-to-shove" phase because it is during this last phase that students come into their own self-agency. Five days before the performance of a production the class titled "Ramblings from the Teenage Mind," I had written in my journal:

> Today it is evident that the show won't be ready. Not with lights, not with anything. I wish I'd said something earlier so we could have worked other pieces. They want more rehearsals, [and they need time] to reflect throughout the process, to give notes. They have no time to warm up and to focus. We crave more time [...] they are passing slips out to their friends to attend the school performance. After school yesterday, Tina stayed to work on her monologue, "In a White Room." She wanted to add blocking and lighting—just like Leslie restaging hers at the last minute.

The next day, I asked the class to talk about where they were in the process. Toward the end of their comments, Tina (the student described in Chapter 3 who hoped to direct *The Shadow Box*) sat in front of the class on my stool and said:

> We're not ready. Some of us care more about this play than others. Some people need to be led, and those who usually lead can't. So, Deb and I have decided that we're going to step up and make this work. We're in charge in front and backstage.

This incident brings up a noteworthy point about altered power relationships. Notice where Tina was sitting when she spoke to the class? Center stage. On my stool. In front of the class. She occupied the space that is traditionally reserved for the teacher. Tina's voice of authority, if uttered by a teacher, represents the privilege of autocratic directing. For some, this example demonstrates typical notions about power and leadership—when one leader steps aside, a replacement (even if that person is a student) is waiting in the wings. But I prefer a different reading. Power is available everywhere, as evidenced by Tina's and Deb's decision to take leadership when none existed. But power is seldom equal when co-authority drives a project. When Tina and

Deb self-defined as leaders, the binary between leader and follower crystallized. But in CODE, power is fluid. Tina and Deb's leadership demonstrated a power surge intended to inspire and motivate their peers in the waning hours of rehearsal, in allegiance to the production that they all owned.

In a post-production reflection, one student commented on my minimized presence as teacher:

> I noticed how you stepped in a little bit more at the end, but you never took over [...] and I liked that. It made each and every one of us realize that this was our project and no one was going to put it together for us. That's when Tina and Deb sort of took the lead, and then we really started to get stuff done. I liked the amount of involvement you had—you were there if we needed you, you always offered advice and notes—but the students were still ultimately in charge.

In a public school setting, teenagers have few opportunities to self-govern. As we guide students to the place where they can feel ultimately in charge, teachers sense when to minimize or maximize co-authority. Developing this sense takes patience. Patience lets a teacher be more willing to listen than speak and more able to ask questions than answer them. Students who follow their own leads as they organize and rehearse a production acquire insight into themselves and others in ways that shape responsible citizenship.

## NOTES

1 Our staff assembled before school on the morning after the 9/11 terrorist attacks. The administrators informed us that classes should be as close to normal as possible. I interpreted this directive as "avoid the topic" because administrators were tacitly discouraging faculty from engaging our students in dialogue. I was teaching *Julius Caesar* to my sophomore English students at the time. Did this mean I should not bring up the raw national event that seethed with retaliation against presumed arrogance and injustice? Three months later, a student team received permission to lead a five-hour social issues workshop, during school hours, that 30 high school students attended. In the workshop, students examined their attitudes on the 9/11 tragedy. For a detailed discussion of the workshop, see Gonzalez (2004).

2 For in-depth discussion on engaging students in critical response toward their work, see Lazarus (2012, 81–86).

3 Increased suicide risk is a concern among students who are lesbian, bisexual, gay, or transgendered. See James Lock and Hans Stiener, "Gay, Lesbian, and Bisexual Youths' Risks for Emotional, Physical, and Social Problems:

Results from a Community-Based Survey," *Journal of Child and Adolescent Psychiatry*, 1 (1999): 297–301.

4 The discussion of boys' emotional well-being is excerpted from Gonzalez, "Navigating Dangerous Waters: Teens, Plays, and the 'Feminist Way' in a Traditional High School Setting," with permission from the publishers. The complete article is included in *Radical Acts*, Ann Elizabeth Armstrong and Kathleen Juhl, eds. (San Francisco, CA: Aunt Lute Press, 2007) (267–69).

5 I learned this exercise from Michael Rohd. In some versions, everyone places their note cards with their comments on a board for all to read.

6 While this agreement can be tacit, fostered naturally by the atmosphere of safe risk-taking, teacher and students might also discuss up front the ways in which the class will differ from others. Whether the agreement for confidentiality is spoken or not may depend upon the make-up of students in the class, including their prior experience and maturity level.

7 The description of my position as teacher under this circumstance is influenced by the role theory that Richard Schechner develops in *Between Theatre and Anthropology* (Philidelphia: University of Pennsylvania Press, 1985). Schechner examines how people perform their social identities and describes all kinds of behaviors as "transitional." He explains that a performer (i.e. teacher) experiences self not directly, but through the medium of experiencing others (i.e. students) by entering the social field. Schechner explains that the way in which "me" (teacher) and "not me" (not teacher) transform into "not teacher … not-not teacher" is through the process of rehearsal (112).

# Chapter 11

## Investigating Student and Teacher Identity

A safe haven is a place where students should be comfortable questioning assumptions about age, class, race and ethnicity, gender, and other areas where social stigmas identify and marginalize. But danger lurks outside the safety of a haven. Within the four walls of a classroom, teacher and students can develop a rapport that encourages diversities rather than manages or "controls" them (Fisher 2001, 44). Protected by the walls, students experience the process of tolerating, accepting, and ultimately respecting the differing perspectives of their peers in the class.

Yet, John Warren contends that "students of color are punished most discreetly by being forced into a school system that reinforces the cultural values, style of interaction, communicative norms and learning methods valued by the culture of power" (2003, 49). Students of color who write about ethnic and racial oppression are especially vulnerable to student and teacher responses that represent mainstream ideology. Teachers who learn to be self-conscious of innate biases and become aware of their own racial/ethnic identities foster a classroom atmosphere that helps students personally relate to, and relay to others, experiences relevant to their own cultural identities.

## POSITIONING STUDENT IDENTITY IN THE CLASSROOM

Citizenship responsibility evolves in CODE classes when students tackle topics that examine forms of oppression in their lives. One of the vignettes emerging from a Play Production course was an autobiographical scene titled "The Question," written by a Latina. The scene asserts that perception of "othered" Americans' cultural identities is driven by assumptions of white privilege. The terms *othered* and *otherness* refer to members of our society whose race, religion, and/or ethnicity distinguishes them from white, Christian, European descendants who comprise the dominant culture in the United States.

In the scene, the author renamed herself Jessica. The scene is set in junior high school, where a white classmate asks Jessica if she is Mexican, because her last name is Lopez. The first half of the scene proceeds:

JESSICA: What? Did you just ask me if I was Mexican?

GREG: Yeah, are you?

JESSICA: Yes, I'm Mexican. Do you have a problem with it?

GREG: No. Can I ask you another question?

JESSICA: What?

GREG: What is it like to be Mexican?

JESSICA: I'm not going to answer that. Don't ask me any more questions.

The second half of the scene mixes fiction with reality, as Jessica imagines rewinding the conversation. Jessica tells a friend about the questions her classmate had asked and enacts the retorts she wished she had given. In the scene's conclusion, when Greg asks what it is like being Mexican, Jessica explains: "Being a Mexican is great since Mexicans have a lot of fun traditions. [...] The holiday I like the most is Easter because my family cracks confetti-filled eggs over each other's heads! Kind of like *this.*" Then Jessica and the other students in the class surround Greg and crack *cascarones* all over his head. In this scene, the Latina publicly asserts pride in her Mexican identity and punishes his ignorance.

## POSITIONING TEACHER IDENTITY IN REHEARSAL

The Latina chose not to play the role of Jessica herself, but instead cast a white student who, the previous autumn, had played multiple small roles in a drama club production of *Simply Maria, Or, The American Dream* by Josefina López (Dramatic Publishing, 1996). *Simply Maria* is an autobiographical one-act play that examines the coming-of-age of a Mexican girl, Maria, whose traditional parents have immigrated to Los Angeles. The clash between the culture of her homeland and U.S. values are politically charged. I, a white high school theatre teacher, staged *Simply Maria, Or, The American Dream* with the Drama Club.[1] I thought students could identify with the coming-of-age theme, the gender stereotypes, and the comedy. For example, in the wedding scene of Maria's nightmare, the ring is a gold dog collar that her husband places around her neck, and the priest says at the end of the ceremony, "You may pet the bride."

Also, I "married Mexican." My children are Mexican American, and I have been personally influenced by Mexican American culture for 35 years. The district where I attended school from kindergarten through high school is an upwardly mobile, very white community nestled between Cleveland and Akron, Ohio. Growing up, I ate lots of homemade noodles. (While German food is ethnic, it is rooted in European white patriarchy, unlike the marginalized otherness of the Mexican culture.) The first time I went to a Mexican restaurant, I asked for a jalapeno pepper, pronouncing the "j" like one pronounces it in my name. On the first day of my first college class in my freshman year, I chose to sit in a chair next to the Latino I would marry some five years later.

Over time, I met members of his extended family and was astounded to discover that five families lived within four blocks of one another; another time I ate scrambled eggs and tortillas on a Sunday evening and listened as his aunt told me the Mexican folktale "La Llorona." Once, I was washing dishes there, and for whatever reason, I washed in the right-hand sink, rinsed in the left, and set the dishes on the far left to dry. One of his cousins laughed at me, "Jeez, Jo Beth, you wash dishes like a Mexican!"

I learned to make tamales with the cousins. When my husband and I moved states away from our families, we would mix, fold, and steam dozens of tamales on Christmas Day to combat the bleakness of Christmas alone. The first year, we used outdated *masa* (corn flour) so the tamales were rancid. We had to throw out 14 dozen tamales. We made 14 fresh batches on New Year's Day. Tamales are an all-day affair, especially when only two people are making them. Eventually, we invited friends over to tamale-making parties where we taught them to spread, fill, and fold—a custom we maintain today. Once, I was irritably offended by the Mexican American I married when, after hours of mixing (fresh) *masa*, folding, and steaming, he ate a few and scowled, "There's something wrong, but I don't know what." Now I recognize that his criticism of our effort stems from a deep respect for the tradition of tamale-making in his family and in his culture.

My sensitivity to and respect for the Latino culture has been shaped by countless incidents that, over time, have complicated my identity as a white woman. At a professional conference a few years ago, I attended a preconference on multiculturalism in educational theatre. At one point, each of us was asked to identify ourselves, and I was suddenly stymied. Of course I am white—but what do I do with all of the rest that has influenced my perspective? That part has helped me identify with Mexican Americans, but I can't pass for one. Because I have lived these thirty-some years with the constant influence of Mexican American culture in my life, I have developed a more critical perspective of whiteness than I would have had I married "white."

One day in mid-July when migrant workers from Texas and Mexico were in nearby fields picking cucumbers, my husband returned from a video store fuming because the clerk had assumed he was a migrant worker. He explained to me that he was making small talk with the clerk while she opened an account for him. When he told her that he was a professor in the university in our town, she asked him when he was going back. Back to the office was his first thought. "Back where?" he asked. "Back to Texas," she clarified. Although my husband had told her he was a college professor, the image of a Latino college professor seemed not to register with her. My husband left the store, having discovered that an interaction with a highly educated Latino male in our community was beyond the framework of the clerk's understanding.

I clearly recognize that this situation would never have happened to me. My relationship with my Mexican American husband has prompted my interest in whiteness theory, which in turn has helped me understand that people of color must employ "survival instincts" on a daily basis to work, learn, and play in a white world. But the white privilege of my birth grants me a visceral ignorance of what it feels like to be suppressed by dominant representations. Because I have no need to "survive" in a white world, I will never understand the codes that others use to read the signals of hegemonic practices. Nonetheless, my personal experiences inculcated a respect for Mexican culture that made me receptive to organizing the *Simply Maria* project.

I look at my Latino students and see them as the cousins on the "married-Mexican" side of my family. I thought the play might speak to them and encourage them to be successful. To that end, I procured a small grant that enabled the playwright to see our performance and interact with the students of our school and members of our community. My motive, then, was political as well as educational. I hoped the project would promote Hispanic Heritage Month in our community and give voice to the Latino members of our school. I hoped that the play would encourage the white students in my drama program, and those in the audience, to explore the otherness of Latina culture. I hoped that the project would draw attention to the high school drama program.

But "good will and an open heart are not enough when one seeks to express cultural experiences which are clearly separate from his or her lived world" (Conquorgood 1985, 4). My students look at me and see "Dr. G.," a white, female, middle-class high school teacher with a Ph.D. and a Hispanic surname. The combination of my education and Latino family can serve to welcome or reject students of color. How students of color respond to me depends upon my ability to listen to them. I cannot truly listen to marginalized students until I recognize that my white privilege invariably creeps between us. Only when I make my whiteness visible can our dialogue begin.

I cannot truly listen to marginalized students until I recognize that my white privilege invariably creeps between us.

My husband reminds me that Latinos are not used to being in the spotlight. Directors should be aware that marginalized actors may experience heightened trepidation, and strategize ways to increase their confidence when preparing for a public theatre performance. Recently, I worked with a group of adults who staged a play in celebration of *Dia de los Muertos*. Enthusiasm was as high as intimidation. After weeks of blocking rehearsals punctuated by nervous self-effacement, a lead actress quit. Undeterred but aware of the encroaching performance date, one of the actors suggested we present the play as a radio drama. This idea released pressure on the remaining actors immediately, for some of them hadn't yet memorized their lines. For the staged radio drama, actors stood before microphones and music stands, on which they set their scripts. When not in scenes, they sat down. To the side was a decorated altar to which actors had contributed items from their own homes, and behind them was an ensemble of vocalists and instrumentalists. The event took place in a community arts center devoted to Hispanic heritage, so the wall behind the performers was colorfully painted with cosmic imagery. During the program, afternoon sunlight streamed through an upper window, flooding the performers in natural light. Actor confidence soared.

This ensemble of Latino actors achieved success due to several interconnected factors. First, the material they were performing was culturally relevant. This point is supported by a survey published in 2005 that asked college students to indicate how important the relevance of their culture is in relationship to curricular content in the process of shaping a safe academic space. Students of color rated culturally relevant content more highly than their white peers (Holley and Steiner 2005, 60).

Second, the event was successful because the performance was held in the Sofia Quintero Art and Cultural Center, a safe space, for its purpose inherently nurtures cultural connection. Third, the event was a success in part because the style of the play adjusted to meet actors' confidence levels. The temporary stage, in fact, wasn't a stage at all, but a corner of the room where actors stood reading their lines on the same level as the audience and drenched in natural sunlight rather than intense stage lights.

## THE CODE CLASSROOM: A "SAFE SPACE" *WITH CONSEQUENCES*

The actress who played Jessica in the Play Production vignette "The Question" had met the playwright of *Simply Maria, Or, The American Dream,* Josefina López, and engaged in cast conversations about the Mexican American experience of otherness. Yet when she rehearsed this role, her interpretation was flat. I asked if she understood why the character was offended by Greg's questions. She responded, "I have no idea."

Perhaps her response was a cover-up for complex feelings she was unable to articulate, or maybe she was trying to maintain her dignity. From a critical perspective, one might interpret this incident as a demonstration of how white privilege can be blind to the existence of social injustice. At the same time, two white students, also in the scene, offered explanations for Jessica's defensiveness based on experiences with their Mexican American friends. The Latina student exercised self-agency by creating a pocket of resistance in a hegemonic institution. Yet when she cast a self-defined clueless white student in the role of herself, it was I who asked why Jessica was offended, and her white peers who explained. Though the scene increased the author's self-agency, she did not engage in dialogue about ethnic difference in real life, deferring instead to her white teacher and peers. This rehearsal moment of "The Question" suggests that if a space is comfortable for white students, it is likely uncomfortable for students of color and for teachers in liminal spaces.

If a space is comfortable for white students, it is likely uncomfortable for students of color.

Christine Sleeter states:

> Whiteness is protected by silence. White people do not have to talk about whiteness or question the personal dimensions of racism very often. If we silence talk about race, we will perpetuate whiteness' silent privilege. White people's voices have always been privileged, even if they are attempting to resist racism.
>
> (1993, 272)

As "The Question" demonstrates, a safe space is actually what some communications scholars call "a safe space with consequences."[2] When the actress playing Jessica answered, "I have no idea," she dismissed the effort to think about cultural difference. It was gratifying to see her white peers offer explanations, but the opportunity to engage in a discussion about Latino sensitivity to ethnic stereotyping halted there.

This situation represents my effort to be polite in the face of potential color conflict. It was easier and safer to avoid confrontation. Ruth Frankenberg asserts that color-blindness is the polite language of race, representing "the effort it takes NOT to 'see,' or at any rate not to acknowledge, race differences" (1993, 142). But this mindset destroys possibilities for students of color to share with their white peers the

At the time, we stopped the discussion to continue rehearsal; we should have stopped the rehearsal to continue the discussion.

richness of their heritages. The practice of ignoring color, or making the visible invisible, suggests to Delpit that "if one does not see color, then one does not really see children." She expands, "Children made 'invisible' become hard pressed to see themselves worthy of notice" (1995, 177). At the time, we stopped the discussion to continue rehearsal; we should have stopped the rehearsal to continue the discussion.

## SEEING THE OPPOSITE REVEALS IDENTITY

One summer, my friend—later to be my husband and whose last name is spelled Gonzalez with a "z" at the end rather than the more common "s"—mailed a letter to me. He addressed it using my maiden name, Enders, but replaced the "s" with a "z," Enderz. I never misspelled his name again.

Most of us raised in environments that condition us to view being white as normal don't see *whiteness* until the white is taken away. Except for usually very personal cases, how long does such sight linger? At one prequel workshop to the Social Issues Theatre course, the topic was diversity.[3] Invited were 40 students from the high school who represented differences in academic achievement, sexual orientation, ethnicity and race, and socio-economic background. At one point in the workshop, a team of students formed a tableau that showed conflict over territory in a high school commons between white and Latino students. Four white actors stood on one side of the turf carrying imaginary books and backpacks, and communicated in body language the attitude "Whatever!" Four Latino actors stood opposite them, imitating gang posturing. Then, an adult in the group asked the white students to take on the postures of the Latino actors and the Latino actors to take on the postures of the white actors.

Observing students commented that until the white and Latino actors reversed postures, they had taken for granted the cultural privilege of the white actors. The image-reversal snapped whiteness into focus, making it instantly obvious to students that the dominant culture normalizes ethnicities in our school. What followed was a 90-minute unplanned discussion about stereotypes in our school. Students who had not spoken up before described how it felt to be identified as gay, Hispanic, or African American, and otherwise "othered." Forty kids who wouldn't say hello to one another in the hallway because they didn't know each other or were from different social cliques sat on the floor, listening to one another's point of view. This, I thought, is a transformative experience! This workshop is a success!

When students debriefed the workshop, they discussed the openness of the conversation that had followed the image-making. One student commented:

> Well, it was really neat to listen to everyone. But, we're high school kids. Nothing is going to change. Maybe we spoke to each other during the workshop, but now we're back at school, and we'll get with our little groups of friends again, and we'll be back in our safe little circles.

I said "Thank you" and let the silence that followed settle.

## STRONG CRITICAL CLASSROOM EXPERIENCE IS AN ONGOING PROCESS

While critical high school teachers may dream that classroom discussion of social, cultural, and racial diversity lead to enlightened future citizens, research shows that such conversations often lead to discomfort, emotional upset, and strained student interactions (Redmond 2010, 4). Redmond explains that:

> the notion of classroom safety thus creates a different, but no less potentially harmful, 'false expectation,' which, when proved artificial, can, in turn, be more damaging than had the conviction [of classroom as safe space] not existed in the first place. (7)

The Social Issues Theatre class that chose the topic of domestic violence was comprised of multiple races and ethnicities. Compared to the demographics of the high school (which is 94 percent white and 6 percent students of color), this particular class was an anomaly, as 44 percent of its students were of color. The class was comprised of drama students and athletes—Latino, African American, white—and four black girls, three of whom had transferred to our rural-suburban-college town from a public school in Detroit. For the first days of class, both groups self-marginalized; those used to the school system sat on one side, those new to it on the other.

Redmond explains that as an African American woman, she had always felt that, despite classroom agreements to treat one another with respect, socially marginalized students "were more cognizant of a different set of pervasive societal rules" (2010, 6). Societal markers such as lesbian, poor, African American, Hispanic, or differently abled, and high school classifications like *cheerleader*, *band dude*, *jock*, *brain*, and *loser*, inform classroom interaction. "Every class participant," Redmond contends, "arrives with individualized personal experiences, understanding of his or her own construction as members of gendered, minoritized, racialized and/or historically marginalized people and personal ideas of what those labels mean when ascribed to others" (7).

This group of disparate students brought varied personal experience to the classroom that I hoped we could mine, but what strategies would we employ? After the first week, two students complained to me in private that they didn't think other students were taking the class seriously, indirectly referring to the students from Detroit who put their feet on one another's legs and lay their heads in one another's lap. Hoping that the work of the course would build community, I encouraged the girls to be patient. Our school's sole African American faculty member was a female administrator who had reprimanded the girls from Detroit more than once. After one student was suspended briefly from class, the administrator assessed that the girls, uncomfortable in our school, developed security by recreating the hallways of their own schools through loud shouting and picking fights. This insight helped me remain sensitive to their initial discomfort and tune in the cultural connections they brought to class. When one of the students suggested we watch Tyler Perry's *Medea's Family Reunion* (2006) for its elements of domestic violence, we did. Students also asked if we could watch Perry's film *For Colored Girls,* adapted from the play *For Colored Girls Who Have Considered Suicide/When the Rainbow is Enuf* by Ntozake Shange (1997), but its violence deterred me. Instead, we read a scene from the script.

As class progressed, students developed rapport. I believe their initial unease with one another wasn't racial as much as it was unfamiliarity with each other and the style and expectations of the class. One day early in the course we warmed up with a game where students non-verbally formed groups that I identified, such as "similarity of shoes" and "form the letter R with three people." When an idea popped into my head, I shouted, "Create a zebra as one whole class!" Immediately, one of the African American students instructed, "OK, stand like this, you guys. Black, white, black, white …" And the class created the zebra. A student's swift and frank assessment of class demographics demonstrated that no one needed to take skin color too seriously. This spur-of-the-moment idea served as a humorous ice breaker for later conversations about race and domestic violence.

As a white teacher in a white-majority school, opportunities to teach a racially diverse class like this are rare. Preconceptions clouded my perception of interpersonal dynamics among students. At the beginning of the course I was concerned that the African American and white students would not get along. What actually transpired is that the African American girls from Detroit had disputes among themselves, from minor verbal jabs in class to family issues outside of class. Lack of trust fed suspicion, until one eventually felt so betrayed that she dropped the class.

By the end of the semester, like students in all theatre-oriented projects, classmates built trust. Their satire and activating scenes were strong, their workshop informative and engaging, their confidence strengthened. The experience of collectively creating dramatic scenes bonded them. In a final reflection, one student wrote:

> When we first started this class, only some of us knew each other, but most of us only knew of each other. I didn't expect to get really close to the people in this class because we were all so different. Once we started working together and stepping out of our comfort zones we became really close, kind of like a little social issues family. We started helping each other, talking together outside of the Theatre Studio, and we became friends as well as classmates. When the workshop was over, we all suddenly realized how much we had grown, how close we had gotten, and that we really didn't want this class to end.

The interaction of students in the Social Issues Theatre class that studied domestic violence reinforces the view that strong critical classroom experience is a richly layered, ongoing process of challenges in the form of confrontation and dialogue, evolving from course materials, teachers, or classmates themselves (MacKeracher 1996).

## UNVEILING WHITENESS IN A "SAFE SPACE WITH CONSEQUENCES"

The murkiness of cultural difference and exchange motivates critical teachers to interrogate our assumptions about the privilege that accompanies white identity and which we embrace almost without thinking. I value learning experiences that open my eyes to my own privilege. While I have a long way to go before I would consider my judgment penetrating, sensitivity to the circumstances of marginalized students has deepened over time, and I am at least quicker to realize oversights. But oversights I still make.

When preparing auditions for *A Piece of My Heart* (Shirley Lauro, 1998) I intentionally cast according to racial and ethnic identity because the racial identities of the characters, based on real women, are richly defined, specific, and central to the stories. In one scene, for example, Steele, an African American intelligence officer, discovers information about the Tet Offensive. She informs her higher-ups, all white male officers, who mock and dismiss her investigation. Later, Steele considers that the triple-threat of her persona—black, female, officer—impeded serious attention to the report. The scene concludes when Steele bemoans, "The rest is history."

To involve as many students as possible, I cast six women in the primary roles, and an additional 30 actresses in six groups to portray the multiple small roles originally scripted to be portrayed by the six primary characters. Each group of actresses reflected one of the six primary characters. The actresses, who we labeled "reflection characters," were visually linked to the primary characters through costume, and to the extent possible, I cast according to ethnicity/race. Throughout the play the reflection characters formed tableaus stylized after the Vietnam Women's Memorial that shifted to reinforce varying emotional undertones as scenes unfolded.

One of the six groups represented Leeann, an Asian American nurse who also portrays a Vietnamese housekeeper named Bien. In the script, Leeann dons a yellow headscarf and carries a pair of clave sticks when she portrays Bien. As Bien, the actress playing Leeann hits the clave sticks together and points to each actor as a signal to speak, controlling them like puppets. Staying true to the concept of sharing secondary roles among reflection-character actresses, I split the secondary role of Bien into two; one actress created character through lines and staging, and the other stood at a distance and clapped and pointed the sticks.

As Steele is obviously African American, Bien is obviously Asian. And this is where the problem arose. The actress who played Leeann was Korean American, and her reflection pool was comprised of three actresses—Elizabeth, her Latina understudy; Brandy, a Latina; and Twyla, an Asian American. Because I consciously cast according to color, I thought it would make sense for Twyla to play Bien. Brandy, the Latina, was cast as Bien to manipulate the clave sticks and Twyla, the Asian American, was cast as Bien to create character through lines and staging. The language of Bien, however, is broken-English. During the read-through, as Twyla read Bien's lines, an uncomfortable chuckle rippled among the actors. We went on.

The next afternoon, Twyla came in to see me. The stereotyped character made her feel very uncomfortable, she said. I asked if she felt playing the role reflected negatively on her and when she replied, "Yes," her eyes welled up. I explained how it was important to cast this play according to racial identity. She explained that it wasn't the play or the character so much as it was the construction of the language, and she asked to work on a production crew instead of perform onstage. In the course of our discussion, I realized that typecasting Twyla as the portion of Bien who spoke diminished the strength of the character. By adhering firmly to principles of democratic casting and racial/ethnic casting consciousness, I diluted Twyla's self-governance of her own racial identity, heightened stereotype, and embarrassed an actress.

Ultimately, Twyla took on a secondary character from a different pool of reflection characters, Brandy portrayed the speaking Bien, and two actresses cast in the principal and understudy roles as Leeann alternated portraying the Bien who controlled the clave sticks. I explained the rationale for the cast change at rehearsal the next day, as I thought it was important for those who had laughed uncomfortably during the read-through to know that I, too, recognized the awkwardness of that casting choice.

This experience prompted a wrestling match with my critical consciousness. I wondered why, working with intention to cast according to color in this play, I got caught once again in a complication relating to racial and ethnic casting. Casting according to color was not rigid, for white actresses—as well as African American, Latina, and Asian—comprised Steele's and Leeann's reflection-character pools. While it was important to cast principals and understudies according to race, I also weighed experience and students' growth potential. Did I compromise a principle by weighing the casting factors of student experience and opportunity against race and ethnicity? Should theatre teachers approach different productions with different objectives, and if so, why? If we view the whole of a theatre program over the span of three- or four-year cycles, we will likely find that we have met various objectives, just not all at the same time. As students enter with temporary membership in our drama programs, the faces of our program change. If we strive to make choices that are socially conscious, true to the script, and most educational for our students, the overall health of our programs will be sustained by equitable opportunities for all our students.

If we strive to make choices that are socially conscious, true to the script, and most educational for our students, the overall health of our programs will be sustained by equitable opportunities for all our students.

## POSITIONING WHITENESS IN PERFORMANCE WHEN THE JOKE IS ON *WHO*?

I am chagrined by the assumptions I continue to make because of ingrained white privilege, and I try to be quick in catching myself. Despite slips, I have grown more attuned to situations that manifest white privilege, wittingly expressed or not, and these situations make me think. At the 2012 International Thespian Festival, I watched an almost impeccable production of Larry Shue's

*The Foreigner* (1985). The context of the play points to the idiocy of white people who are ignorantly afraid of difference and whose commitment to white supremacy is made to look foolish. The cast was skilled and featured several award-winning National Forensic League competitors. The set was beautiful, the comic timing spot-on, the characters boldly exaggerated, and the pace controlled. The show was fabulous. So what was wrong?

During curtain call, the actors who play the Klan-member townspeople in Act II enter dressed in their Ku Klux Klan costumes—starched white robes and eye-holed hoods. Simultaneously, the actors sweep off their hoods, and the actor in the middle of the seven Klansmen is a black male. The white actors react as if surprised, the black actor looks at the audience, then gestures with a shrug as if to say, "What? So you're surprised to see me here?" or "Don't I belong here?" or perhaps, "What do you *think* I'm doing here?" I suspect that actors of color perform in *The Foreigner* frequently, and that the curtain-call staging was not unique to the production I saw. A well-staged farce that deals specifically with the fear of foreigners deepens insight and sparks creativity. Therefore, this choice invited the festival audiences to critically contemplate ethnic and racial identity.

However, treating issues of race lightly or obliquely can generate more discomfort than upfront serious dialogue. Leda Cooks points out that white teachers and students express frustration, confusion, and concern when ethnic jokes are made because of their racial implications. She contends:

> While most research on the topic has examined white subjects identifying racial others as targets of abusive humor, little attention has been paid to the reception of joke telling by "antiracist" whites, their reports of intervention into racist actors of joke telling, or the perceived costs of doing so. Even more difficult for white students who wish to address racist acts and their own white privilege are situations in which people of color seem to act in self-deprecating ways.
>
> (Cooks 2007, 233–34)

One could read the actor's guffaw as a reinforcement of African American comic stereotypes, or reclaiming identity, as when one African American refers to another with the "n"-word. Perhaps the action demonstrates that the Klan no longer poses the threat it once did, because an African American male costumed as a Klan member standing in the middle of a row of white actors dressed in Klan robes diminishes the Klan's power. The choice was strong, however interpreted. While those watching were not informed about how the idea evolved, perhaps it is not a call for white people to make; it is a choice that African Americans should decide.

## NOTES

1 For a descriptive analysis of whiteness theory in relationship to the Drama Club's production of *Simply Maria, Or, The American Dream*, see Gonzalez, Cantú, and González (2007).

2 Ellsworth (1989) addresses in detail the notion of safe spaces (106–10). For the phrase "safe space with consequences," I acknowledge the participants of the preconference "Moving Forward, Looking Back: Communicating Whiteness Within Pedagogy," part of the National Communication Association, Chicago, November 9, 2004.

3 The Drama Club received grants to sponsor and facilitate workshops for junior high and high school students that we held during the school day in a local park building. We also received grant money to bring in well-known guest artists, including artist/advocate Michael Rohd (see Rohd 1998) and Augusto Boal, world-renowned for his development of Forum Theatre. For a detailed description of Boal's terminology, see the glossary in Schutzman and Cohen-Cruz (1994).

# Chapter 12

## Preparing for the Audience

If high school theatre programs present thought-provoking and even discomforting theatre, some audience members will feel unsettled as they encounter cultural assessments that rub against the conservative norm. Because I encourage students to produce and occasionally publicly perform edgy material, sometimes as a course requirement, I must likewise acknowledge and respect school district policies that govern so-called sensitive topics. Many high schools have banned the use of guns in plays, and plays produced in high schools in more conservative districts are forbidden to mention rape or homosexuality ("Censorship vs. Freedom of Artistic Expression"). In 2012, a drama club in northeastern Ohio was denied permission to stage *The Foreigner* due to the Klan presence in the show. Simply put, artist/educators working within the confines of traditional high school settings face censorship. At the 2000 International Drama in Education Research Institute (IDIERI) Conference in Columbus, Ohio, Kathleen Gallagher asked, "At what junctures can teachers give up power and still work within the institutional setting?" (personal comment, July 24, 2000). Teachers must have faith to deal with moments of risk in mature, responsible ways. CODE enables teens to explore the exciting precipice while keeping foremost in their minds the point that theatre is not theatre without an audience to whom they must be responsible.[1]

## WORKING THROUGH THE AUDIENCE "FEAR FACTOR"

To what audiences are high school theatre students and their teachers accountable? If one purpose of theatre is to challenge the status quo through confrontation with big, tough issues, then the insular space of the classroom or rehearsal makes the work more susceptible to scrutiny by parents and administrators. This is because closed doors invite curiosity bordering on suspicion and heighten adults' fears of teenagers' interest in controversial issues. When the Drama Club produced *Simply Maria, Or, The American Dream*, the father of the female cast member who portrayed Jessica in "The Question" picked her up from rehearsal. He observed part of a scene where Maria, played by another actress, is captivated by her dawning sexuality. She looks at herself in a full-length mirror and runs her hands along the curves on her body. Her mother enters, notices her daughter's activity and scolds, "Maria what are you doing? Sex is dirty!" The next day the parent called the principal and complained that the Drama Club was producing a play that contained masturbation.

The parent's judgment of a moment in a scene taken out of context parallels the same powerful fear of teenage girls' sexuality that the central character's mother expressed. Because the principal had read the play and we had discussed the content, she was aware that the scene was not about masturbation, but about an adolescent girl's awakening sexuality. My principal told the parent, "High school theatre isn't what it used to be." Her response reinforces the point that a supportive administrator contributes to students' success when theatre teachers' pedagogy deviates from the mainstream.

Eventually the parent realized that he had taken the scene out of context, but he was still disconcerted because he felt the play was not suitable for his daughter's younger siblings. Drama is an effective tool for infusing adolescents with the confidence and skills needed to communicate insights and experiences about issues important to them with clarity, wit, and poignancy. But when teens speak words and their bodies create images that school officials, parents, or community members consider off limits, teacher and students enter an educational zone "under construction."

> When teens speak words and their bodies create images that school officials, parents, or community members consider off limits, teacher and students enter an educational zone "under construction."

Teens themselves are aware of danger areas. Students in Social Issues Theatre who were investigating the topic of driving while intoxicated wrote a scene in which teens goad Kathy, a friend who drove to their party, into performing a keg stand. (A keg stand is when a person stands on his or her hands and, aided by friends, drinks beer upside down from a tube connected to a keg of beer. Most teens know that this technique causes alcohol to affect the drinker more quickly.) When students suggested that this is how Kathy should get drunk, the question crossed my mind, "What would the principal, superintendent, or parents think if they walked into the Theatre Studio while teens were acting out a keg stand?" The students were unfazed by the ramifications of incorporating a keg stand into the scene. However, the actress who performed the keg stand made sure that the character's name, Kathy—which was her own name—was changed when students performed the scene again for a community event that the class was invited to. Kathy was concerned that the choices the character made would imply that *she*—the actress—made those choices.

On the threshold of risk, teachers and students—in pockets of programs in schools across the country—choose productions and staging strategies that expand the definition of high school theatre. Ron Santoro describes a situation that led two boys, one playing a man and one playing a woman, to kiss tenderly onstage. Santoro directed *Antigone* in the mid-70s at an all-boys school. Because only one girl had tried out (through auditions with another school), his drama students decided to do the show with all guys. When the two boys learned that the characters they were cast to play were supposed to kiss, Santoro suggested, "Let's not decide on that just yet."

As rehearsals progressed, Santoro observed these two actors standing close to each other, as if trying to approach that place on their own. The opening of the show was near. During one rehearsal, at the kissing moment, Santoro made a smooching sound with his lips. Then he told the boys that during performances they'd have to be strong enough to block out those kinds of noises, which might come from the audience.

By opening night, the two boys were able to kiss with an expression of simple intimacy. And the audience? "You could hear a pin drop," Santoro remembers, then added, "Those boys were very brave." Reflecting further, Santoro asserts, "I believe high school students are quite capable of tackling challenges like this. It's the audience we need to address our worry for" (personal comments, August 8, 1997).

"I believe high school students are quite capable of tackling challenges like this. It's the audience we need to address our worry for."

It is valuable to discover those adults who welcome teen actors' edgy choices. One audience member sensitive to LGBTQ issues commended an intriguing relationship she noticed in the prologue to *Aida*. Two actresses held hands while meandering among the museum's displays. Were the actresses instructed to do this, she asked me? Not at all, I replied, for the girls had made the choice spontaneously. The audience member returned to watch the closing performance and was disappointed that the actresses were not holding hands in this performance.

Adults who advocate against oppression respect teens' commitment to tough issues. To gather research for a Social Issues Theatre class that chose to learn about human trafficking, I registered for a conference on the topic. In a session led by state representative Teresa Fedor, who is primarily responsible for the passage of the Safe Harbor Act in Ohio, I explained that it was the goal of my high school students to bring the topic to the attention of their peers, through drama. Fedor responded:

> Yes, and thank you! We can't forget to ask the children to help [spread awareness about sex traffickers]. The youth are missing from the solution. We can't be graphic with them, but we've got to talk about it with them. Even better, they need to talk with each other.
>
> (Fedor, personal comment, September 28, 2012)

Throughout situations like these, theatre teachers must remain cognizant of the difference between *controversial* and *inappropriate*. Controversial topics are issues about which people hold strongly felt but differing points of view. When writers/performers apply shock treatment to controversial issues, the content easily becomes inappropriate. One need only think of Howard Stern and Rush Limbaugh to realize how quickly a choice can turn detrimental to one's career. I don't want my drama program to suffer the same fate. What I want for my drama program is permission to progress with the times, cautiously nudging students and their audiences toward dialogue on tacit social issues.

Throughout situations like these, theatre teachers must remain cognizant of the difference between *controversial* and *inappropriate*.

## WHEN EMOTIONS AREN'T ENOUGH: INTEGRATING FACTS FOR HEALTHY DIGESTION OF CONTROVERSIAL MATERIAL

In classroom discussions and play rehearsals, it is not surprising to discover students being passionately expressive about controversial topics with which they identify. However, untempered by fact and logic, emotions heighten when participants exchange differing viewpoints on sensitive subjects. Guest speakers whose expertise provides stable grounding for students as they investigate topics in Social Issues Theatre are necessary components of the course. So, too, are experts who share information and experiences that relate to the subject matter of co-curricular theatre productions. Experts who are familiar with the students, the school, and/or the community are especially effective communicators. When experts insensitive to the lived experiences of their audiences rely upon emotion unbalanced by reason to address a social problem, the effort may result in miscommunication, anger, and disconnection. Presenters may be classroom teachers, teen performers, or guests from outside the school district. No matter the circumstance or the location, I believe that presentation of potentially penetrating content is best conveyed in an intimate atmosphere and with background knowledge of one's audience. A single experience especially reinforced this point for me.

In the midst of a rash of teen suicides at our high school, the Drama Club presented *Eric and Elliott* (Dwayne Hartford, 2004) for six different audiences over the period of a year. Each performance was followed by a structured talk-back led by a health-care professional.[2] As an additional approach to addressing issues that might cause depression or bullying, our school sponsored Challenge Day, an off-campus, day-long school event developed by a company from California and highlighted on *The*

*Oprah Winfrey Show* (Harpo Productions, 2006). Intended to bring to the surface problems that inhibit participants from maintaining strong, healthy relationships with family, friends, and faculty, Challenge Day is intense and emotionally draining.

Faculty had been asked to participate with students in Challenge Day. On the springtime morning of the workshop, I stepped into a local coffee shop and encountered a retired teacher who asked if I'd heard about one of my former sophomore English students; he had committed suicide the night before. This student was the fifth of seven students who committed suicide over the course of four years. Midway through the workshop, held in an expansive church multi-purpose room and involving 150 participants, one of the presenters began to tell a detailed story, underscored with music, to demonstrate a personal circumstance in which he experienced regret. This was to prepare participants for an exercise afterward during which they would be asked to apologize to someone for an action they'd committed.

> What I want for my drama program is permission to progress with the times, cautiously nudging students and their audiences toward dialogue on tacit social issues.

When the speaker arrived at the moment in the story when he came across his dead brother, he said, "I don't want to even describe what it looked like to see my brother hanging." The fact is that he didn't have to describe the scene. Administrators were present in the room who, just the year before, had sadly faced a similar experience when a student hanged himself in a restroom during school hours. At least one student was also present who had discovered a friend who had nearly died of hanging the previous autumn. Students began passing a box of tissues, because as one student later lamented, "Challenge Day guilts you into feeling bad about yourself." The presenter challenged us to tell others how much we care about them because "just one word might help someone else make a better choice." Participants stood up and mingled, then hugged. I hugged many students, including the actors and crew members of *Eric and Elliott*. Then I escaped into the kitchen, pulling a colleague with me to whom I expressed my emotion.

I was angry. That school year, our faculty, staff, and students had put time and effort into learning that 90 percent of suicides are the result of clinical depression, and that for the majority of people who are clinically depressed, no amount of words from others will save them. We had learned the signs of depression and identified ways to help potential victims seek help. The emotional ride that Challenge Day participants experienced contradicted the information that we had learned. Amplifying teens' feelings, unaccompanied by accurate information, does more than manipulate, it creates danger, for our unmonitored students returned to school emotionally bruised. When dealing with controversial topics, we need to remind our students, as well as ourselves, to think with objectivity as well as compassion.

Challenge Day, for communities that can fund it, can be an effective tool for opening lines of communication. But follow-up is necessary. Challenge Day leaders flew in one day and out the next, leaving students to ruminate on their personal faults and transgressions. By contrast, Social Issues Theatre workshops, in a student's words, "focus on the issues, and how you can help." Students recognize the difference between pure emotion and information, and the value of sharing information "with a spoonful of sugar." One student claimed, "People think that teens will react only emotionally about issues that we have in our community. People don't expect us to *learn* about them in a fun and educational way." Intimate and closely moderated environments encourage teens to fully contemplate decisions that protect their welfare and secure their well-being.

"People think that teens will react only emotionally about issues that we have in our community. People don't expect us to *learn* about them in a fun and educational way."

A description of how students explore options when the driving while intoxicated activating scene stops illustrates the point. The point of crisis at which that scene ends is when the protagonist Roxanne resists driving home with the now-inebriated Kathy. During the five-hour workshop, participants came up with nine possible ways for Roxanne to get herself home without riding in a car driven by Kathy. In order, the suggestions included:

- 1st Action: Roxanne calls her father, Rusty.
  Denied: Rusty is passed out and unable to drive.

- 2nd Action: Roxanne calls her friend Doug, to whom she had lied after Kathy invited her to the party.
  Denied: Doug says his mother won't allow him to drive after midnight.

- 3rd Action: Roxanne asks Kathy to give her the keys so she can drive Kathy's car home.
  Denied: Kathy says no.

- 4th Action: Roxanne asks to borrow Kathy's cell phone to call Kathy's mother.
  Denied: Kathy's mother denies that Kathy is drunk.

- 5th Action: Roxanne asks Brian, an acquaintance at the party, for a ride home.
  Denied: Brian can't leave because he fears someone will take his beer.

- 6th Action: Roxanne asks Maria, the party's host, to give her a ride home.
  Denied: Maria can't leave the party.

- 7th Action: Roxanne considers walking home.
  Denied: Roxanne thinks better of it; it is after midnight and the house is several miles out of town.

- 8th Action: Roxanne asks Maria to loan her money for a cab.
  Denied: Maia says she needs the money to clean the carpet from the keg stand and no one else at the party offers any money.

- 9th and Final Action: Roxanne calls a cab and decides to get money from her father's bedroom after she gets home.

The procedural tools of issues-based theatre that I glean and adapt from assorted sources guide students as they lead one another through interrogation of protagonists' dilemmas. The difference between a driver's-education class, message play, or even Challenge Day and a Social Issues Theatre workshop is that no one is standing before them to teach. Adults assist in the dissemination of crucial information that students identify as categories of knowledge they lack, but *no adult tells them what choices to make*. The students who could drive had already seen grisly photos and been drilled with facts in their driver's-education classes; still, some of them risked drinking and driving. Students need an influence stronger than "teacher's knowledge" to motivate them to think twice; teens need time to mine knowledge with those most likely to influence them, their peers.

Teens need time to mine knowledge with those most likely to influence them, their peers.

When teacher and students explore together, a positive energy of uncertainty propels the classroom because the suspense of drama is naturally invigorating. Discovered knowledge may include facts and statistics, expert testimony, anecdotal evidence, and examples, but the most significant comprehension stems from listening to multiple viewpoints. From this experience, students realize they can think for themselves. One student commented, "The two different drivers showed opposing viewpoints. Before the workshop I hadn't realized that people might react in such ways to the situations."

Both feminist—unknowable—(Ellsworth 1997) and masculinist—rational—(Scholnick 2000), CODE courses kindle an androgynous sort of reflection that awakens the deep insights necessary for personal growth and self-agency. At the end of the semester, a member of the Social Issues Theatre class that explored domestic violence considered how her activating scene "demonstrated a perfect example of how hard it is for families to cope with family cruelty. Abuse hurts everyone." Another contemplated the stage of denial that occurs within the cycle of abuse. Having learned about the cycle of abuse in a class presentation by a member of the county sheriff's department, the student commented, "I was glad we showed denial in our scene. It gave everyone something to think about, and prepared them for if they ever saw such denial in their own lives, especially with something as obvious as abuse." When teens examine controversial topics in depth, the emotive, disorganized, threatening discourse of controversy occurs in concert with the rationale of cognition.

Students leave a Social Issues Theatre workshop, and occasionally a strong theatrical performance, jazzed and thinking. Yet, I am left with burning questions: How long-lasting is the impact of an issues-based theatre workshop? Does a single workshop experience prompt students to change their behavior in a risky situation? How do we assess an unconventional learning experience in light of institutionalized standards and political mandates measured only through standardized tests that still leave some children behind, and make breathless many in the "race to the top" that others shall surely lose?

I believe that, as educators, we want to know we have made differences, and this is what drives us to teach. But long-term impacts are more difficult to ascertain in the public school because standardized, formal assessments that speak to a majority of teachers and administrators are not applicable to many qualitative aspects of theatre education, much less Social Issues Theatre work. Anecdotal evidence and student voices and behavior validate the effectiveness of learning in these circumstances more powerfully than evaluating and comparing standardized test results. Nevertheless, in the political environment that surrounds us, theatre teachers must commit to advocating on behalf of our classes and programs, and never stop our efforts to convince detractors that theatre education in all its facets—quantifiable and qualitative—transforms students' lives.

Perhaps the best way to find out the degree to which students acknowledge the effect of participating in Social Issues Theatre work is to ask them longitudinally how their work as adolescents in the alternative pedagogy has affected them.[3]

## THE RESPONSIBILITIES OF DEMOCRATIC TEACHING INCLUDE PREPARING FOR THE AUDIENCE

New challenges await a critical theatre teacher when the performance space of a play with edgy content changes from a make-shift classroom that comfortably seats 40 audience members to a state-of-the-art performing arts center with seating for over 700. When we decided to perform Act I of *A Piece of My Heart* by Shirley Lauro (1998), the opportunity to share the educational experience with the entire student body was available.

*A Piece of My Heart* at its core is a play that raises the profile of women who served in Vietnam, and by extension honors all women in the military, past and present. As such, it is a radical production, because females who served in Vietnam were ignored even more so than men who returned from service. The leader of The Vietnam Women's Memorial Project, Diane Carlson Evans, justified the need for the monument, assessing:

> Historically, women who have served humanity during America's struggles and wars are not included in the artistic portrayals. They slip into history unrecognized and forgotten, compounding the myth that either they did not serve or their service was not noteworthy. They, too, had disappeared off the landscape of the Vietnam era.
>
> (Carlson 1982)

To promote awareness of the position of women in the military, and to honor Veteran's Day, we performed two matinees in early November, one for upper and another for lower classmen. Talk-backs by former Vietnam-war nurse and author Mary Reynolds Powell followed both performances. The overriding goal of the matinees was to validate women's experience in Vietnam; this was a critical effort toward leveling women's service with men in the minds of our students.

However, our effort was thwarted by a fateful oversight. Providing background information and shaping student's aesthetic perception of a play (or any school presentation, for that matter) that students are mandated to see should be standard assembly procedure in schools. But this is not a practice in our school; taking time to front-load an all-school event absorbs class time reserved for core content and requires buy-in from all teachers. In my earnest desire to challenge students to ponder the contributions of women who served in Vietnam, perform a play for the entire school in the Performing Arts Center for the first time, advocate for high school theatre in general, and impact all students through the power of serious drama, I neglected to make an exception to the norm. I did not ask teachers to describe the context of the play to their students. I did not take into account the behavior students might exhibit who would be watching a serious drama disconnected from historical context or the theatrical aesthetic. I did not query my principal about where students would sit or who would monitor their behavior. They were, it turns out, allowed to sit anywhere in the house, so naturally they sat with friends. Teachers were encouraged to attend but not all of them did, and most who did sat in a cluster behind the students. During the performance, we turned off the houselights. (What were my administrators and I [not] thinking?)

Moments of intensity punctuated the play, including a violent kiss, loud recorded explosions, blackouts, and the line, "You shouldn't be in a fucking war;" characters were often on the brink of emotional collapse. Furthermore, directing choices abstracted the staging: reinforcing themes, teams of actresses formed tableaus in the background throughout the play; actors playing soldiers who died remained standing, signifying death by turning their backs to the audience.

Unsupervised students reacted to these elements with laughter, bordering at times on derision. In one scene, the character Sissy confronts a horrific injury—a soldier's foot is torn from his leg. The scene ends when she cries, "I can't, I can't, I can't!" A boy sitting just two seats from me, obviously disengaged, retorted, "I bet you can." I pulled another disruptive student from the group and delivered him to our newly hired assistant principal who was nervously pacing the aisles. When yet another student made a rude comment, I looked him directly in the eyes and said "Shut ... Up." Students next to him jeered, a response that threw me back to my first year of teaching when I was learning—the hard way—how to earn classroom control.

Why had I romanticized the Performing Arts Center as a place where the uninformed student body would respectfully appreciate, by virtue alone, our artistic product and the beautiful theatre in which we presented it? Why did I naively assume that students, untrained in theatre etiquette, would flock to the auditorium eager to watch their peers act in a play they knew nothing about? bell hooks suggests that, rather than stable and self-contained as represented by our ideal image, the notion of place is an evolving construct (hooks 2009). Why did I not take it upon myself to alter conditions of the space?

> I ignored an important precept: traditional conditions require traditional forms of control.

Absorbed with logistics related to guest speakers and tech-week details, I did not consider best practice when it comes to audience reception. I ignored an important precept: traditional conditions require traditional forms of control. Instead of using the matinee as a means to empower students, we ushered students into an unsafe space, cultivating discomfort by forcing them to witness difficult content for which they didn't understand the context. Rather than forming *community* in the new theatre, actors performed in conditions that actually encouraged audience members to disconnect from the event. Gruenewald states:

> Human communities, or places, are politicized, social constructions that often marginalize individuals. [...] If place-based educators seek to connect

> place with self and community, they must identify and confront the ways that power works through places to limit [our] possibilities.
>
> (2003, 315)

In this situation, students' ignorance of their purpose in this space fueled their ability to control, and destroy, the aesthetic experience we were so eager to share with them.

Behavior worsened. Sitting in the front row was a group of male athletes. During one of the monologues delivered by the actress who played Steele, one boy muttered to a friend, "That "n"-bitch can't act." Though the actress didn't hear the remark, others onstage did, and they met me after the show in tears. I informed my principal immediately. He interrogated and subsequently punished the offending student, commenting, "I will not have a student disrespected onstage."

Short of turning on the house lights (which didn't occur to us) or stopping the play altogether, we couldn't change student behavior. Only when our guest speaker came to the stage to speak did students realize that the stories they had seen unfold in the play were real. In an e-mail, the former Vietnam War soldier who had written a letter to the editor after the killing of Saddam Hussein (see Chapter 3), wrote:

> I was a little distressed with how the freshmen and sophomores reacted and behaved. But I think there were a number of reasons for that. First and foremost the cast was made up of peers who they all knew. I don't think the noise and laughter would have been so prevalent had the cast been made up of adults. [...] I don't believe most of the members of the audience were able to grasp the depth of the situations which lead to the show of temper, the drinking, the drug use and the passing relationships that are so much a part of the combat experience.
>
> (Arnold, e-mail correspondence, September 10, 2011a)

Many students apologized for their peers' behavior. Others, chagrined, nevertheless recognized that performance conditions encouraged their impudence. One 17-year-old boy confessed that he was one of the kids who'd been laughing during the performance. His rationale? "Well, when a novice actor is speaking and you don't even know what it is you're supposed to be watching ..." We had made it easy for students to behave with disrespect.

One student unconnected to the production submitted a pointed editorial to the school newspaper, chastising her peers. "I thought we had all graduated third grade, where a kiss was considered the end of the world," the writer admonished. "Apparently, some of you failed to progress past that stage in your development." The day the school paper came out, the assistant principal called a student down for an infraction; it was the same rudely behaving student I had removed from his seat during the performance. On an impulse, the administrator read him the entire editorial. In an act of shared authority, the administrator, using the student writer's words, admonished the offender by describing the hurtful impact of poor theatre manners on performers and audience alike.

In the editorial, the student suggested that administrators devise a strategy for seating students at events such as this to curb immature antics. A new format successfully modified conditions for the next all-school assembly, which celebrated Black History Month. Students sat with their classes in assigned seats, teachers were required to sit with their classes, and the house lights remained at half. Behavior improved immensely.

Although my students and I were disheartened by their peers' behavior during the matinee performances, critical insight puts the challenges of this experience into perspective. Acquisition of a new performing arts center requires a process of transition not only for those who produce events to showcase, but also for audiences. Training a large student body to collectively practice theatre etiquette may be an impossible goal to achieve; and there are likely more effective ways to infuse aspects of our theatre program into the curricular framework of our school. Stevenson identifies social change as a dynamic process, full of junctures and disjunctures, continuities and discontinuities. With this awareness, he advises, "a critical pedagogy of place (broadly defined) can be commensurate with the disjunctures or divergences with which we must live and from which we must learn" (Stevenson 2008, 358).

## POSTSCRIPT

After speaking at the matinees of *A Piece of My Heart*, we thanked Mary and gave her a dog tag on a chain, engraved with the year, our school's name, and the title of the play. That's when she shared that she had been so angry when she came home from the war that she threw away her dog tags, along with everything else that reminded her of the war. Except her fatigues. She said she was proud of the nursing work she had done, so she kept them.

We accepted an invitation to perform the play at the Ohio Thespian Conference the following spring, and Mary attended. To thwart potential disappointment if their audience was small, I told the cast, "Even if only 30 audience members attend the performance, those 30 students will be exceptionally attentive because they will have chosen to attend this show above other options." (I'm glad I'd warned them, because 30 people attended the show.) Prior to house opening, we rearranged chairs so audience members were as close to the performance area as possible. By the third scene, some were sitting on the edges of their seats. At the play's conclusion, there was silence. Then, two boys in the front row leaped to their feet and began to applaud. Mary spoke to the small crowd afterward. At one point, she turned to the cast and crew and told them that the intensity of their performance *this* night, in *this* intimate space, took her right back to Vietnam. Then she looked at me and said wistfully, "I should've worn my fatigues."

The difference in student behavior between the school matinees and the state conference performance points to the significance of the performance environment. If the theatre is a sanctuary that harbors the creative spirit, it is important that students who enter that sanctuary do so with respect for the performance they are about to see. A state-of-the-art performing arts center provides students opportunities for advanced training and a chance to showcase their best efforts for all of their peers. It also becomes a site for new tensions that challenge critical theatre teachers to discover fresh avenues by which students can practice resistance against oppression and discover self-agency.

## NOTES

1 My thinking on accountability to an audience is informed by comments made by Bruce Fox, Dennis Mills, Mary Lawlis, Christine Jackson, and Steve Russell, contributing members of the panel presentation "Developing a Statement That Establishes the Rights, Freedoms, and Responsibilities of Teachers in Regard to Public Performances by Students" at 2004 IDEA, the 5th World Congress of Drama/Theatre and Education in Ottawa, Canada. The educators spoke individually about ways to promote the rights of theatre teachers to explore difficult or controversial themes, events, and ideas.

2 For insight on addressing the topic of suicide with audiences, see Gonzalez and Donnelly (2008).

3 Omasta calls for long-range studies in the conclusion of his report on the Educational Theatre Association's 2012 Survey of Theatre Education in United States High Schools. He states that the field would benefit from "longitudinal research that tracks student involvement with arts education experiences literally from birth through their adulthood to explore any long-term impacts theatre and drama experiences might have" (2012, 26).

# Epilogue

A recent report about Barack Obama's second-term education agenda begins, "Soaring campaign-year aspirations to close the achievement gap and boost college graduation rates to the highest in the world may have to fall back to earth—at least temporarily—as lawmakers tackle ..." and concludes with a quote from Senator Tom Harken stating in an email, "While the administration's efforts to grant waivers are helpful for states operating under the tenets of No Child Left Behind, these fixes are temporary and piecemeal" (Lederman 2012). National efforts toward achieving equity in education operates in temporary stages.

Local efforts to support theatre arts education operates in temporary stages, too. During the autumn that Obama was campaigning for re-election, our school district was campaigning for a levy to raise income taxes. As a campaign strategy, a PTO parent attended many school events that fall and, prior to each, read a statement describing the school's need for increased funding. I remember thinking earlier that summer as I contemplated fall play titles that if our fall production was strong, perhaps it, too, would influence voters to support the levy. I was partially right and also very wrong. The day before the election and two days following the close of our fall play, a letter to the editor appeared with the headline, "Levy Talk Spoils Drama Club Play" (Letters to the Editor 2012). In the letter, the writer indeed praised the production. But then he proceeded to complain about the pre-show levy speech and criticize the school's levy request. While I hope that quality performances influence voters to support students' theatre arts education, I cannot control how audience members react; some may use our best efforts to suit their own agendas. The levy failed. Twice.

Yet I have faith that this failure is temporary, and that I will continue to explore high school theatre arts with critical awareness in the new Performing Arts Center even if I must work with limited hours, constrained funds, or fewer students. But if my program is cut, no matter what I teach or where, I am committed to practicing a liberatory pedagogy. I will make a *place* for it. As a liberatory teacher, I will continue to seize moments that engage students whose voices are marginalized by race, academic status, class, ethnicity, gender, and a host of other alienating aspects of the high school social structure—whether on a new state-of-the-art stage or in an English classroom. I will continue to question why some moments escape my grasp.

A liberatory pedagogy attempts to reveal inequities and lead all students toward critical consciousness, with the hope that they can influence communities to take action for social change—be it a levy to support the schools or a policy that provides equitable conditions in the work place. High school theatre students have already made an impact on the Broadway Cares About AIDS Project. At the 2012 International Thespian Festival, Broadway Cares chairman Joe Norton announced that Thespian troupes across the country collectively donated over one million dollars to Broadway Cares. Norton told International Thespian Festival delegates that this amount marked the largest contribution to Broadway Cares About AIDS from any single organization, ever.

As a teacher of liberatory high school theatre education, I try to be open to students who help me understand elements of their lives that I misunderstand, or do not know. A pedagogy is successful not when the work that arises from it is previewed by the media, applauded by a conference screener, or when its strengths are used as a backdrop for lambasting a school levy campaign. A pedagogy is successful when it draws students toward topics and exercises that make them face one another's differences; it is successful when the experiences themselves viscerally involve and sustain student interest, and seedlings of critical awareness emerge.

A student in the Social Issues Theatre class that explored the subject of human trafficking reported that she was appalled one afternoon while shopping for a Halloween costume. She overheard a father say to his young son, "This pimp costume will make you look *boss*." Through research, the student had recognized that Toledo, Ohio—a city just 20 miles up the road from our school—is the fourth-largest hub in the nation for sex trafficking per capita. She had found out that conditions of modern slavery exist in every country in the world today, and discovered ways that women and men are exploited and manipulated by labor and sex traffickers globally. This knowledge helped the student develop a sensitivity to casual comments that glorify pimp culture. After sharing this anecdote with the class, the student added that she wouldn't have thought twice about the conversation she overheard if it weren't for participating in Social Issues Theatre. Discussion among students began.

As teachers, we must become diligently aware of these critical moments, and provide time for extended student engagement in critically conscious thinking as we plan our rehearsal schedules and classroom activities. Engagement is an intense, incomplete process that occurs between people. bell hooks asserts that "the engaged voice must never be fixed and absolute but always changing, always evolving in dialogue with a world beyond itself"

(1994, 11). True engagement takes us into the unknown, where energy fuses self-knowledge and student artistry to create small, but not inconsequential, stages toward social change. We and our students stand at the footlights of these stages temporarily. Teens will graduate and move on, and our teaching conditions vary as levies pass … and fail. But in nooks of time and pockets of space, students and their teachers can practice social equity in rehearsals and theatre classrooms one day at a time.

# Works Cited

*Aida* Opinions. 2009. Web. 31 March–1 April.

Arnold, Steve. 2011a. E-mail Correspondence. 10 September.

——— 2011b. Letters to the Editor. *Sentinel-Tribune*. 25 April.

*Arts at the Core: Recommendations for Advancing the State of Arts Education in the 21st Century*. 2009. National Task Force on the Arts in Education Final Report. New York: The College Board. (3).

*Arts Education in Public Elementary and Secondary Schools 1999–2000 & 2009–2010*. 2012. National Center for Education Statistics. Washington, DC: U.S. Department of Education. (46–51).

Averill, Gage. 2003. *Four Parts, No Waiting: A Social History of American Barbershop Harmony*. New York: Oxford University Press.

Ballanca, James and Ron Brandt, eds. 2010. *21st Century Skills: Rethinking How Students Learn*. Bloomington, IN: Solution Tree Press.

BarackObama.com. 2009. In *Arts at the Core: Recommendations for Advancing the State of Arts Education in the 21st Century*. National Task Force on the Arts in Education Final Report. New York: The College Board.

Barbules, Nicholas C. and Rupert Berk. 1999. "Critical Thinking and Critical Pedagogy: Relations, Difference, and Limits." In *Critical Theories in Education*. T. Popkewitz and L. Fendler, eds. New York: Routledge.

Behar, Ruth. 1986. *The Vulnerable Observer*. Boston, MA: Beacon Press.

Belenky, Mary Field, Blythe McVicker Clinchy, Nancy Rule Goldberger and Jill Mattuck Tarule. 1986. *Women's Ways of Knowing: The Development of Self, Voice and Mind*. New York: Basic Books.

Bennett, Jeff. 2001. *Secondary Stages: Revitalizing High School Theatre*. Portsmouth, NH: Heinemann.

Berlak, Ann C. 2004. "Confrontation and Pedagogy: Cultural Secrets, Trauma, and Emotion in Antioppressive Pedagogies." In *Democratic in Education: Troubling Speech, Disturbing Silence*. Megan Bohler, ed. New York: Peter Lang. (123–44).

Berry, Gordon L. and Joy Keiko Asamen. 2001. "Television, Children, and Multicultural Awareness." In *Handbook of Children and the Media*. Dorothy G. Singer and Jerome L. Singer, eds. Thousand Oaks, CA: Sage Publications.

*Black. White*. 2006. Six-Part Reality TV Show. Ice Cube and R. J. Cutler, producers. FX Cable Channel.

Boston Women's Teachers' Group. 1983. "The Other End of the Corridor: The Effects of Teaching on Teachers." *Radical Teacher*. 23 (Spring): 3.

Breon, Robin. 1995. "Show Boat: The Revival." *The Drama Review*. 39 (2): 86–105.

Britzman, Deborah P. 1991. *Practice Makes Practice: A Critical Study of Learning to Teach*. Albany, NY: State University of New York Press.

Brook, Peter. 1984. *The Empty Space*. New York: Atheneum Press.

Brown, Cindy. 1999. "A Nice Way to Make a Living: Reflections on the Career of an Experienced Theatre Teacher." *Youth Theatre Journal*. 13: 26–42.

Bush, Max. 2011. American Alliance for Theatre and Education Conference Presentation. Chicago, IL. 30 July.

——— 2006. *Kara in Black*. Woodstock, IL: Dramatic Publishing.

Carr, Paul R. 2011. *Does Your Vote Count? Critical Pedagogy and Democracy*. New York: Peter Lang.

"Censorship vs. Freedom of Artistic Expression." 1994. In *Ohio Marquee*. Winter. Diana E. Vance, ed. Web. Accessed 22 December 2004.

Chapman, Jennifer, Heather Sykes, and Anne Swedberg. 2003. "'Wearing the Secret Out:' Performing Stories of Sexual Identities." *Youth Theatre Journal*. 17: 27–37.

Chow, Esther Ngam-Ling, Gang-Hua Fan, Chadwick Fleck, Joshua Joseph and Deanna M. Lyter. 2003. "Exploring Critical Feminist Pedagogy: Infusing Dialogue, Participation, and Experience in Teaching and Learning." *Teaching Sociology*. 31 (3): 259–75.

Christian, Pamela. 2012. E-mail correspondence. 12 July.

Clinchy, Blythe McVicker. 1996. "Connected and Separate Knowing: Toward a Marriage of Two Minds." In *Knowledge Difference, and Power: Essays Inspired by Women's Ways of Knowing*. Nancy Rule Goldberger, ed. New York: Basic Books.

Conquergood, Dwight. 1985. "Performing as a Moral Act: Ethical Dimensions of the Ethnography of Performance." *Literature in Performance*. 5 (2): 1–13.

Conrad, Diane. 2004. "Popular Theatre: Empowering Pedagogy for Youth." *Youth Theatre Journal*. 18: 87–106.

Consortium of National Arts Education Associations. 1995. *Opportunity-to-Learn Standards for Arts Education*. Tempe, AZ: Arizona State University.

Cooks, Leda M. 2007. "The Joke's On You?" In *Whiteness, Pedagogy, Performance*. Leda M. Cooks and Jennifer S. Simpson, eds. Lanham, MD: Lexington Books.

Cowan, Allison Leigh. 2007. "Play About Iraq War Divides a Connecticut School." *New York Times*. 24 Mar. Web. Accessed 7 June 2012.

Delpit, Lisa. 1995. *Other People's Children*. New York: The New Press.

DeMarisco, Jonette. 2002. E-mail Correspondence to the AATE High School Network List-serv. 9 November.

Denevi, Elizabeth. 2004. "White on White: Exploring White Racial Identity, Privilege, and Racism." In *Independent School Magazine*. National Association of Independent Schools. Web. Accessed 3 January 2005.

Dever, Jeff. 2010. "Letters to the Editor." *Sentinel-Tribune*. 5 May.

Doust, Abigail. 2004. Telephone Conversation. 13 August.
Duncan, Arne. 2009. Letter to School and Education Community Leaders. Washington, DC: U.S. Department of Education.
Ellis, Dawn. 2012. "Good News, Bad News." *Teaching Theatre*. 24 (1): 31–43.
Ellsworth, Elizabeth. 1997. *Teaching Positions*. New York: Teachers College Press.
——— 1989. "Why Doesn't This Feel Empowering? Working Through the Repressive Myths of Critical Pedagogy." *Harvard Educational Review*. (297–324).
Evans, Diane Carlson. 1982. "Moving A Vision: The Vietnam Women's Memorial." Web. Accessed 4 August 2012.
Fedor, Theresa. 2012. Personal Comment at the Human Trafficking, Prostitution and Sex Work Conference sponsored by Second Chance. Toledo, OH. 28 September.
Fisher, Bernice. 2001. *No Angel in the Classroom*. Lanham, MD: Rowman & Littlefield Publishers.
Frankenberg, Ruth. 1993. *White Women, Race Matters: The Social Construction of Whiteness*. Minneapolis, MN: University of Minnesota Press.
Freire, Paulo. 1970. *Pedagogy of the Oppressed*. New York: Continuum.
Fronek, Susan. 2011. E-mail Correspondence. 9 May.
Gallagher, Kathleen. 2000. Personal Comment. 6th Annual IDIERI Conference. Columbus, OH. 24 July.
Gallagher, Rori. 2008. "'Rent' Gets A High School Makeover." *All Things Considered*. National Public Radio. 4 December.
Garan, Elaine. 1994. "Who's in Control? Is There Enough Empowerment to Go Around?" *Language Arts*. 71 (3): 192–99.
Gilligan, Carol. 2006. "Mommy, I Know You." *Newsweek*. 30 January. (53).
Gonzalez, Jo Beth. 2014. "Developing 'Dramatic Metaphor' To Teach Concepts of Science." In *The Reflective Teaching Artist*. Dan Kelin and Katie Dawson, eds. Bristol: Intellect.
Gonzalez, Jo Beth. 2010. "A Fresh Approach to Using Understudies." *Teaching Theatre*, Educational Theatre Association. 21 (4): 37–42.
——— 2009. "The Cast List: A Better Way to Say 'You Didn't Get the Part.'" *Teaching Theatre*, Educational Theatre Association. 20 (2): 29–32.
——— 2004. "Social Issues-Based Theatre Workshops: Stimulating Teens' Critical Thinking." *Inquiry: Critical Thinking Across the Disciplines*. 23 (2): 4–22.
——— 1995. "The Chorus and Contemporary Youth Theatre." *Stage of the Art*, American Alliance for Theatre and Education. 7 (3): 20–23.
Gonzalez, Jo Beth and William O. Donnelly. 2008. "When It Matters Most: Creating Post-Show Talk-Backs." *Teaching Theatre*. 19 (3): 30–36.
Gonzalez, Jo Beth, Rosalinda Cantú, and Alberto González. 2007. "Staging Whiteness: Possibilities for Resistance and Revelation in a High School Production of *Simply Maria, or, The American Dream*." In *Whiteness, Pedagogy, Performance*. Leda M. Cooks and Jennifer S. Simpson, eds. Lanham, MD: Lexington Books.

Goode, Eric. 2011. "World War I Returns to Center Stage." *New York Times*. 24 July.
Gore, Jennifer. 1993. *The Struggles for Pedagogies*. New York: Routledge.
——— 1992. "'What We Can Do For You! What Can "We" Do For 'You?'": Struggling Over Empowerment in Critical and Feminist Pedagogy." In *Feminist and Critical Pedagogy*. Carmen Luke and Jennifer Gore, eds. New York: Routledge.
Green, Jesse. 2005. "The Supersizing of the School Play." *New York Times*. 8 May.
Greenleaf, Robert. 1970. "The Servant as Leader." In "Servant-Leaders are the Best Leaders During Times of Change" by Kent M. Keith. *Branches Magazine*. 21 (6). Web. Accessed 1 July 2012.
Gruenewald, David A. 2003. "The Best of Both Worlds: A Critical Pedagogy of Place." *Educational Researcher*. 32 (4): 3–12.
Hacker, Andrew. 2012. "Is Algebra Necessary?" *New York Times* Sunday Review, Opinion Page. Web. Accessed 9 September 2012.
Heins, Marjorie. 2001. *Not in Front of the Children*. New York: Hill and Wang.
Hesford, Wendy. 1999. *Framing Identities: Autobiography and the Politics of Pedagogy*. Minneapolis, MN: University of Minnesota Press.
Holley, Lynn. C. and Sue Steiner. 2005. "Safe Space: Students' Perspectives of Classroom Environments." *Journal of Social Work Education*. 41 (1): 49–64.
Holt, John. 1982. *How Children Fail*. New York: Delta.
hooks, bell. 2009. *Belonging: A Culture of Place*. New York: Routledge.
——— 2003. *Teaching Community: A Pedagogy of Hope*. New York: Routledge.
——— 2000. *Feminist Theory: From Margin to Center*. Cambridge, MA: South End Press.
——— 1998. "Feminisim: A Transformative Politic." In *Race, Class and Gender in the United States*. Paula S. Rothenberg, ed. New York: St. Martin's Press.
——— 1994. *Teaching to Transgress: Education as the Practice of Freedom*. New York: Routledge.
Jakubowski, Lisa and Livy Visano. 2002. *Teaching Controversy*. Halifax, Nova Scotia: Fernwood Publishing.
Kalb, Claudia. 1999. "Schools on the Alert." *Newsweek*. 23 Aug. (43).
Katz, Jackson. 2000. *Tough Guise*. Videocassette. Produced by Sut Jhally through the Media Education Foundation.
Keith, Kent M. 2009. "Servant-Leaders are the Best Leaders During Times of Change." *Branches Magazine*. 21 (6). Web. Accessed 1 July 2012.
Kenway, Jane and Helen Modra. 1992. "Feminist Pedagogy and Emancipatory Possibilities." In *Feminisms and Critical Pedagogy*. Carmen Luke and Jennifer Gore, eds. New York: Routledge.
Kohli, Wendy. 2000. "Teaching in the Danger Zone." In *Democratic Social Educations: Social Studies for Social Change*. David W. Hursch and E. Wayne Ross, eds. New York: Falmer Press.
Kreisberg, Seth. 1993. "Educating for Democracy and Community: Towards the Transformation of Power in Our Schools." In *Promising Practices in Teaching*

*Social Responsibility*. Sheldon Berman and Phyllis La Farge, eds. Albany, NY: State University of New York Press.

Kumagai, Arno K. and Monica L. Lypson. 2009. "Beyond Cultural Competence: Critical Consciousness, Social Justice, and Multicultural Education." *Academic Medicine*. 84 (6): 782–87.

Lather, Patti. 1992. "Post-Critical Pedagogies: A Feminist Reading." In *Feminisms and Critical Pedagogy*. Carmen Luke and Jennifer Gore, eds. New York: Routledge.

Lauro, Shirley. 1998. *A Piece of My Heart*. New York: Samuel French, Inc.

Lazarus, Joan. 2012. *Signs of Change: Revised and Amplified Edition*. Bristol: Intellect.

——— 2004. *Signs of Change: New Directions in Secondary Theatre Education*. Portsmouth, NH: Heinemann.

Lederman, Josh. 2012. "Loose Ends to Drive Obama's Next Term Education Agenda." *Sentinel-Tribune*. 19 November.

Lement, Wendy and Bethany Dunakin. 2005. *And Justice For Some*. Portsmouth, NH: Heinemann.

Lenning, Mary. 2011. Personal Interview. 27 June.

Letters to the Editor. 2012. "Levy Talk Spoils School Play." *The Sentinel-Tribune*. 5 November.

Little, Jennifer. 2010. "Applying Ourselves to the Human Drama." *Teaching Theatre*. 22 (1): 27–32.

López, Josefina. 1996. *Simply Maria, Or, The American Dream*. Woodstock, IL: Dramatic Publishing Company.

Loschert, Kristin. 2004. "The Play's the Thing." *NEA Today*. 23 (3): 22–23.

Luke, Carmen. 1992. "Feminist Politics in Radical Pedagogy." In *Feminisms and Critical Pedagogy*. Carmen Luke and Jennifer Gore, eds. New York: Routledge.

McCammon, Laura and Johnny Saldaña. 2011. *Lifelong Impact: Adult Perceptions of their High School Speech and/or Theatre Participation*. Unpublished Monograph.

McInerney, Peter John Smyth and Barry Down. 2001. "'Coming to a *Place* Near You?' The Politics and Possibilities of a Critical Pedagogy of Place-Based Education." *Asia-Pacific Journal of Teacher Education*. 39 (1): 3–16.

McIntosh, Peggy. 1998. "White Privilege: Unpacking the Invisible Knapsack." In *Race, Class and Gender in the United States*, Paula S. Rothenberg, ed. New York: St. Martin's Press.

MacKeracher, Dorothy. 1996. *Making Sense of Adult Learning*. New York: Culture Concepts.

McNay, Lois. 1992. *Foucault & Feminism*. Boston, MA: Northeastern University Press.

McNeil, Linda M. 1986. Contradictions of Control. New York: Routledge.

Maher, Frances A. and Mary Kay Thompson Tetreault. 2001. *The Feminist Classroom*. Lanham, MD: Rowman & Littlefield Publishers.

Mandell, Jan and Jennifer Lynn Wolf. 2003. *Acting, Learning and Change.* Portsmouth, NH: Heinemann.

Mayberry, M. and Rees, M.N. 1999. "Feminist Pedagogy, Interdisciplinary Praxis, and Science Education." In *Meeting the Challenge: Innovative Feminist Pedagogies in Action.* M. Mayberry and E.C. Rose, eds. London and New York: Routledge. (193–214).

Mencer, Sandy. 2011. Social Issues Theatre Class Presentation. 28 February.

Ng, Roxanna. 1995. "Teaching Against the Grain: Contradictions and Possibilities." In *Anti-racism, Feminism and Critical Approaches to Education.* Roxanna Ng, Joyce Scane, and Patricia Staton, eds. Westport, CT: Bergin and Garvey Press.

Norris, Joe. 1995. "The Use of Drama in Teacher Education: A Call for Embodied Learning." In *Creating a Theatre in Your Classroom.* North York, Ontario: Captus Press.

Omasta, Matt. 2012. "A Survey of School Theatre." *Teaching Theatre.* 24 (1): 9–28.

"Opportunities-to-Learn Standards for Arts Education: Dance, Music, Theatre, Visual Arts." 1995. Consortium of National Arts Education Associations. (34–37.)

Orner, Mimi. 1992. "Interrupting the Calls for Student Voice in 'Liberatory' Education: A Feminist Poststructuralist Perspective." In *Feminist and Critical Pedagogy.* Carmen Luke and Jennifer Gore, eds. New York: Routledge.

Orr, David W. 1992. *Ecological Literacy.* Albany, NY: State University of New York Press.

Palmarini, Jim. 2012. "Research Matters." *Teaching Theatre.* 24 (1): 29–30.

Redmond, Melissa. 2010. "Safe Space Oddity: Revising Critical Pedagogy." *Journal of Teaching In Social Work.* 30: 1–14.

Ressler, Paula. 2002. *Dramatic Changes: Talking About Sexual Orientation and Gender Identity with High School Students.* Portsmouth, NH: Heinemann.

Roberts, Dan. 1997. *DUI=DOA.* Tallahassee, FL: Eldrige.

Rohd, Michael. 1998. *Hope is Vital: Theatre for Community, Conflict and Dialogue.* Portsmouth, NH: Heinemann.

Ruitenberg, Claudia. 2005. *Deconstructing the Experience of the Local: Toward a Radical Pedagogy of Place.* Philosophy of Education Yearbook. (212–220).

Saldaña, Johnny. 2012. "Theatre Finds A Way." *Teaching Theatre.* 24 (1): 44–46.

Santoro, Ron. 2002. E-mail Correspondence to the AATE High School Network List-serv. 2 September.

——— 1997. Personal Comment at the American Alliance for Theatre and Education National Conference. Charlotte, NC. 8 August.

Scholnick, Ellin Kofsky. 2000. "Engendering Development: Metaphors of Change." In *Toward a Feminist Developmental Psychology.* Patricia H. Miller and Ellin Kofsky Scholnick, eds. New York: Routledge.

Schutzman, Mady and Jan Cohen-Cruz, eds. 1994. *Playing Boal.* New York: Routledge.

"The Science of Theatre." 2012. *Pro Excellentia.* Spring. Cleveland, OH: The Martha Holden Jennings Foundation.

Seidel, Kent. 1991. "Theatre Education in United States High Schools: A Survey Report." *Teaching Theatre*. Educational Theatre Association. 3 (1).

Shor, Ira. 1992. *Empowering Education*. Chicago, IL: University of Chicago Press.

Simon, Scott. 2011. "Cancelling the School Play Won't Avoid 'Kismet.'" *Weekend Edition Saturday*. National Public Radio. 24 Sept.

Sizor, Theodore. 1984. *Horace's Compromise: The Dilemmas of the American High School*. Boston, MA: Houghton Mifflin.

Sleeter, Christine. 1993. "How White Teachers Construct Race." In *Race, Identity and Representation in Education*. Cameron McCarthy and Warren Chrichlow, eds. New York: Routledge.

Stevenson, Lauren M. and Richard J. Deasy. 2005. *Third Space*. Washington, DC: Arts Education Partnership.

Stevenson, Robert B. 2008. "A Critical Pedagogy of Place and the Critical Place(s) of Pedagogy." *Environmental Educational Education Research*. 14 (3): 308–24.

Strut and Fret. 2012. "'Maine,' 'Beauty' at the Top of the Survey." *Dramatics*. Cincinnati, OH: Educational Theatre Association. (14).

Survey of Theatre Education in United States High Schools 2011–2012. 2012. Educational Theatre Association and Utah State University. *Teaching Theatre*. Educational Theatre Association. 24 (1).

Swarms, Rachel L. 2012. "Meet Your Cousin, the First Lady: A Family Story, Long Hidden." *New York Times*. 16 June. Web. Accessed 24 June 2012.

Tache, Diane. 2010. Personal Interview. 29 June.

Tatum, Beverly. 1997. *"Why Are All the Black Kids Sitting Together in the Cafeteria?" and Other Conversations About Race*. New York: Basic Books.

Taylor, Dana. 2011. "It's Technical: New Standards in Technical Theatre Education." *Teaching Theatre*. Educational Theatre Association. 21 (2): 30–34.

Taylor, Phillip. 2003. *Applied Theatre*. Portsmouth, NH: Heinemann.

*Thespians*. 2011. Documentary. TigerLily Media, producer. Tampa, FL: Maven Films.

Vincent, Norah. 2006. *Self-Made Man*. New York: Viking Press.

Wallace, Miriam. 1999. "Beyond Love and Battle: Practicing Feminist Pedagogy." *Feminist Teacher*. 12 (3): 184–97.

Warren, John. 2003. *Performing Purity*. New York: Peter Lang.

Worthman, Christopher. 2004. "Our Public and Private Selves: Fostering Dialogism and Student Perspective Taking." *Discourse: Studies in the Cultural Politics of Education*. 25 (3): 365–73.

# Index

A

activating scenes 139, 176, 190
actor/crew binary 85 *see also* binaries
added time 113–14
administrative support 18–19, 43–4, 46, 76–7, 184
admirable competition 109
age, and power 12
*Aida* 61–5, 185
*Anatomy of Gray* 106, 111, 112
*Antigone* 185
*Anything Else Would Be Substandard* 156, 160
artistic vision 73, 74, 77–9, 83
artistry, students 13, 53–4, 75, 79–84, 117
audience 190–5
  fear factor 183–6
  performance and 190–5
  play choice and 32–3, 36–8, 43, 45, 50, 77–8, 148
  support and 60, 82
  students as 191–2, 194
Aurora, Colorado 153–4
authority 9, 12–13, 19, 74–5, 87n.2, 159–62
  co-authority 73, 75
  democracy and 91–2, 93–5
  directing and 74, 79, 85, 93–5, 161
  of teacher 8, 13, 85, 86, 91–2, 94, 143
autobiography 151–3, 168

B

*Bang Bang You're Dead* 32
barbershop music 58, 59
*Beauty and the Beast* 86, 129–30
Behar, Ruth, quoted 159
Bennett, Jeff, quoted 37
Berlak, Ann, quoted 61, 62–3, 64, 65
"The Best Drunk Driver" 150 *see also* driving while intoxicated
bias,
  of students 25, 154
  of teacher 15, 51, 96, 139–40, 167
binaries 16, 91
  actor/crew 85
  creativity/technology 128–9
  democracy and 85, 86
  leader/follower 86, 161–2
  science/theatre 130, 131–2
  teacher/student 84–5
black heritage 58–9, 172–3 *see also* Hispanic heritage
Black Poetry Ensemble 65
blackface 56–7, 58
*Black. White* 63–4
Boal, Augusto 139, 180n.3
bonding 10–11, 153, 154
boys, emotion and support 154–6, 163n.4, 185
Breon, Robin, quoted 50, 51, 59
Britzman, Deborah P., quoted 12, 41, 76–7, 92, 139–40
Broadway Cares About AIDS 200
Brook, Peter, quoted 128
Brown, Cindy, quoted 18
budgets 5, 117, 129–30, 199–200
bullying 32, 52, 140–1, 144n.1, 186
Bush, Max 41–3, 45
  quoted 39–40

C
Carr, Paul R., quoted 51, 55
casting 52–3, 95–100, 114
  color and 50, 55–7, 58, 61–2, 177–8
  double-casting 104–5, 106–7
  ensembles 104–5
  gender and 57, 71, 73
  *A Midsummer Night's Dream* 94–6
  *A Piece of My Heart* 176–8
  power and 104
  racial/ethnic 176–9
  rehearsals and 95, 99, 111–12
  rejection and 81, 97–8
  three As 105
  *Twelfth Night* 103–5
  *West Side Story* 55–7, 99
  *see also* principals; star system; stereotypes; understudies
CCPOC (critically conscious production-oriented classroom) 9
censorship xii, xiii, 6–7, 31, 36–46, 183
Challenge Day 186–8, 189
change 5, 14–15, 34–5
  physical/venue 5–6, 18, 49, 117, 120–1
  plays 34, 37
  problems with 34–5
  students and 74–5, 128, 143
  *see also* social change
Chapman, Jennifer, quoted 38
character development 50, 108–9, 111
Christian, Pamela, quoted 119–20
class *see* social class
classrooms xiii, 8–9, 24–6, 28n.1 and 2, 171–3, 174
  access 34–5
  communication and 74, 154–5
  criticism in 97, 99, 174–6
  democracy in xiii, 8, 35, 97
  *see also* place
co-authority 73, 75 *see also* authority
co-governance 73, 126–8
co-operation 13, 84, 104, 153
CODE (critically oriented drama education) 9
  reflective practice and 149–62
collaboration 8, 13, 46, 80–2, 131
  leadership and 51, 54–5
  musical theatre 51–2, 53
  with other subjects 130–2
  principal/understudy 104, 106, 108
  set design 72–4, 84
color, and casting 50, 55–7, 58, 61–2, 177–8 *see also* black heritage; Hispanic heritage; privilege; race/racism; whiteness
color-blindness 172–3
Columbine High School 153, 154
commitment 44–6, 54, 141
  student 92, 106, 109, 158
  teacher 157
communication 123
  in the classroom 74, 154–5
  student 24, 81, 92–3
  teacher 16
competition 13, 94–5, 99–100, 104, 109, 112
compromise 37, 75, 79–84, 93, 98, 122
conflict 74, 122
  play choice and 43, 64
  students and 64–5, 92–3, 157–8, 173
  teachers and xii, 37, 41, 74, 94–5
consciousness *see* critical consciousness; social consciousness
consciousness-raising 153–6
control xii, 73–5, 140
controversial topics 7, 32, 40, 43–6, 138–42, 154, 186–90, 195n.1 *see also* plays, choice of
Cooks, Leda, quoted 179
copyright 34
creative spirit 18, 128, 195
creativity 10, 129, 141

creativity/technology binary 128–9
see also binaries
critical consciousness 8–9, 18–19, 31–4, 139, 178, 200
rehearsals 24, 55–7, 200–1
critical directing 49–52 *see also* directing
critical inquiry 6, 33, 51, 57–60, 139 *see also* research
critical pedagogy xiii, 6–7, 8, 15, 19, 118 *see also* pedagogy
critical reflection 25, 26–7 *see also* reflective practice
critically conscious production-oriented classroom *see* CCPOC
critically oriented drama education *see* CODE
criticism 41
in the classroom 97, 99, 174–6
public 31, 33
from students 26, 54–5, 80, 83, 92
cultural borders 61–5

**D**

*Dames at Sea* 32
Dance of the Robe 62, 63, 64
*Danny and the Deep Blue Sea* 40
Danville Community High School 41
dating violence 139, 151 *see also* violence
Delpit, Lisa, quoted 173
DeMarisco, Jonnette, quoted 38
democracy 9, 16, 95–6
authority and 91–2, 93–5
binaries and 85, 86
classroom xiii, 8, 35, 97
pedagogy and 153
students and 75–7, 80, 83–4
teaching and 8, 13, 73, 74–7, 80–1, 93–7, 191
time constraints and 77
demographics, students 174–5
design *see* production design; set design; Theatre Design class
dialogue 122, 141–2, 153
"Best Drunk Driver" 150
*Kara in Black* 42–3
"The Question" 168
Dickinson, Bonnie, quoted 39, 40
directing,
authority and 74, 79, 85, 93–5, 161
critical 49–52
student 36–7, 99, 161
*see also* musical theatre
discipline 143, 191–2
diversity 16, 120, 167, 173–4
casting 55–7, 61, 62
domestic violence 139, 174, 175, 190 *see also* violence
double-casting 104–5, 106–7 *see also* casting
Doust, Abigail, quoted 159
dramaturgy, and identity 57–60
driving while intoxicated 139, 147–50, 154, 157–8, 184, 188–9
*The Drowsy Chaperone* 53

**E**

education
effects of 118
power and 15, 139–40, 153
research 10, 143–4, 174, 195n.3
Ellsworth, Elizabeth, quoted 12, 15, 41, 142, 180n.2, 189
emotional expression 51, 94, 153–6, 174, 187–8
boys and 154–6, 163n.4, 185
engagement 9, 63, 158, 200–1
ensembles 110–12, 114
casting 104–5
understudies and 106
equality 107–8, 161–2 *see also* inequality
*Eric and Elliott* 43, 46n.2, 186

ethnicity 16, 55–7, 61, 167, 172, 176–9 *see also* identity
evaluation 25–8, 53, 55, 96–7, 98–9 *see also* grades
Evans, Diane Carlson, quoted 191
exclusion 34, 50, 52, 58, 120 *see also* involvement
experts, use of 38, 148–9, 186–7

**F**
"Fagzilla" 150
fear factor 183–6
Fedor, Teresa, quoted 185
feminism, and science teaching 130
feminist leadership 122–3, 142 *see also* leadership
feminist pedagogy 6–7, 35, 142–3, 155–6 *see also* pedogogy
*Fiddler on the Roof* 33–4
*For Colored Girls Who Have Considered Suicide/When the Rainbow is Enuf* 175
*The Foreigner* 179, 183

**G**
Gallagher, Kathleen, quoted 183
Gallagher, Rori, quoted 32
gender 12, 156, 168, 175
  casting and 57, 71, 73
Gilligan, Carol, quoted 155–6
*The Girl in the Mirror* 32
*Good Boys and True* 32
grades 8, 24, 27–8 *see also* evaluation
Green, Jesse, quoted 129–30
Greenleaf, Robert, quoted 121–2
Gruenewald, David A., quoted 17, 192–3
*Guys and Dolls* 53, 98, 103, 106
"Guys Like Me" 156

**H**
Hacker, Andrew, quoted 141
*Hairspray* 56
hegemony 16, 49–50, 59–60, 170, 172–3 *see also* privilege; whiteness
Hesford, Wendy 152
hierarchies 49–52, 60, 62, 121
Hispanic heritage 169, 170–1, 172–3 *see also* black heritage
Hochschild, Jennifer L., quoted 59
homophobia 32, 38, 149, 150
homosexuality 32, 36–9 *see also* sexuality
honesty 54, 151, 153–6
hooks, bell, quoted 8, 122, 152, 192, 200
Hughes, Jan, quoted 154
human trafficking 185, 200
humor 110, 151, 155, 160, 179 *see also* satire

**I**
identity120, 173–4
  dramaturgy and 57–60
  students xi, 155, 167–8
  teachers 95, 168–71
  *see also* ethnicity; whiteness
improvisation 33, 111–12
inequality 8, 15, 62–3, 118 *see also* equality
involvement 53–4, 65, 78–9, 106, 122–3, 162 *see also* exclusion
issues-based theatre 142, 189–90
"It Made Me Think" stories 157

**J**
Jakubowski, Lisa, quoted 154
*James and the Giant Peach* 63, 127–8
Johnstown High School 31, 33

**K**
*Kara in Black* 39–40, 41–4, 45, 46n.1
*The Katrina Project: Hell and High Water* 45–6
Katz, Jackson, quoted 156

*Kismet* 31
Kreisberg, Seth, quoted 74–5

**L**
language 36–8, 106–8, 177–8
  Shakespearean 105, 106, 112
leader/follower binary 86, 161–2 *see also* binaries
leadership 120, 121, 161
  collaboration and 51, 54–5
  feminist 122–3, 142
  servant-leadership 121–2
  student 40, 161–2
  teacher 86
  *see also* power
Lenning, Mary, quoted 119, 121, 129
liberatory pedagogy 152–3, 199–200 *see also* pedagogy
listening 25, 26–7
Little, Jennifer, quoted 45–6

**M**
McCammon, Laura, quoted 143
management 23, 123–6
Mandell, Jan, quoted 32, 34, 157–8
marginalization 6–7, 34, 50, 51–2, 120, 130, 170–1, 174–5 *see also* whiteness
masculinist teaching 142–3, 189 *see also* teaching
masculinity 156 *see also* gender
mathematics 73, 127, 130–1, 141
*Medea's Family Reunion* 175
Mencer, Sandy, quoted 16
*A Midsummer Night's Dream* 71, 72–5, 79, 94–6, 83–4, 87n.3
*Miss Saigon* 50
Morris, Tom, quoted 43
moving statues 78–9
*Much Ado About Nothing* 77–81, 91–3
muscle memory 107–8
*The Music Man* 57–60, 63, 124
musical theatre 33–4, 49–52, 53, 129 *see also* plays, choice of; theatre

**N**
national trends 10–11, 127, 130
negotiation 15, 72, 74–5, 87n.2, 123
New Albany High School 129–30
Ng, Roxanna, quoted 17
Norton, Joe, quoted 200

**O**
*Oklahoma* 31
Omasta, Matt 143–4, 195n.3
"Oppression" 151–3
oppression 27–8, 33, 63, 138–9, 140, 167, 195
original scripts 32, 138–9, 147–9, 152
ownership, student 54–5, 78–81, 104–5, 138, 151, 159–60

**P**
Palmarini, Jim, quoted 144
parents 99–100
partnership 103–14
pedagogy 49, 117–19
  critical xiii, 6–7, 8, 15, 19, 118
  democratic 153
  feminist 6–7, 35, 142–3, 155–6
  liberatory 152–3, 199–200
  place-based 17–18, 28n.2, 49, 117–19, 120, 194
  of the unknowable 41
  *see also* teaching
Peitz, Michael, quoted 32
performance,
  accessibility 51–2
  audience and 190–5
  set design and 82–4
  understudies and 103–14
*A Piece of My Heart* 45, 176–8, 191, 194

place,
safe space 171–3, 176–8, 180n.2
significance of 5, 17, 23–4, 192–3, 195
*see also* classrooms; theatre
place-based pedagogy 17–18, 28n.2, 49, 117–19, 120, 194 *see also* pedagogy
plays,
audience and 32–3, 36–8, 43, 45, 50, 77–8, 148
changing 34, 37
choice of 31–4, 36–9, 41–3, 64, 106, 184–5
political 39–40
writing workshops 57
*see also* musical theatre; Play Production class; scripts
Play Production class 9, 138–9, 147, 153, 155–6, 167, 171
teacher authority and 159–60
*see also* plays; production design
political plays 39–40 *see also* plays
Powell, Mary Reynolds 191, 194–5
power 7, 9, 10–11, 26, 61, 72, 121, 161–2
casting and 104
in education 15, 139–40, 153
student 33, 84–5, 91–3
teacher 8, 11–12, 14, 74–5, 94, 157
of theatre xi, 18, 49–50, 60, 191–3
*see also* leadership; strength
principals, and understudies 103–4, 105–14, 178 *see also* casting
privilege 11, 15–16, 57–60, 63, 118–20, 173–4 *see also* color; hegemony; social class; whiteness
production design,
*Much Ado About Nothing* 79–81
*The Winter's Tale* 81–2
*see also* Play Production class; set design
production research 41, 57, 61–2, 138, 147–9, 151, 153, 185, 200

**Q**
"The Question" 167–8, 171–2

**R**
race/racism 16, 58–9, 64, 139, 167, 172–3
barbershop and 58
casting and 56–7, 176–9
Social Issues Theatre class 174–6
*see also* color; stereotypes
"Ramblings from a Teenage Mind" 162
Redmond, Melissa, quoted 17, 120, 174–5
reflection characters 177–8
reflective practice 6, 24–7, 45–6, 92, 189
CODE strategies 149–62
rehearsals 8–9, 24, 59–60
casting and 95, 99, 111–12
critical consciousness 24, 55–7, 200–1
space for 51–2, 119
student responsibility 160–2
teacher identity 168–71
time for 64–5, 113–14, 173
for understudies 100, 104, 106, 107–8, 114
rejection 81, 97–8 *see also* casting
*RENT* 32
research,
for productions 41, 57, 61–2, 138, 147–9, 151, 153, 185, 200
on theatre education 10, 143–4, 174, 195n.3
*see also* critical inquiry
responsiblities,
students 37, 76, 99, 114
teachers 37, 39–40, 72–3, 190–1, 195n.1

Ressler, Paula, workshops 11, 38
rigging system 122–4, 131
see also technology
risk taking xii, xiii, 12, 18–19, 45–6, 125–6, 157–8, 161, 183, 184–5
Rohd, Michael 163n.5, 180n.3
Ruitenberg, Claudia, quoted 17, 120

S
"Sadtown Zombie Puppet Theatre" 151
safety 17, 157–8, 163n.6, 167, 171
technology and 123–4, 126, 132n.1
*see also* security
safe space with consequences 171–3, 176–8, 180n.2
Saldaña, Johnny, quoted 38, 143
Santoro, Ron, quoted 38, 39, 184–5
satire 149–51, 176 *see also* humor
scheduling 113–14, 122–3 *see also* time constraints
Scholnick, Ellin Kofsky, quoted 141, 142, 189
science/theatre binary 130, 131–2
*see also* binaries
scripts,
controversial 138–9
student-written 43–4, 138–9, 148–62
teacher-fed 147–8
*see also* plays; Social Issues Theatre class
security 14, 41, 82, 159–60, 175
*see also* safety
*Seeing Eye to Eye: A Glimpse of Reality* 155
self-agency 8, 18–19, 73, 128, 141
examples 40–1, 152, 161–2, 172
self-disclosure 8, 25, 151–3, 157, 158–9
self-image 24, 130, 141, 154
servant-leadership 121–2 *see also* leadership
set design 53–4, 72–3, 75–6, 79–81, 84–5
*James and the Giant Peach* 127–8
*A Midsummer Night's Dream* 71–5, 79, 83–4, 87n.3
*Much Ado About Nothing* 77–81
performance and 82–4
*The Winter's Tale* 75–6, 81–2
*see also* production design; Theatre Design class
sexting 140
sexuality, in plays 16, 181–2, 184 *see also* homosexuality
*The Shadow Box* 36–7, 43
shadowing 108–10
Shor, Ira, quoted 14, 143
*Simply Maria, Or, The American Dream* 168–72, 183–4
single-sex productions 185
Sleeter, Christine, quoted 172
social change 6–7, 8, 16, 27–8, 41, 194, 201
personal commitment and 44–6
students and 95–7, 139
*see also* change
social class 12, 36, 57–8, 170 *see also* privilege
social consciousness 153–6
Social Issues Theatre class 9, 147, 153, 157, 188, 189–90
dialogue in 141–2
impact 190, 200
issues addressed 173–6, 184–6
race/racism and 174–6
satire and 149–51
student-written scripts and 43–4, 138–9, 148–62
teacher authority and 159–60
teacher-fed scripts 147–8
workshops 139, 147, 149, 162n.1, 173–4, 176, 190
*Spring Awakening* 32
star system 50, 52–3 *see also* casting

stereotypes 12, 31, 50, 55–7, 61–5, 173, 177–8 *see also* casting; race/racism
Stevenson, Lauren M., quoted 11
Stevenson, Robert B., quoted 17, 194
strength
 of students 53–4, 82, 92, 105, 114, 176
 of teaching 95–7, 157–9
 *see also* power
students,
 artistry 13, 53–4, 75, 79–84, 117
 as audience 191–2, 194
 bias 25, 154
 change and 74–5, 128, 143
 commitment 92, 106, 109, 158
 communication 24, 81, 92–3
 conflict and 64–5, 92–3, 157–8, 173
 criticism from 26, 54–5, 80, 83, 92
 democracy among 75–7, 80, 83–4
 demographics 174–5
 directing and 36–7, 99, 161
 identity xi, 155, 167–8
 interaction 176
 leadership and 40, 161–2
 ownership 54–5, 78–81, 104–5, 138, 151, 159–60
 power and 33, 84–5, 91–3
 rehearsal and 160–2
 responsibility and 37, 76, 99, 114
 social change and 95–7, 139
 strength of 53–4, 82, 92, 105, 114, 176
suicide 5, 32, 43, 155, 162n.3, 186–7, 195n.2
support, of audience 60, 82
Swedberg, Anne, quoted 38
switching out 111, 112–13
Sykes, Heather, quoted 38

**T**
Taylor, Dana, quoted 124
Taylor, Phillip, quoted 25, 26
teacher/student binary 84–5 *see also* binaries
teachers,
 authority 8, 13, 85, 86, 91–2, 94, 143, 159–60
 bias 15, 51, 96, 139–40, 167
 commitment 157
 communication 16
 conflict and xii, 37, 41, 74, 94–5
 dominance 71–3
 identity 95, 168–71
 interventions 75–6
 job security 40
 leadership and 86
 Play Production class and 159–60
 power and 8, 11–12, 14, 74–5, 94, 157
 preconceptions 175–6
 rehearsal and 168–71
 responsiblities 37, 39–40, 72–3, 190–1, 195n.1
 self-disclosure and 158–9
teaching,
 democracy and 8, 13, 73, 74–7, 80–1, 93–7, 191
 masculinist 142–3, 189
 strength of 95–7, 157–9
traditional methods 142–3
*see also* pedagogy
technical knowledge 122–3, 124–6
technology
 creativity and 128–30
 rigging system 122–4, 131
 safety and 123–4, 126, 132n.1
 training/education 124–7
Tedesco, Guy, quoted 130
terminology 106–8 *see also* language
theatre
 issues based 142, 189–90
 newness and transition 6, 17, 28n.1, 49, 119–20, 121–2, 125
 power of xi, 18, 49–50, 60, 191–3
 *see also* musical theatre; place

Theatre Design class 9, 74, 82, 92–7, 126–8 *see also* set design
Theatre of the Oppressed 139
*Thespians* 40
time constraints
democracy and 77
rehearsals 64–5, 113–14, 173
*see also* scheduling
"Tough Guise" 156
tradition 14, 17, 33, 34–8, 94–5, 97–100, 142–3
trust 25, 92, 149, 153–6, 157, 176
*Twelfth Night* 103–6, 112–14

**U**

understanding 14, 26–7, 41–4, 74, 79, 141–2, 200
understudies 106–7
ensembles and 106
performance and 103–14
principals and 103–4, 105–14, 178
rehearsals 100, 104, 106, 107–8, 114
*see also* casting

**V**

Vincent, Norah, quoted 154
violence 156, 175
dating 139, 151
domestic 139, 174, 175, 190
in school 32, 154
Visano, Livy, quoted 154
voice 9, 84, 157–9
*Voices in Conflict* 39, 41
vulnerability 25, 92–3, 157–9

**W**

*War Horse* 43
war themes 39–46, 191–5
warm ups 111–12
*West Side Story* 55–7, 99
whiteness 8, 62, 169–70, 172–3, 176–9 *see also* color; hegemony; identity; marginalization; privilege
Wilton High School 39, 41
*The Winter's Tale* 75–7, 81–2
Wolf, Jennifer Lynn, quoted 32, 34, 157–8
workshops
African Dance 65
bullying 140–1
Challenge Day 186–8, 189
ensembles 111–12
homophobia 38
playwriting 57
Social Issues Theatre 139, 147, 149, 162n.1, 173–4, 176, 190
*Twelfth Night* 105
Worthman, Christopher, quoted 142
*The Wrestling Season* 32

www.ingramcontent.com/pod-product-compliance
Lightning Source LLC
LaVergne TN
LVHW060728310826
846742LV00016B/52